INTRODUCTION

Welcome to a world where the mystique of the wolf comes alive amidst the serene beauty of nature. Within the pages of this book, you will embark on a journey into the depths of the forest, where surreal landscapes and majestic creatures intertwine in a mesmerizing display of artistry and symbolism.

The wolf, revered as a totem animal in many cultures, stands as a symbol of strength, freedom, and resilience. Throughout history, it has captivated the human imagination, embodying the untamed spirit of the wilderness. In these pages, we celebrate the spirit of the wolf, depicting it in its natural habitat with unparalleled detail and reverence.

Each design within this collection is a testament to the intricate beauty of nature and the boundless creativity of the human spirit. From the depths of the forest to the cascading waterfalls and beneath the glow of the full moon, the wolf roams freely, its presence commanding attention and awe.

What sets this collection apart is its emphasis on originality and uniqueness. Every design is meticulously crafted, offering a fresh perspective on the timeless symbol of the wolf. Surreal landscapes blend seamlessly with intricate details, creating an otherworldly atmosphere that is both captivating and unforgettable.

To further enhance your tattooing experience, we have included numbered stencils for each design. This ensures ease of identification and application, allowing you to bring these mesmerizing designs to life with precision and confidence. Additionally, a printable PDF is provided, offering maximum detail and shadow representation, ensuring flawless execution of your chosen tattoo.

As you explore these pages, allow yourself to be drawn into the world of the wolf, where imagination knows no bounds and the beauty of nature reigns supreme. Whether you are an artist seeking inspiration or simply a lover of the wild, let these designs transport you to a realm where the spirit of the wolf roams free and untamed.

BOOK OWNER

COPYRIGHT

No part of this publication may be reproduced, distributed, or transmitted in any form or by any means, including photocopying, recording, or other electronic or mechanical methods, without the prior written permission of the author and sole copyright owner, **Alex Metsovas (Alex Mets)**.

This prohibition includes, but is not limited to:

- **Digital Distribution:** Uploading to websites, file-sharing platforms, social media groups, or cloud storage for public access.
- **AI Training:** The use of any content from this book for machine learning or artificial intelligence training is strictly prohibited.
- **Unauthorized Resale:** Any form of commercial exploitation beyond the specific licenses granted below.

Limited License for Tattoo Artists & Painters: The lawful purchaser of this book is granted a limited, non-transferable license for **personal and professional artistic use only**:

1. **Tattooing:** You may photocopy or print stencils from this book for the sole purpose of applying a tattoo to yourself or a client.
2. **Reference Art:** You may use the images as a printed reference to create original physical paintings or artworks.

Strictly Prohibited: Digital redistribution of the downloaded PDF or any portion of this book is a violation of international copyright laws and will be prosecuted. Brief quotations are permitted only if they include a direct link to the author's official buying page

Copyright © 2024 Alex Metsovas DivineTattooDesign

ISBN: 9798320309927

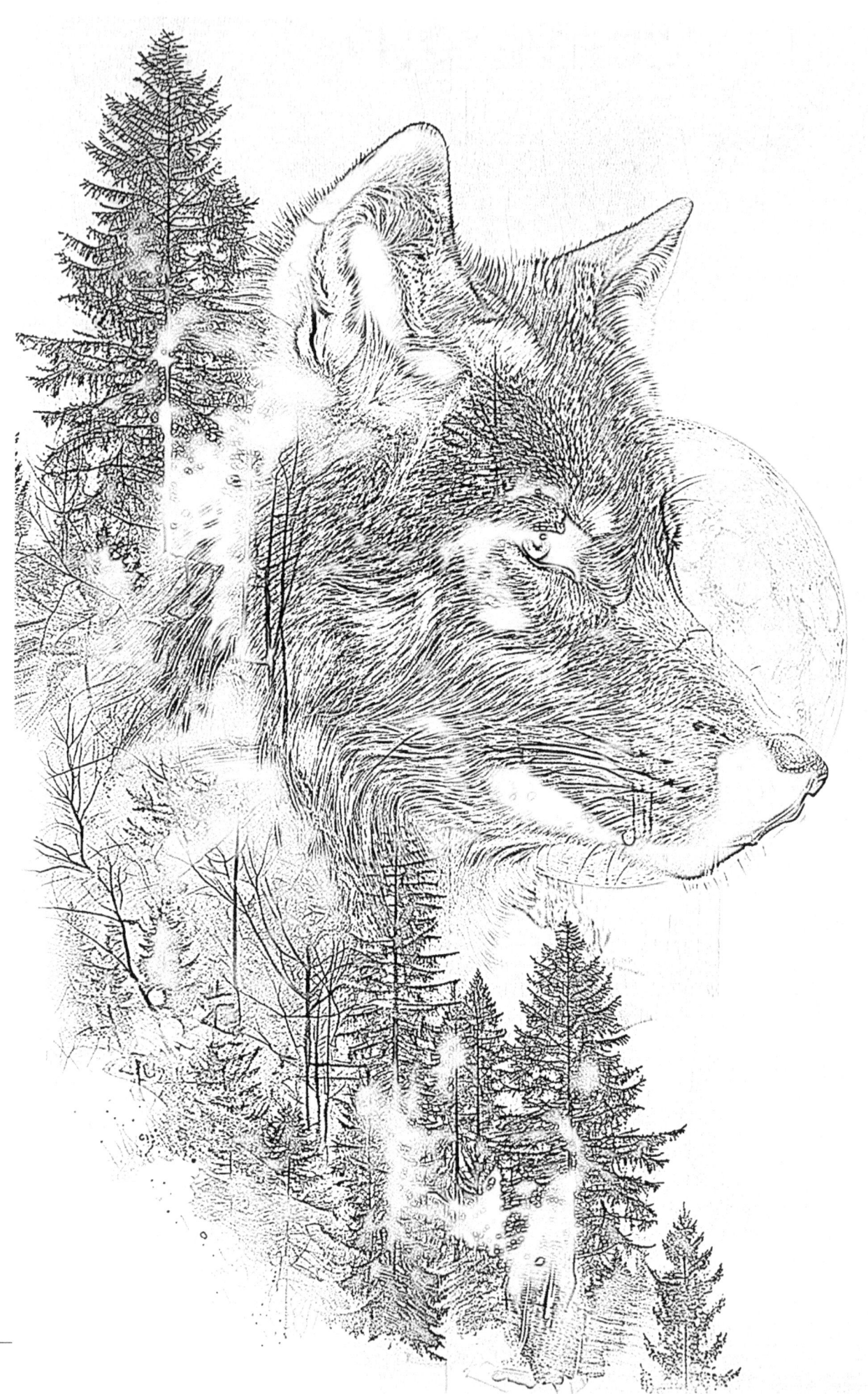

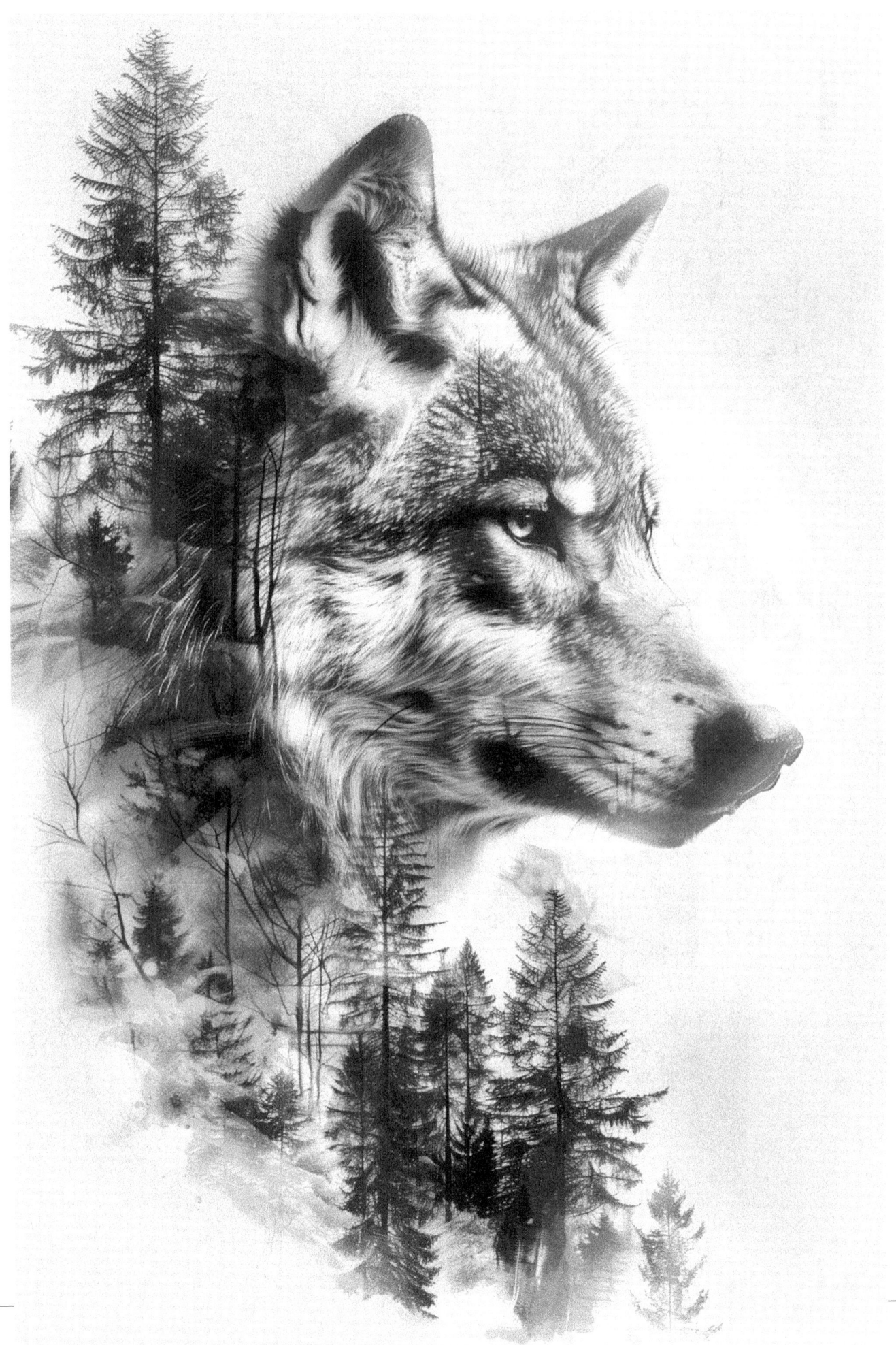

1

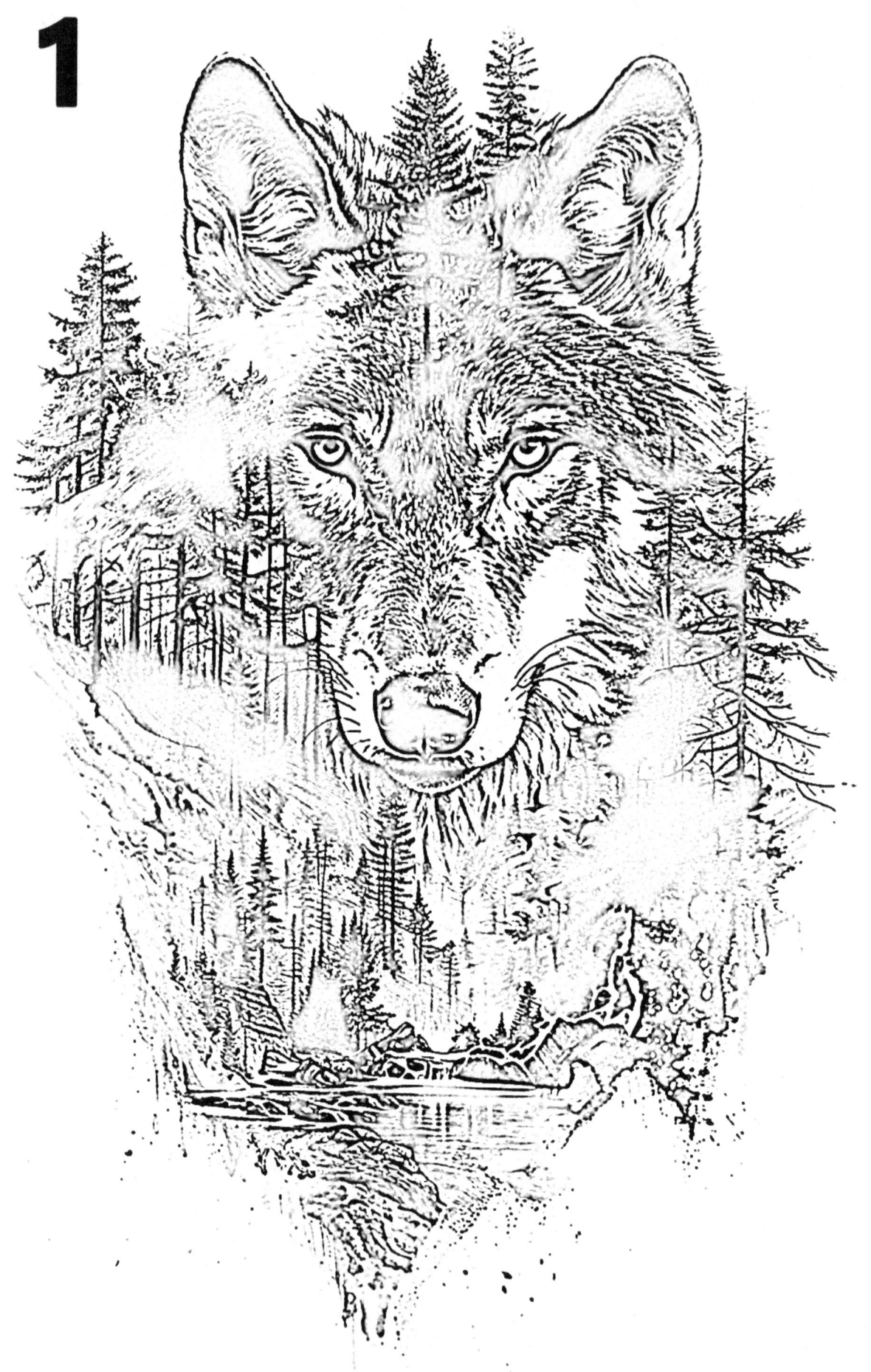

1

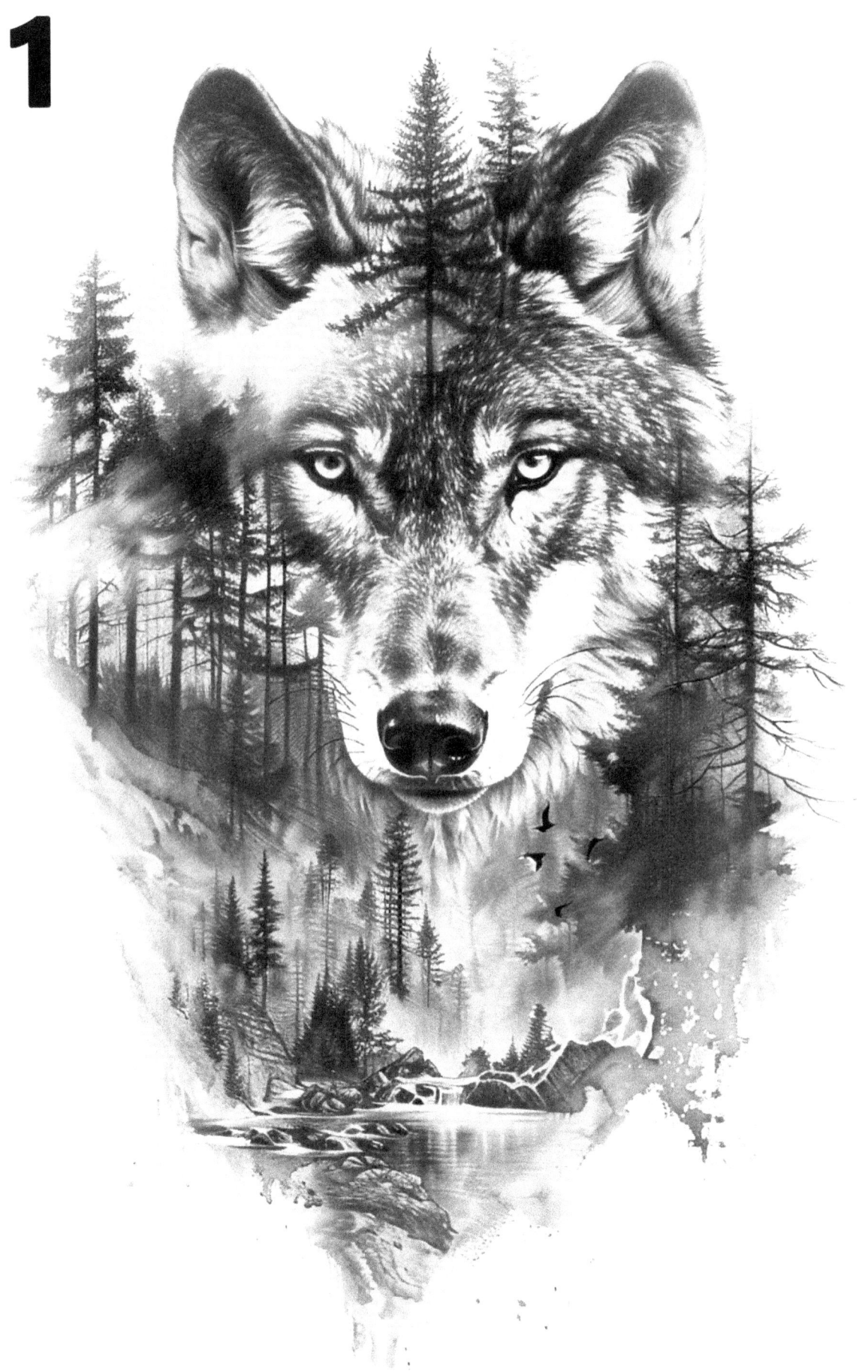

2

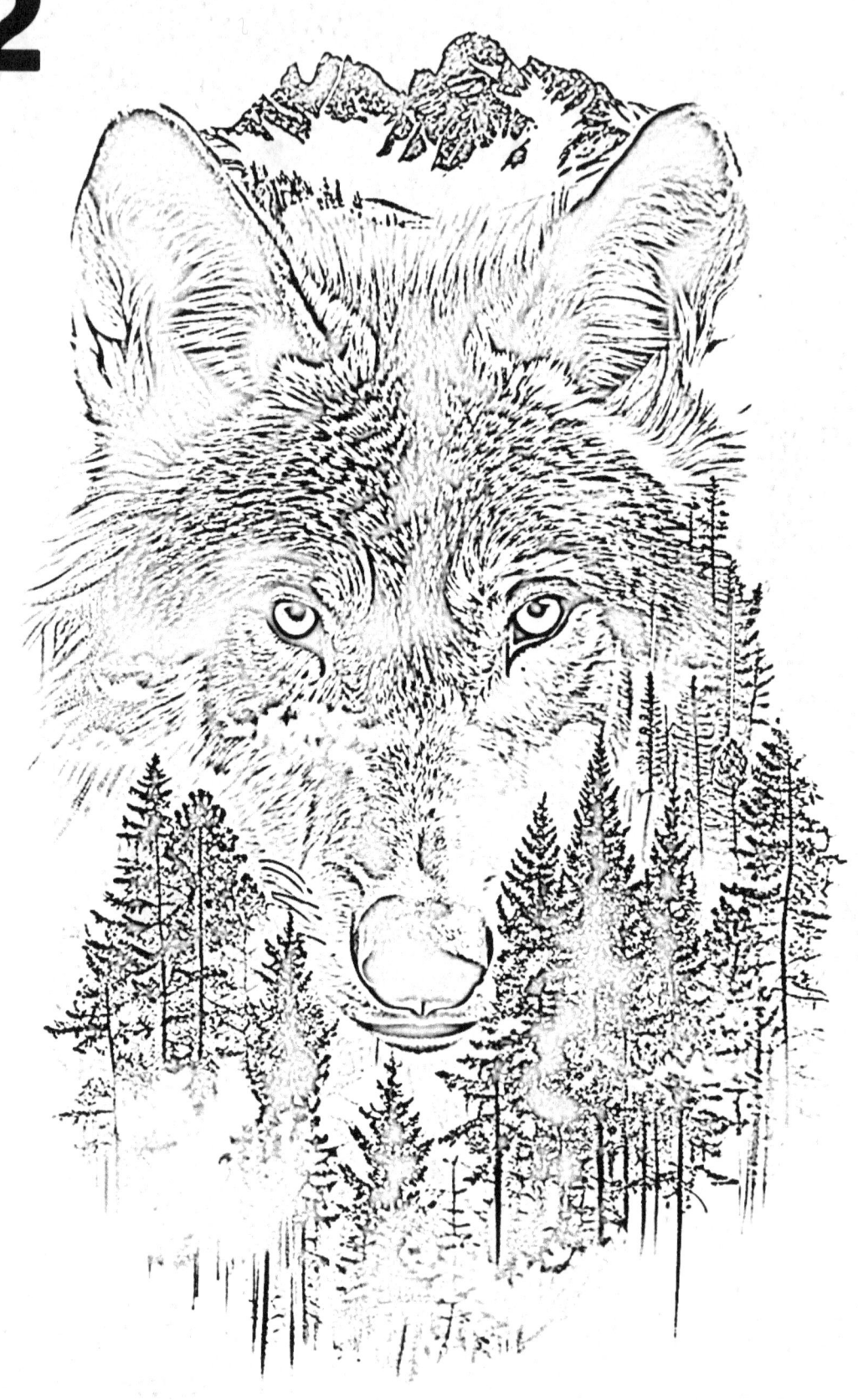

2

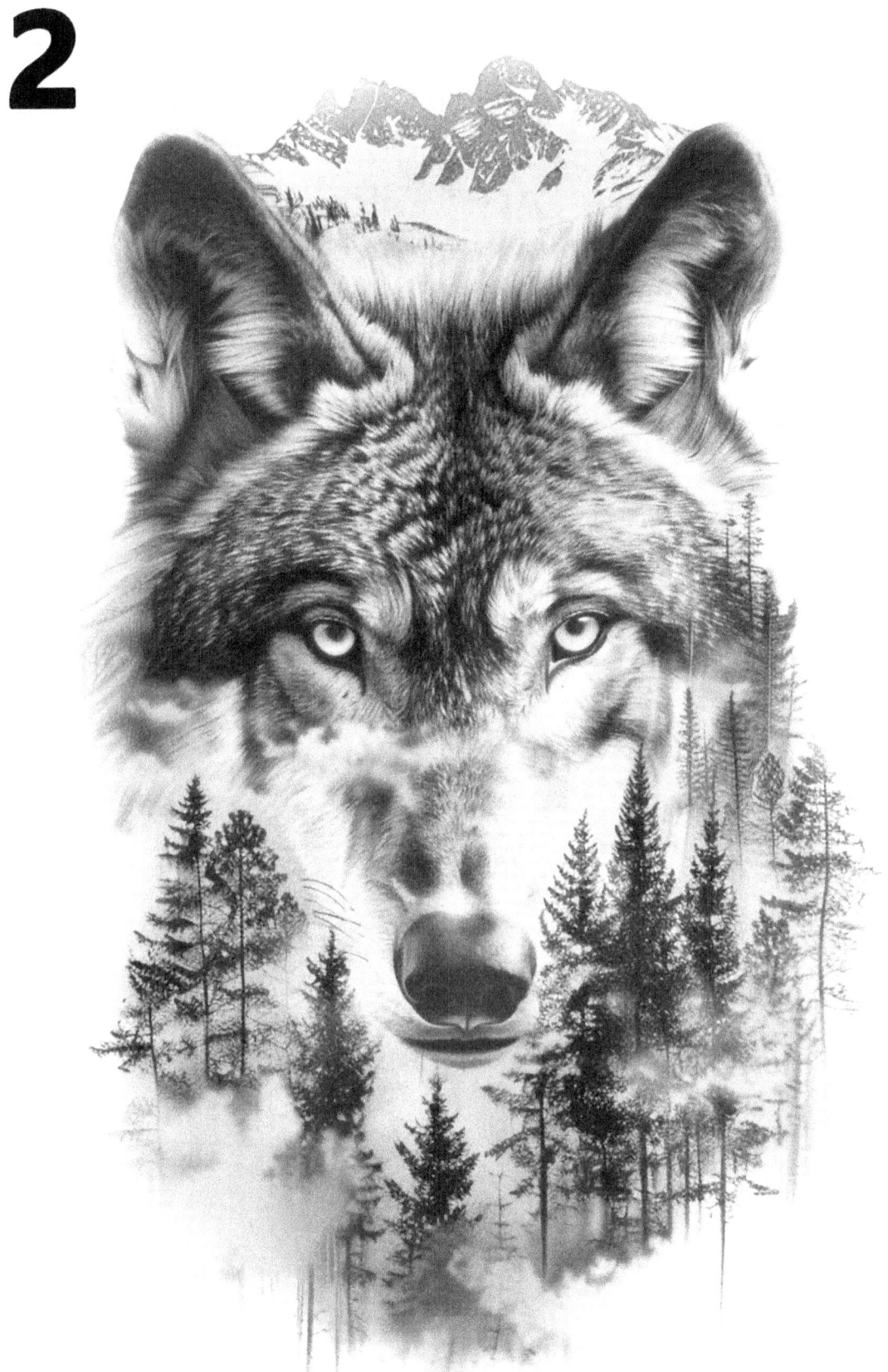

3

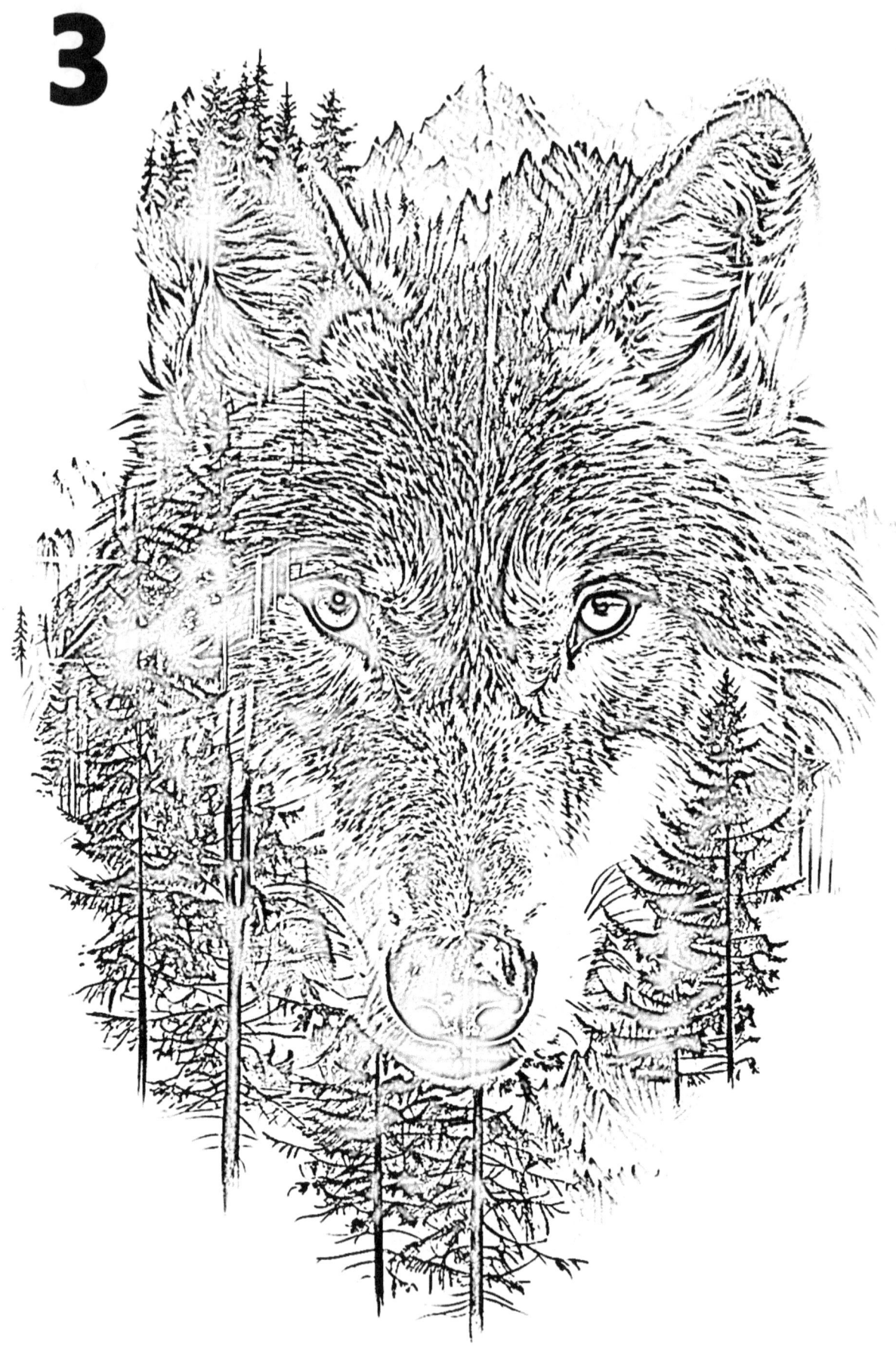

3

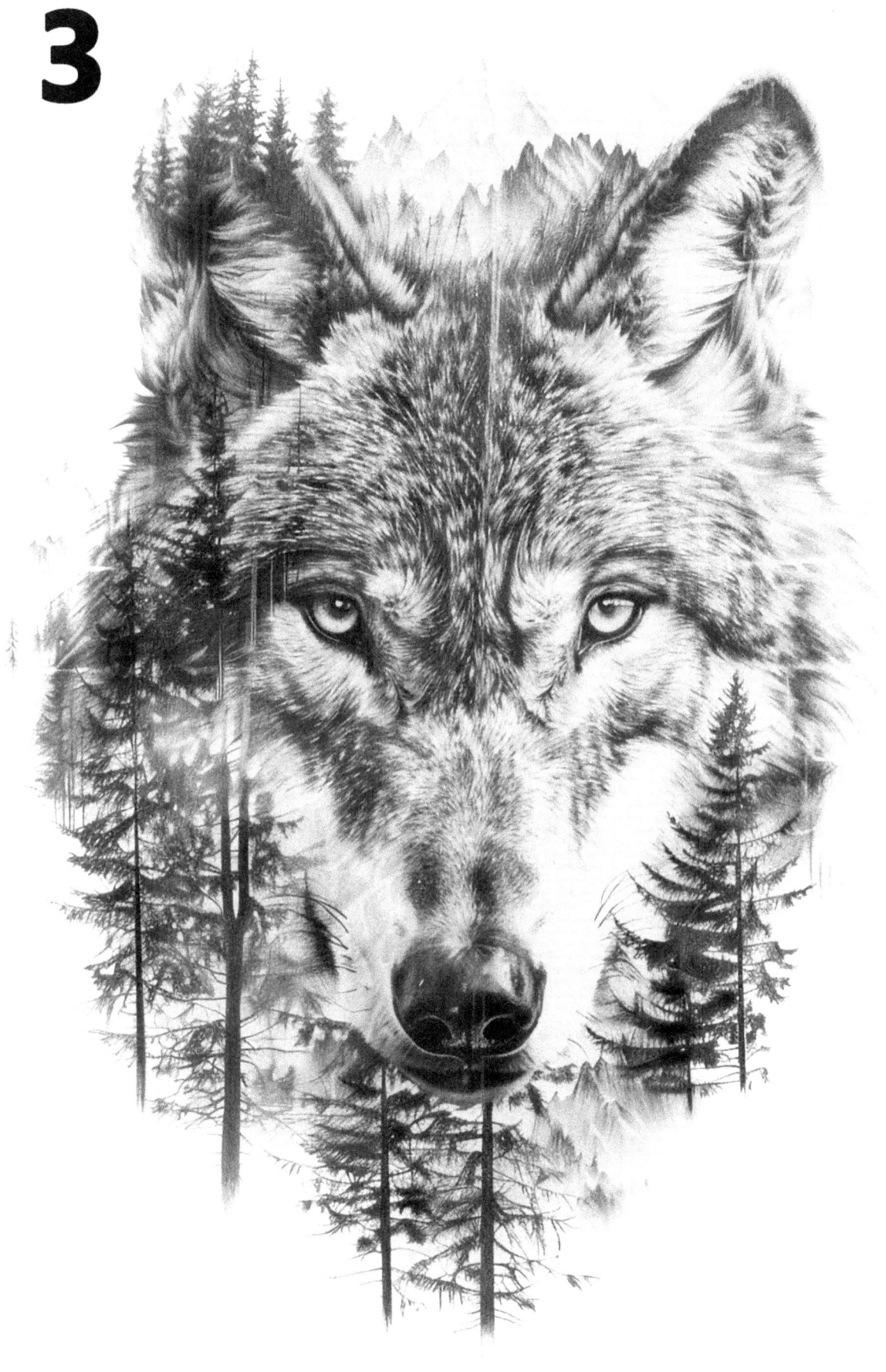

4

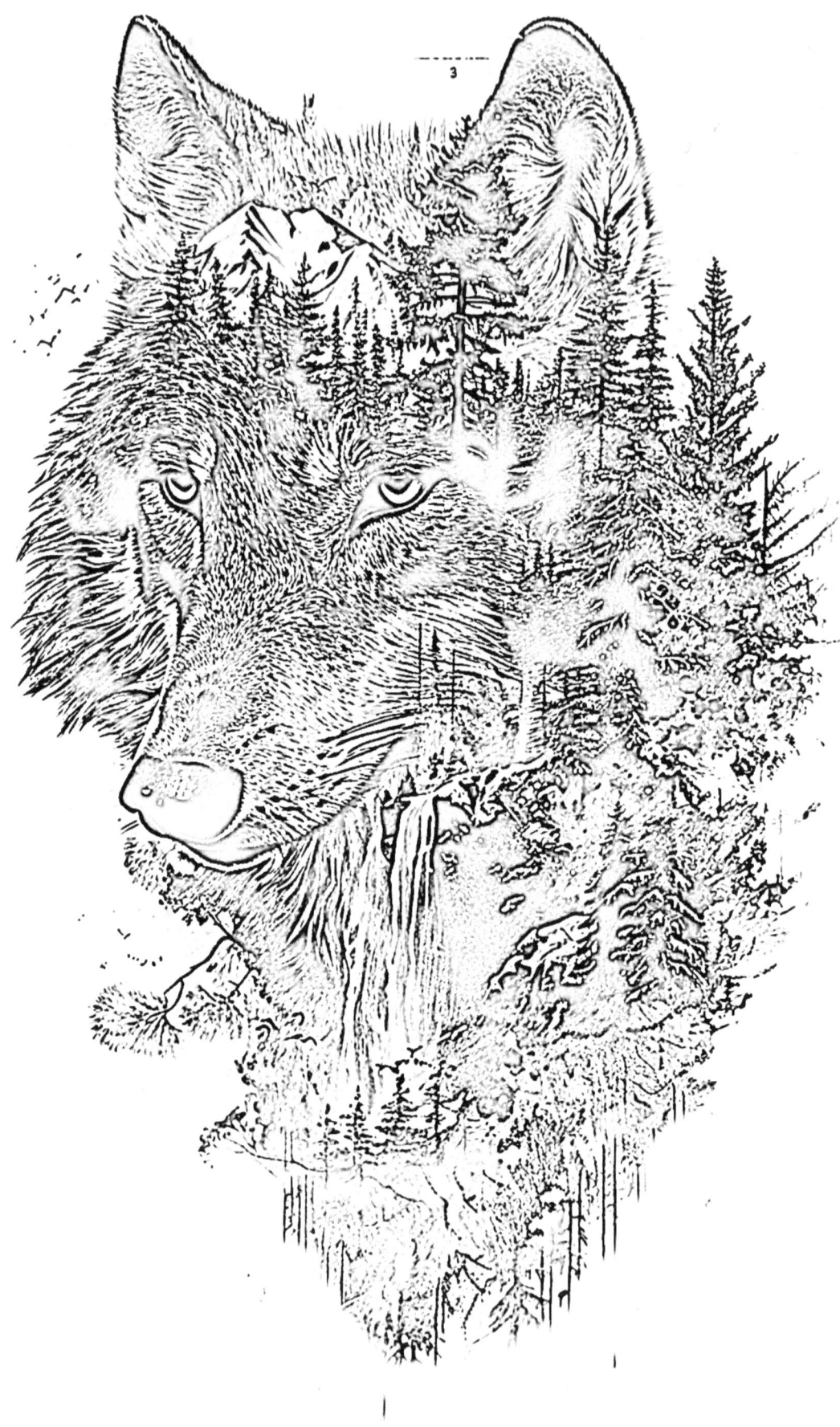

4

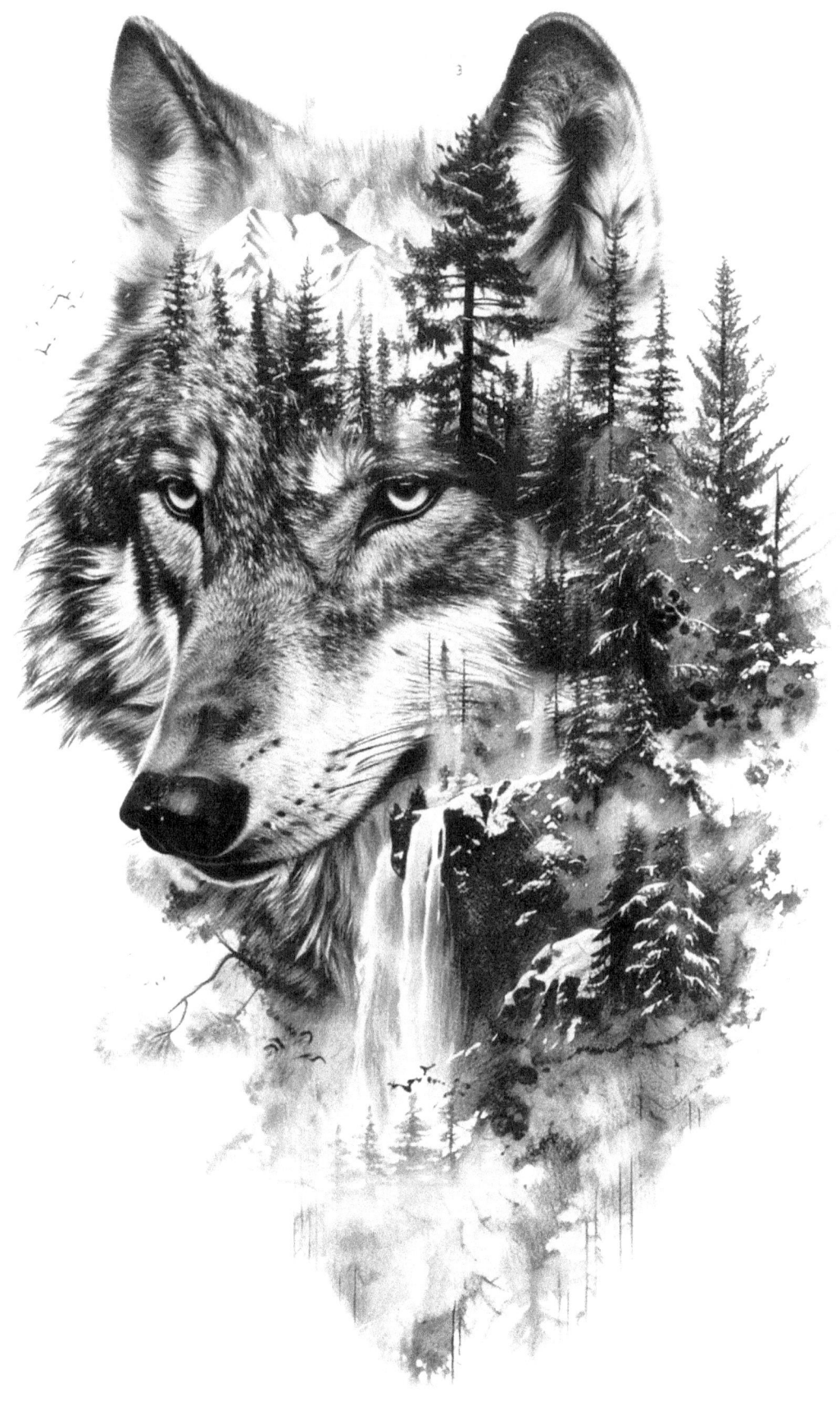

5

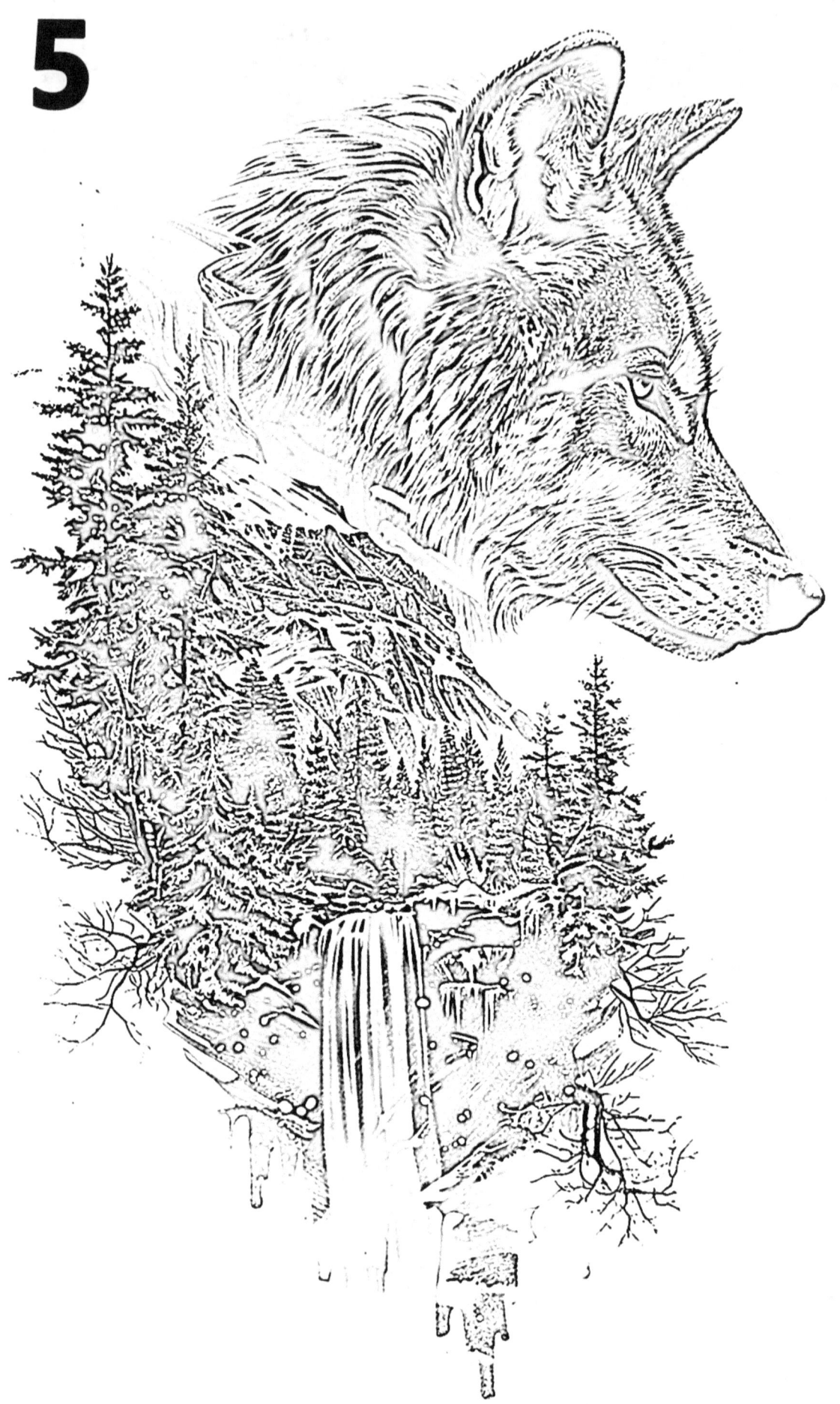

5

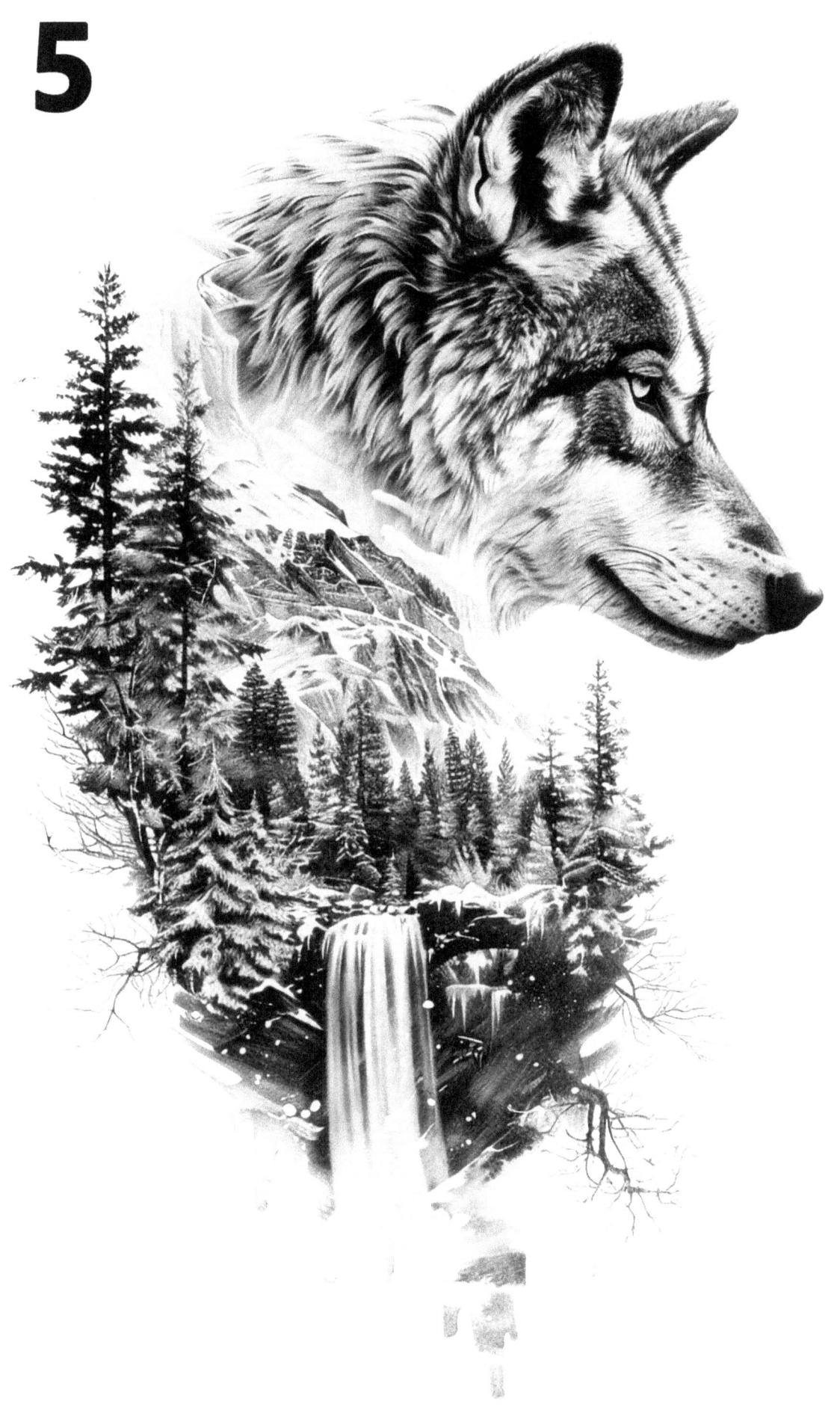

6

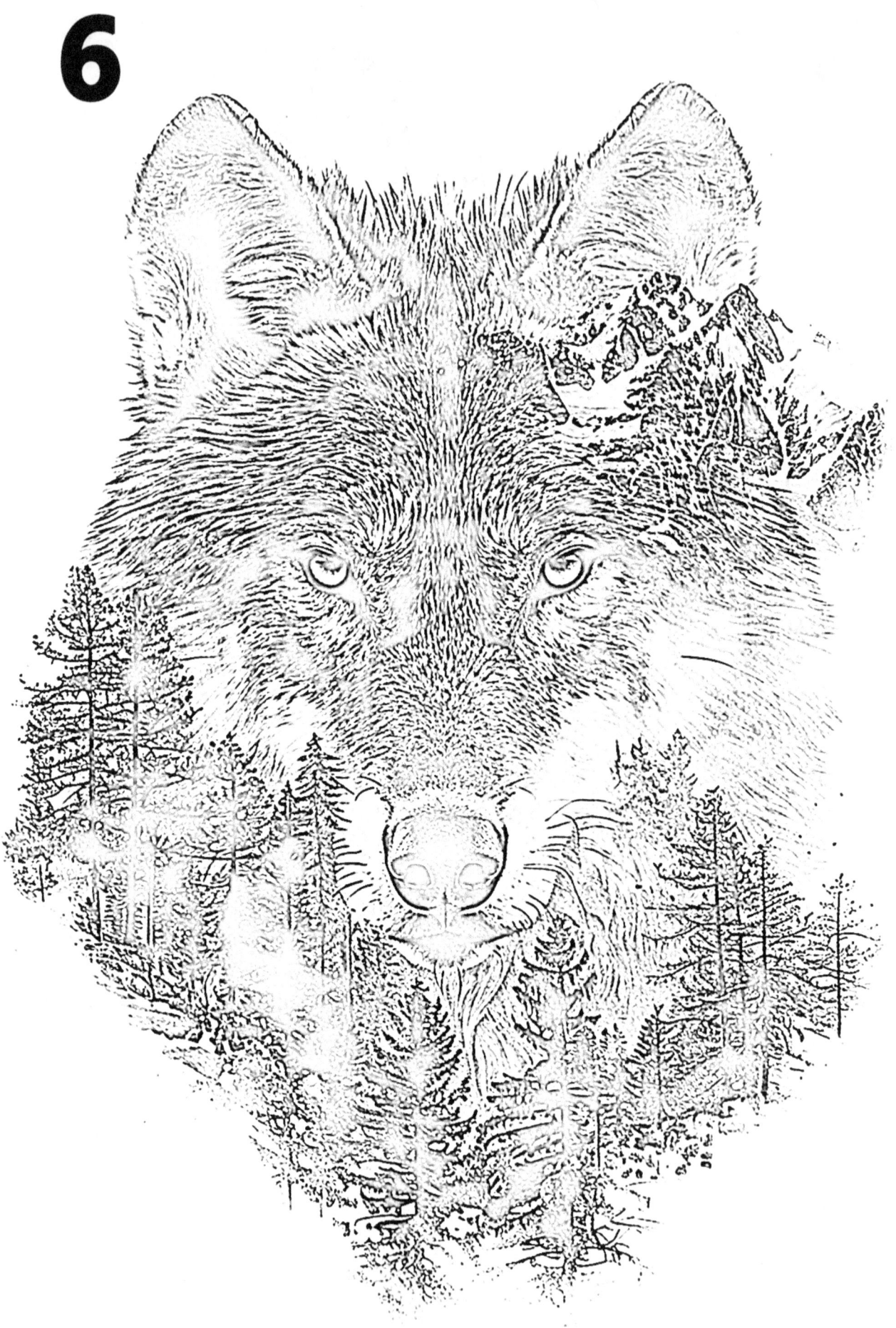

6

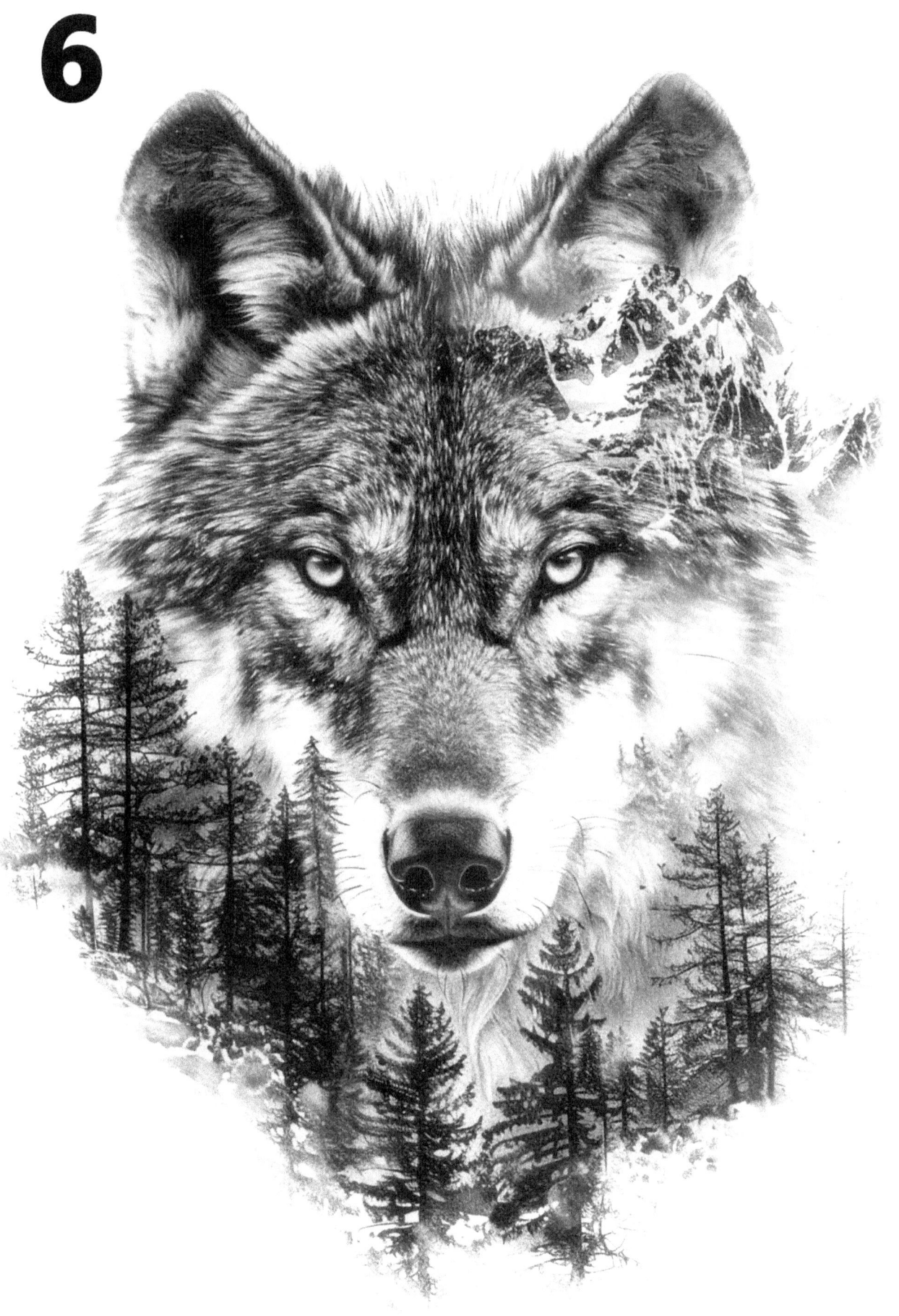

7

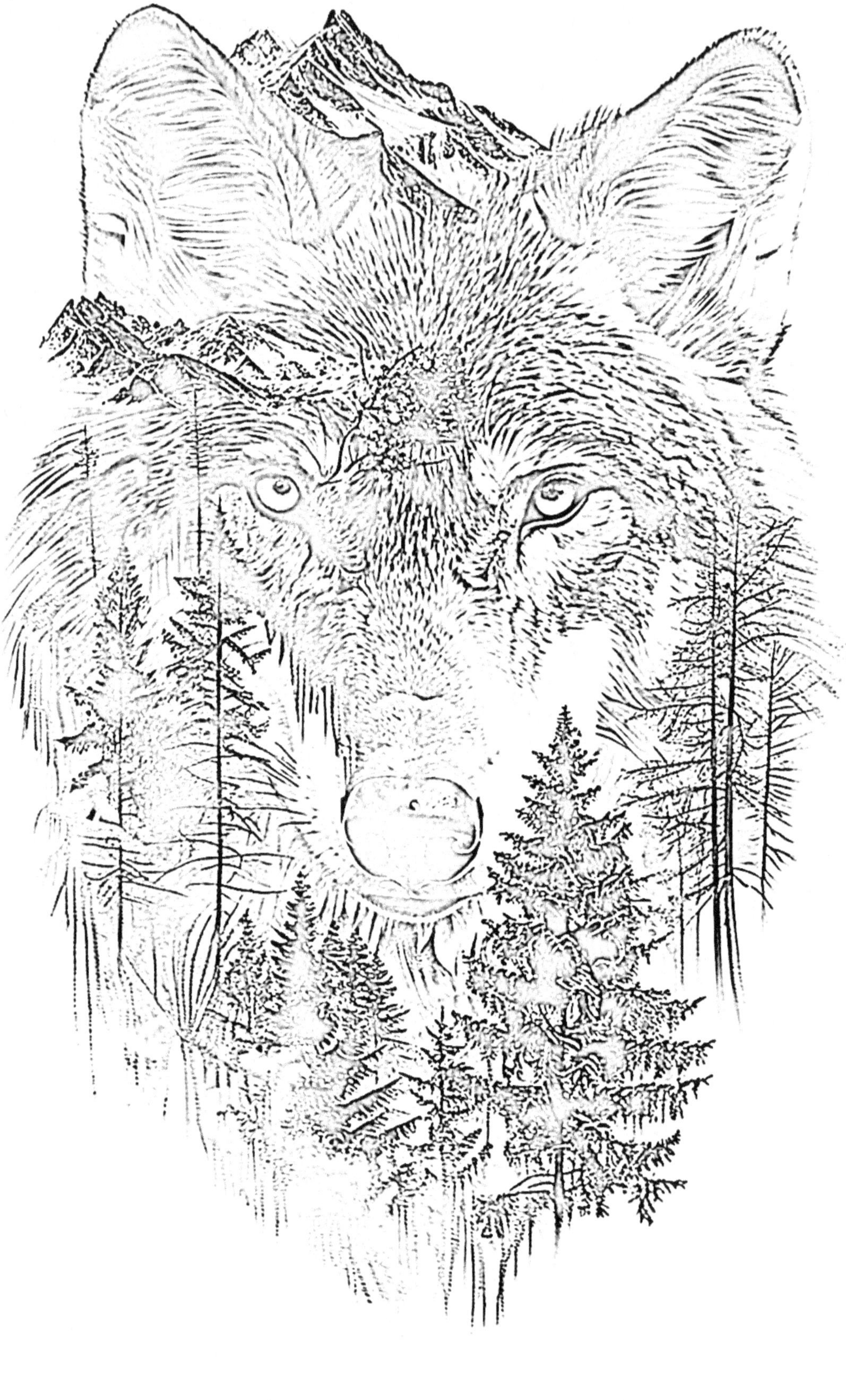

7

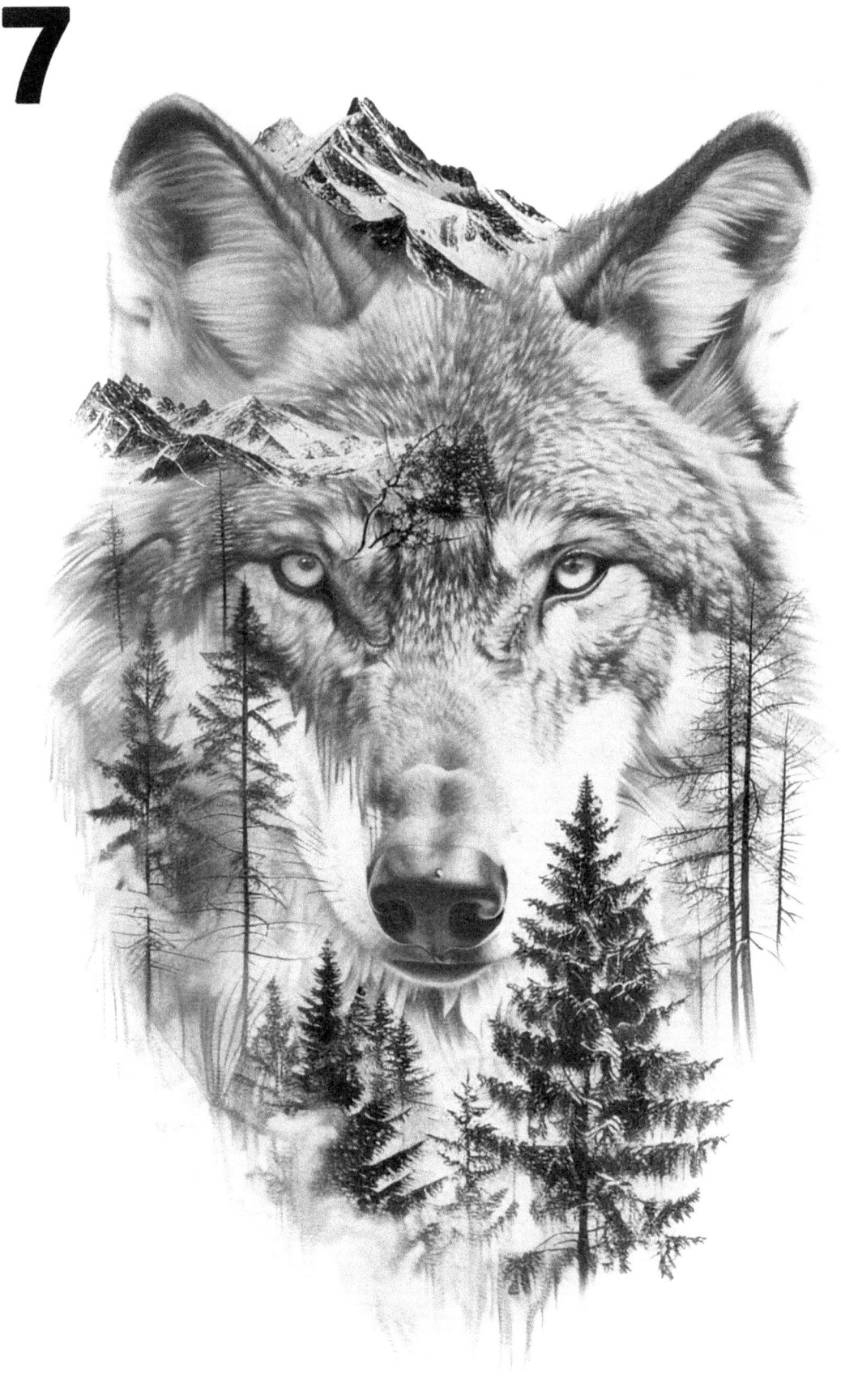

8

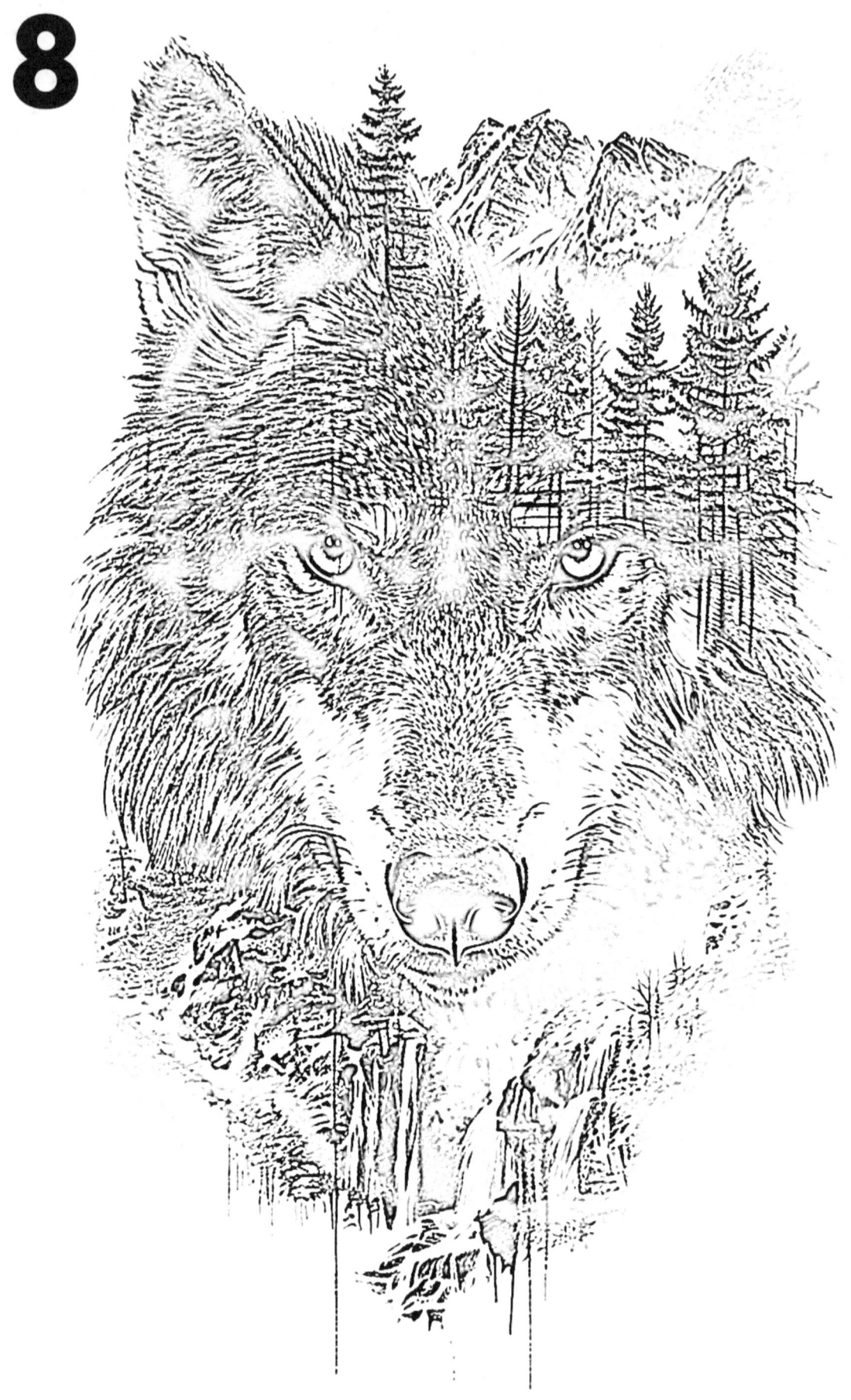

8

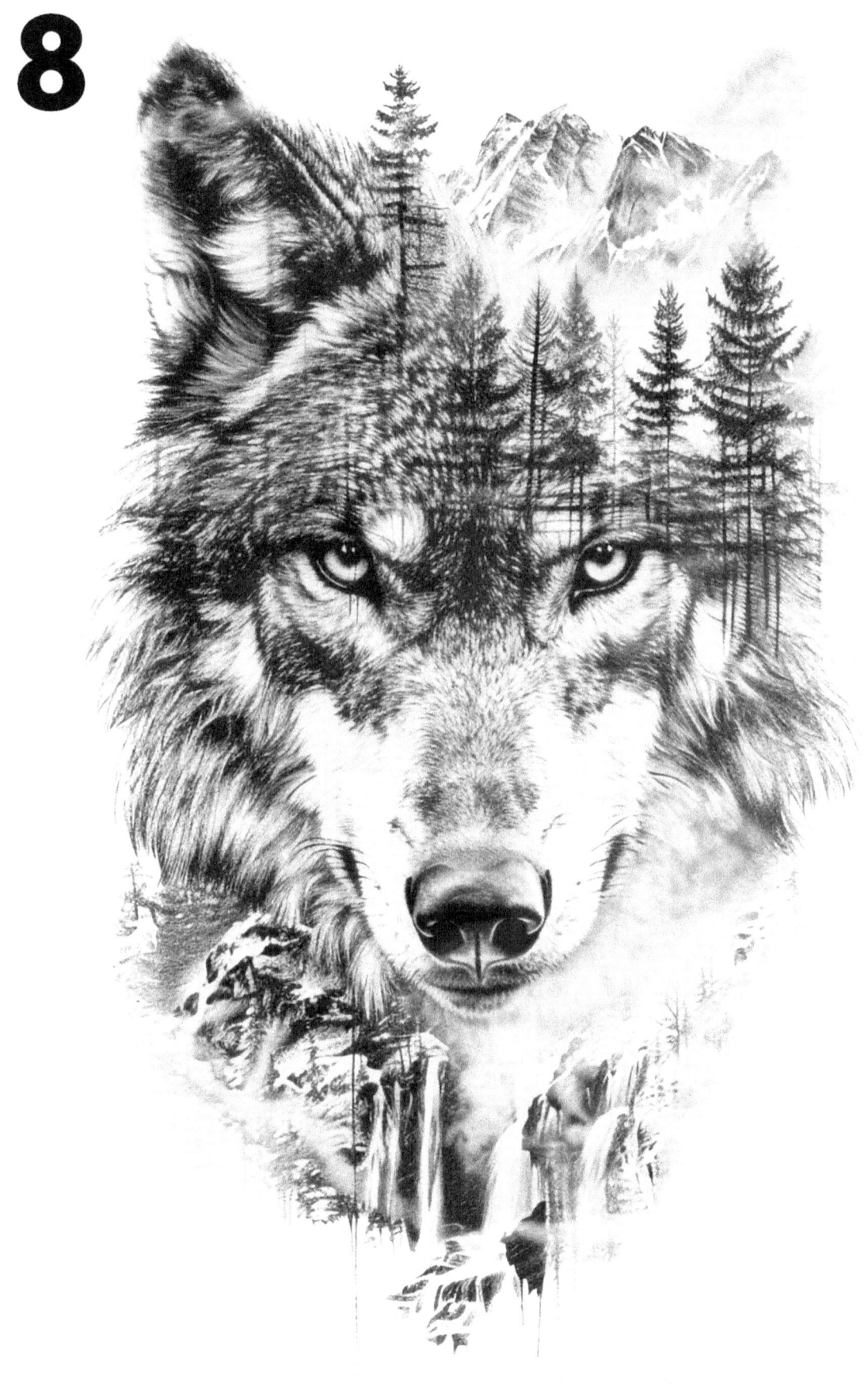

9

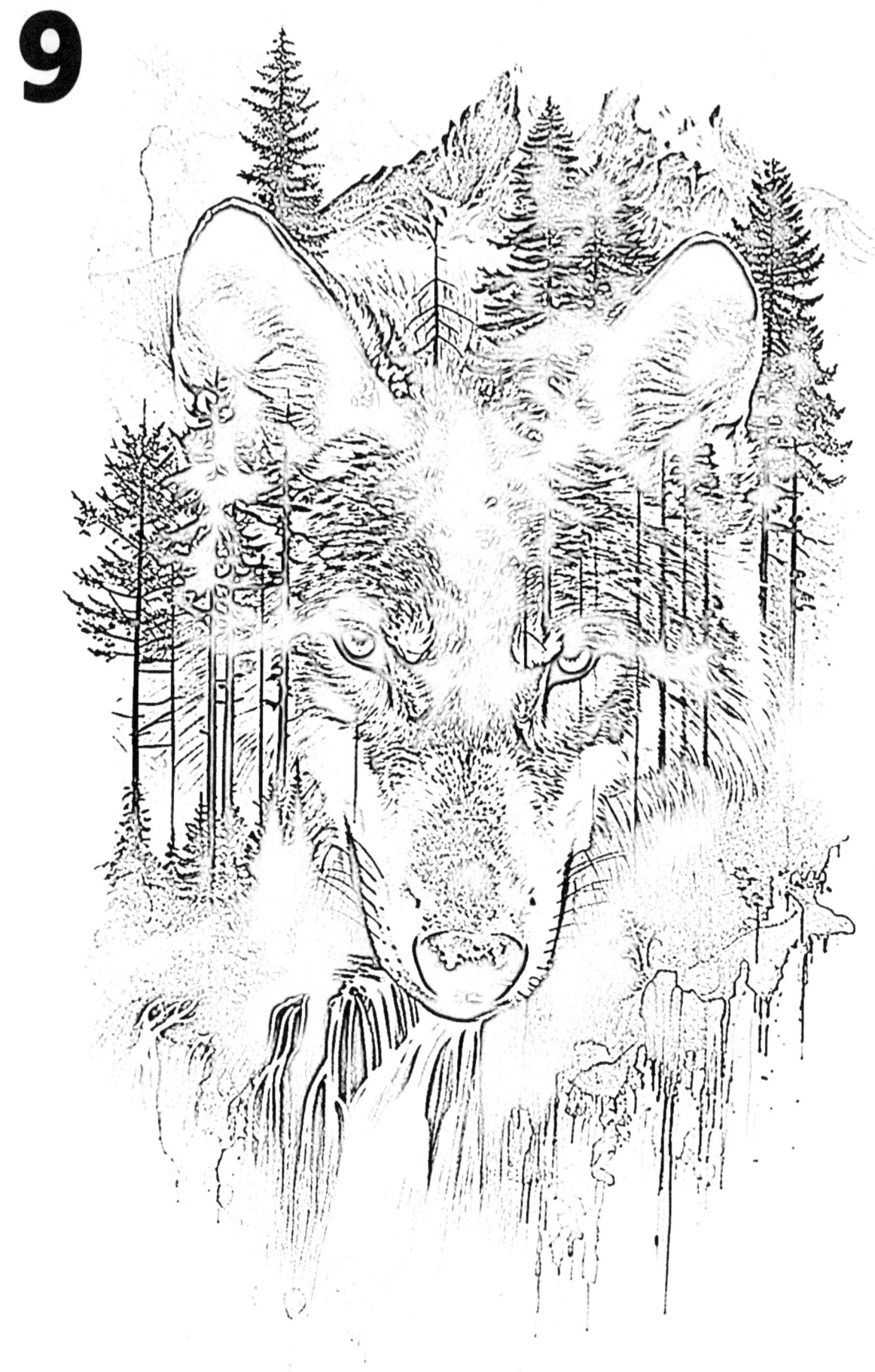

9

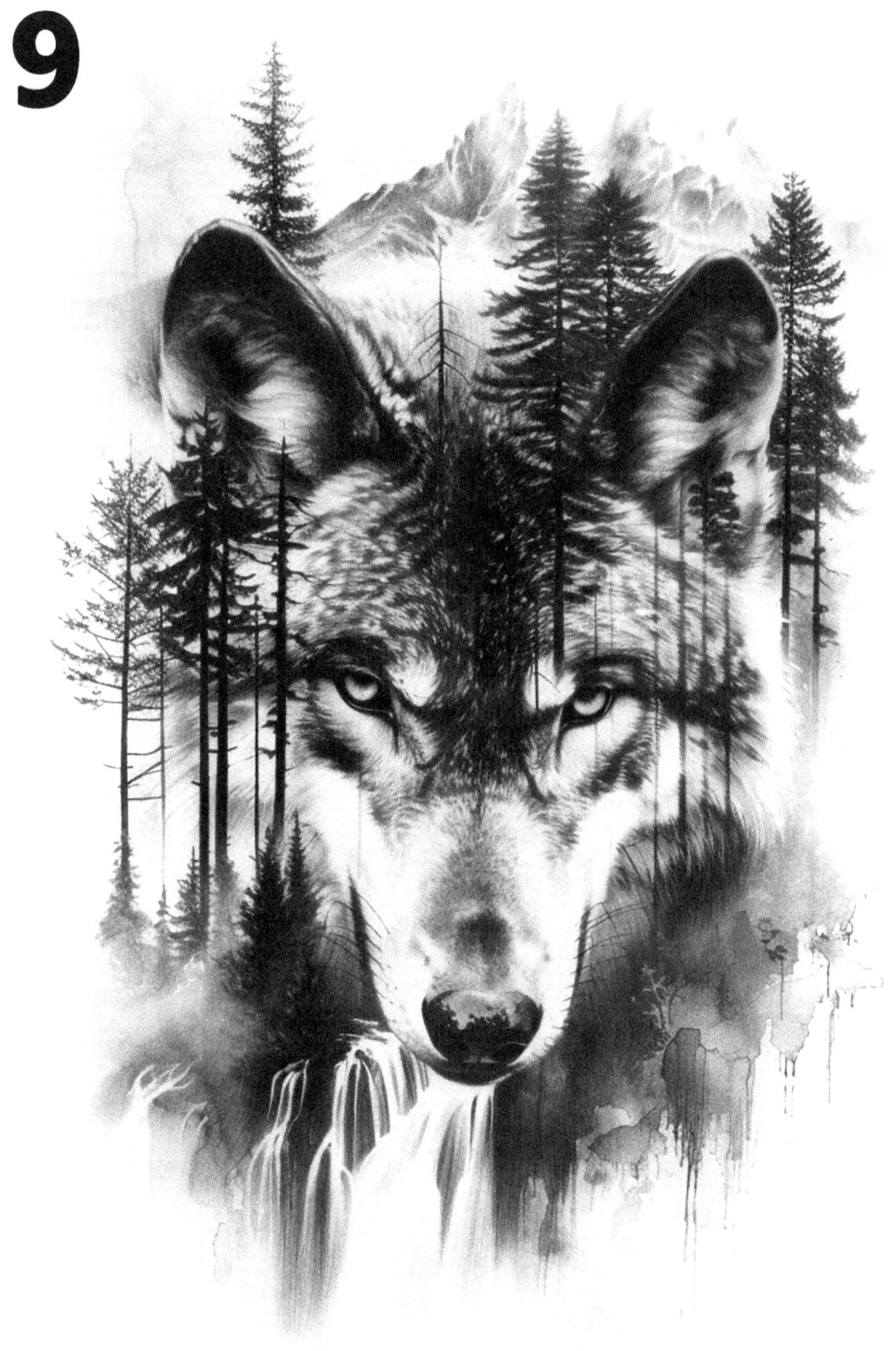

10

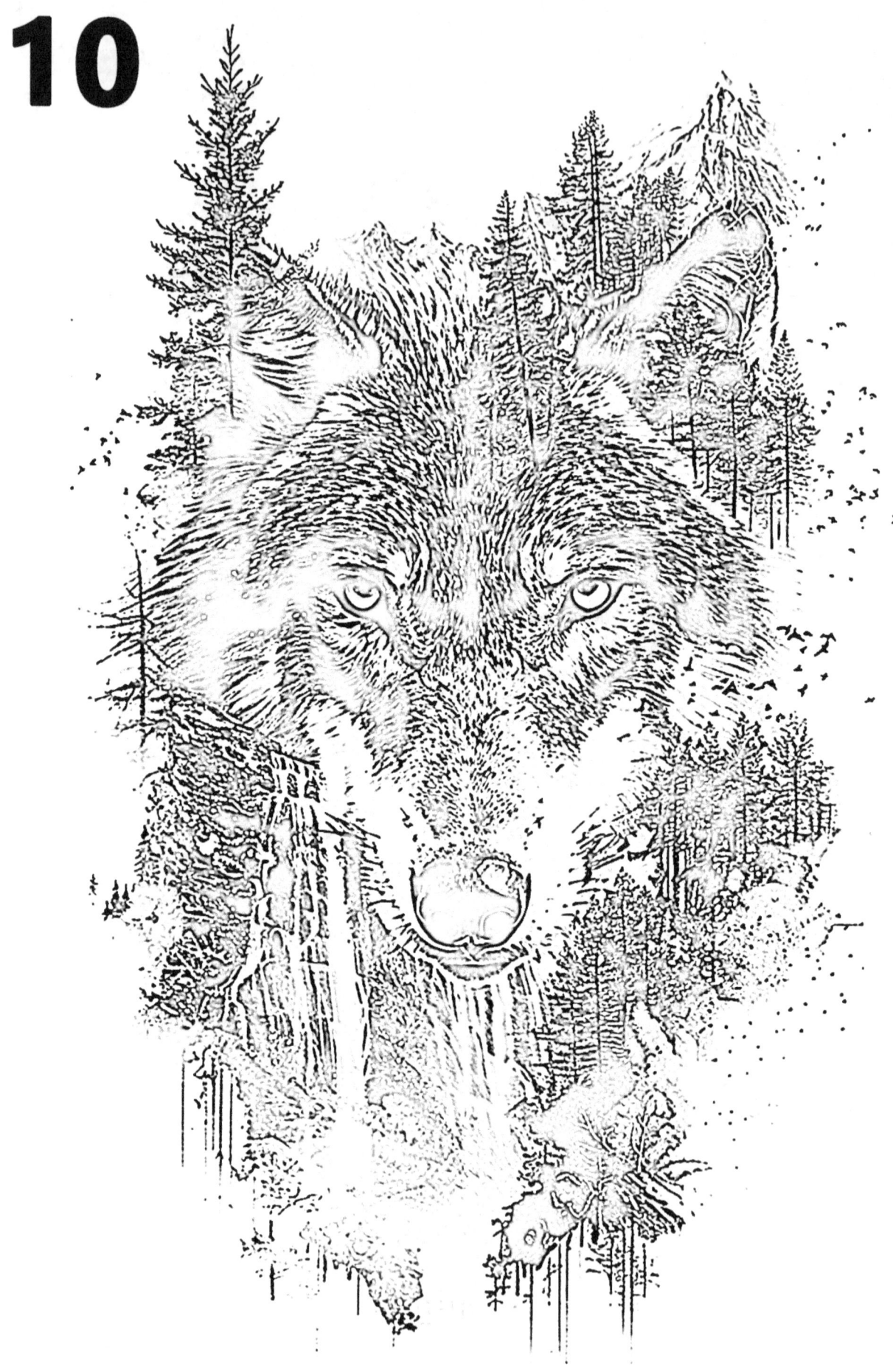

10

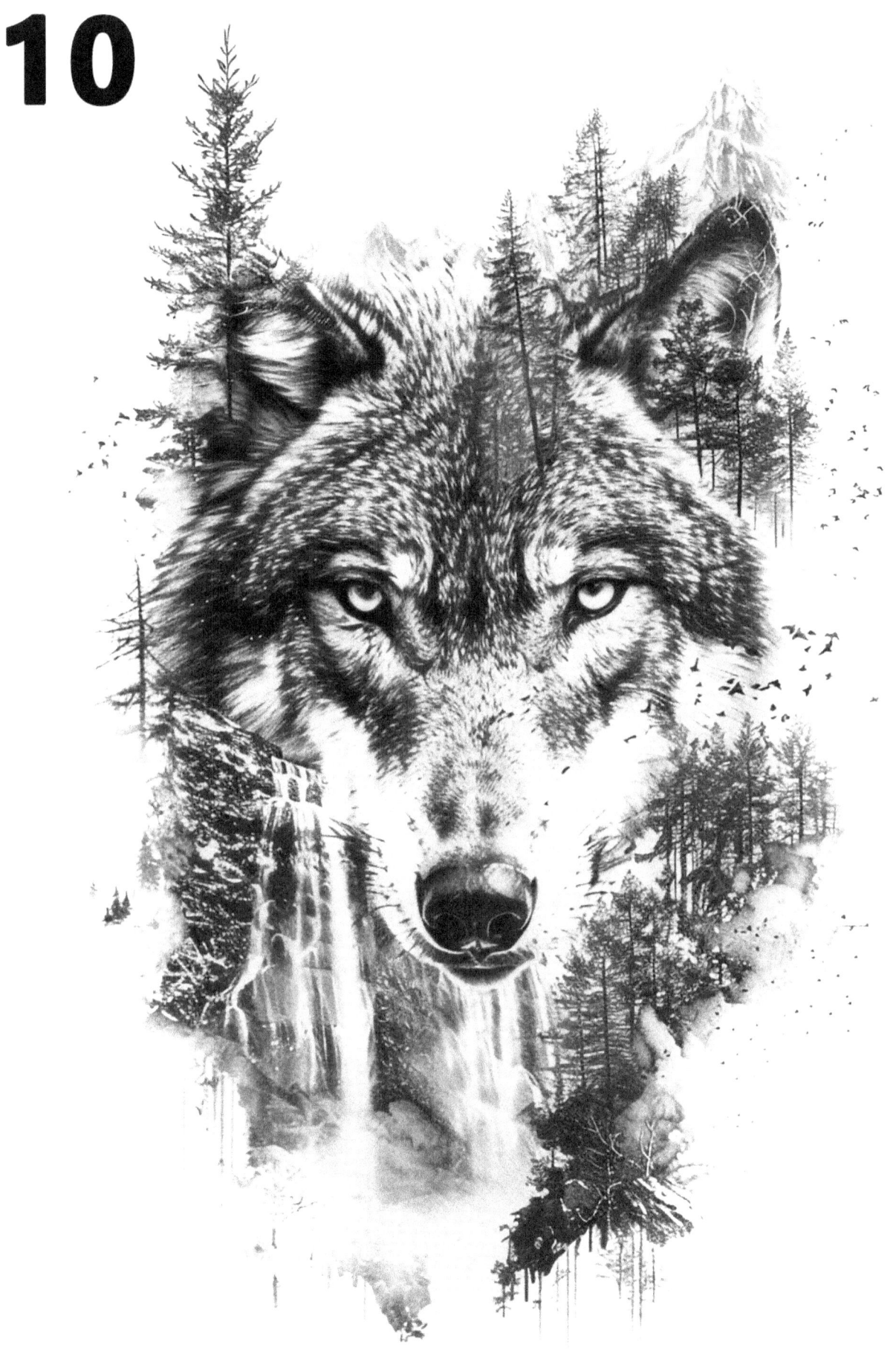

11

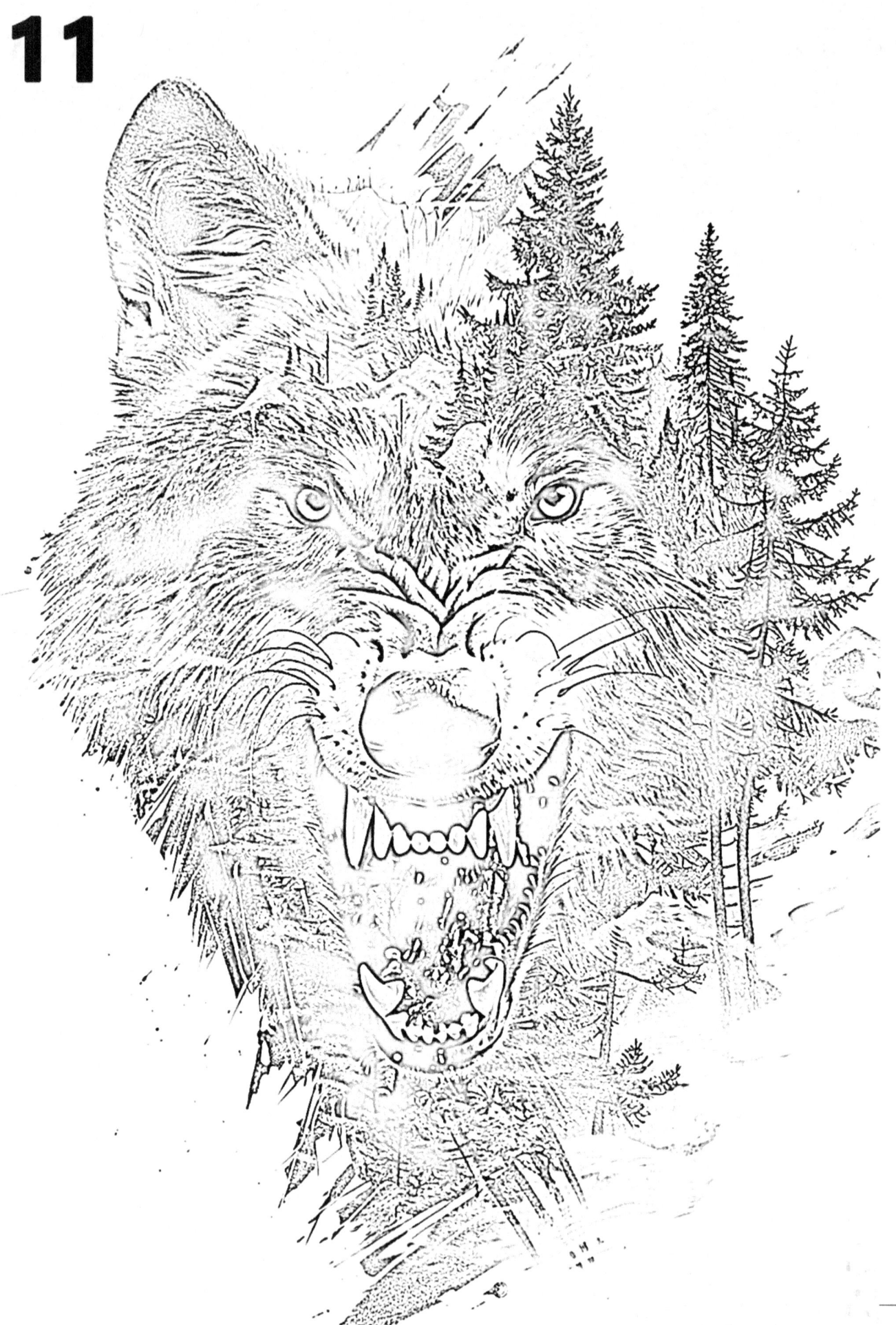

11

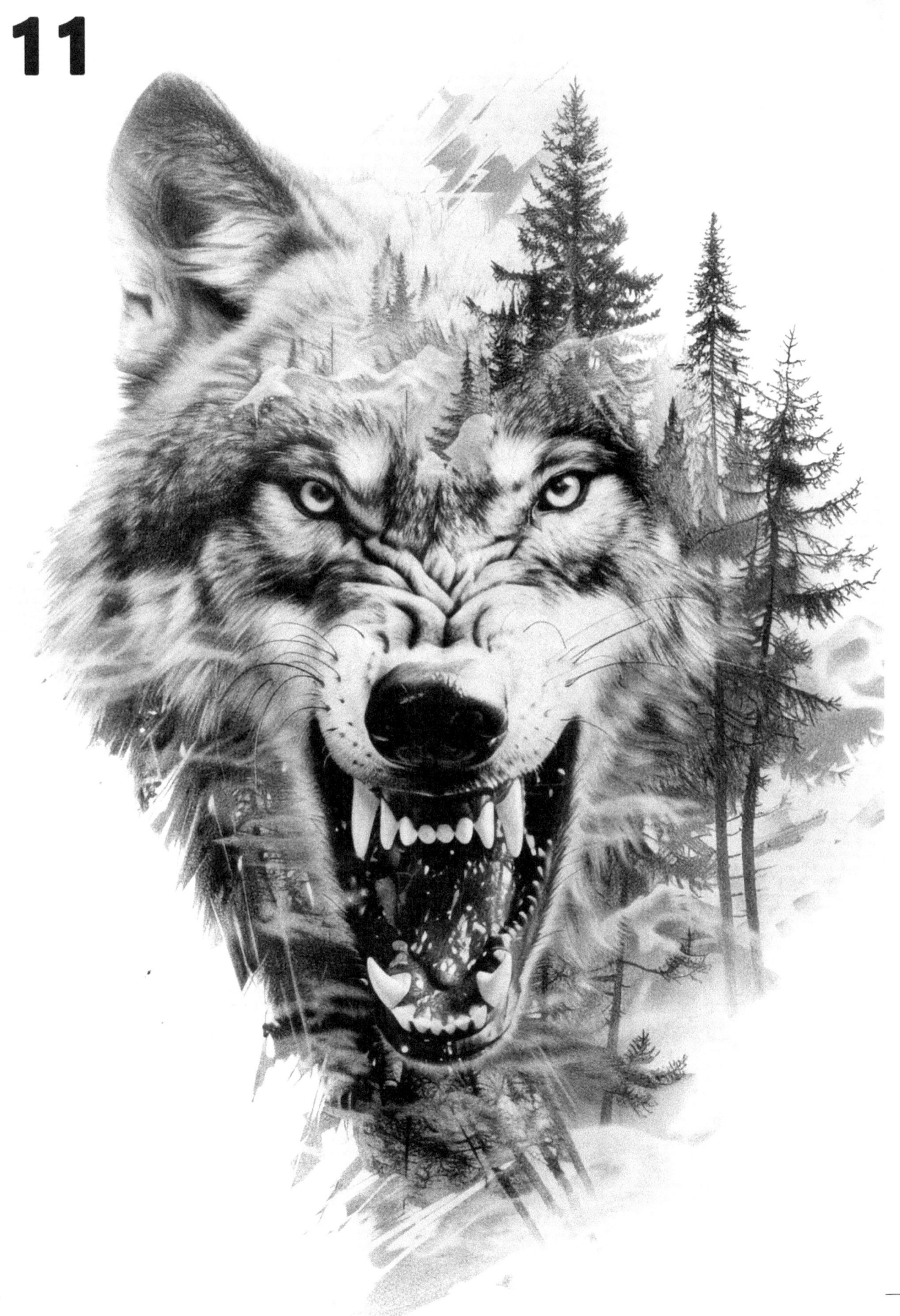

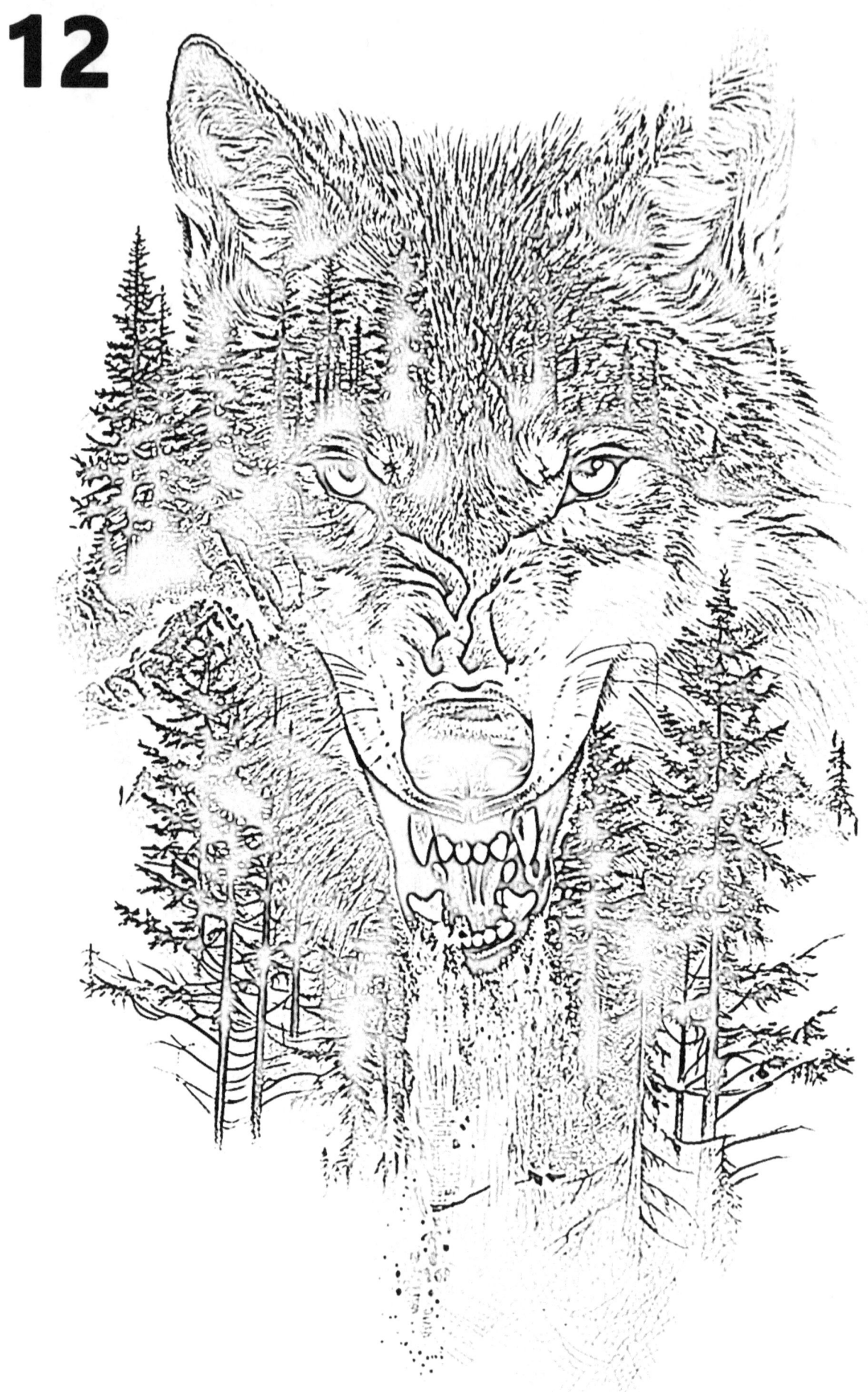

12

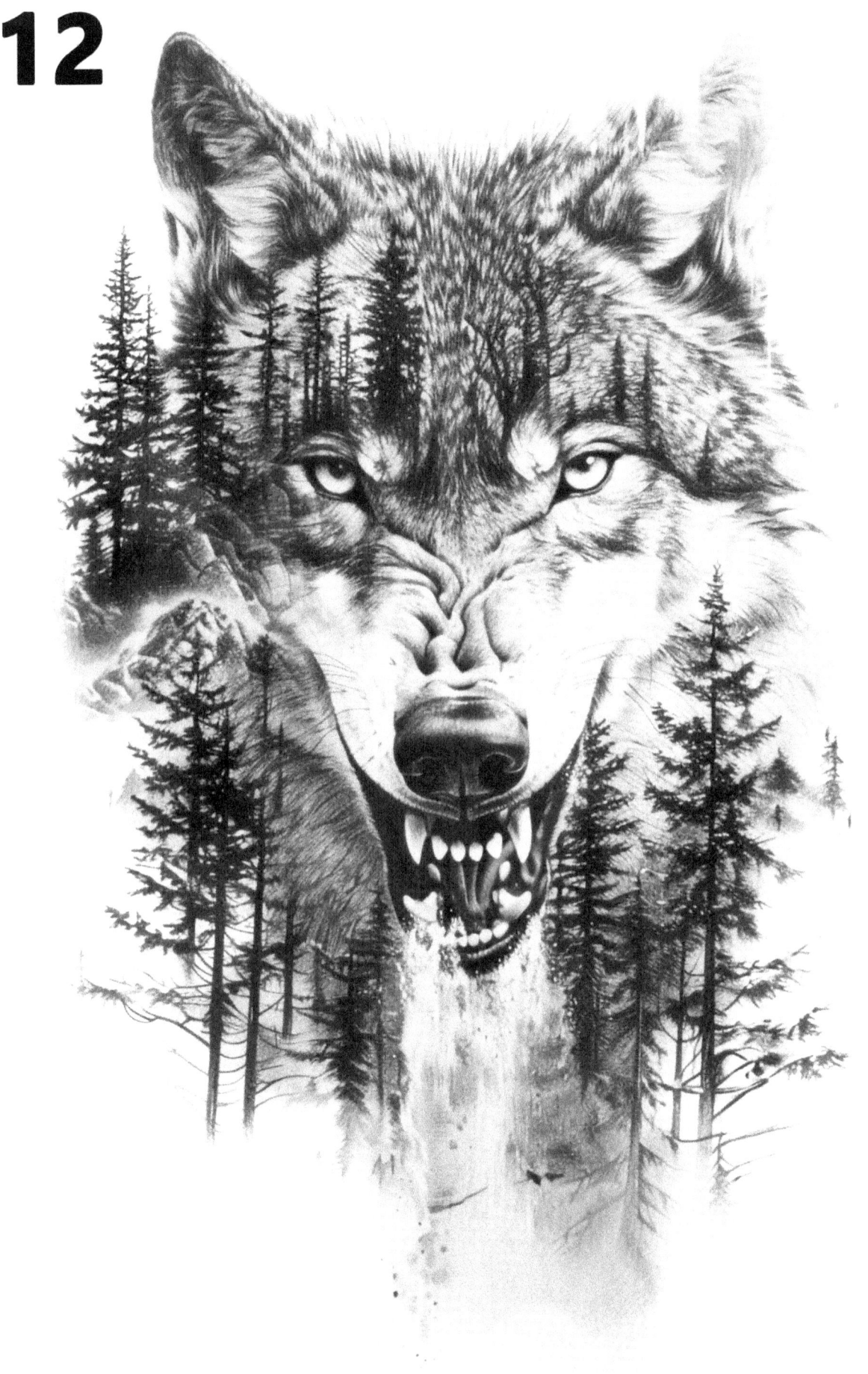

13

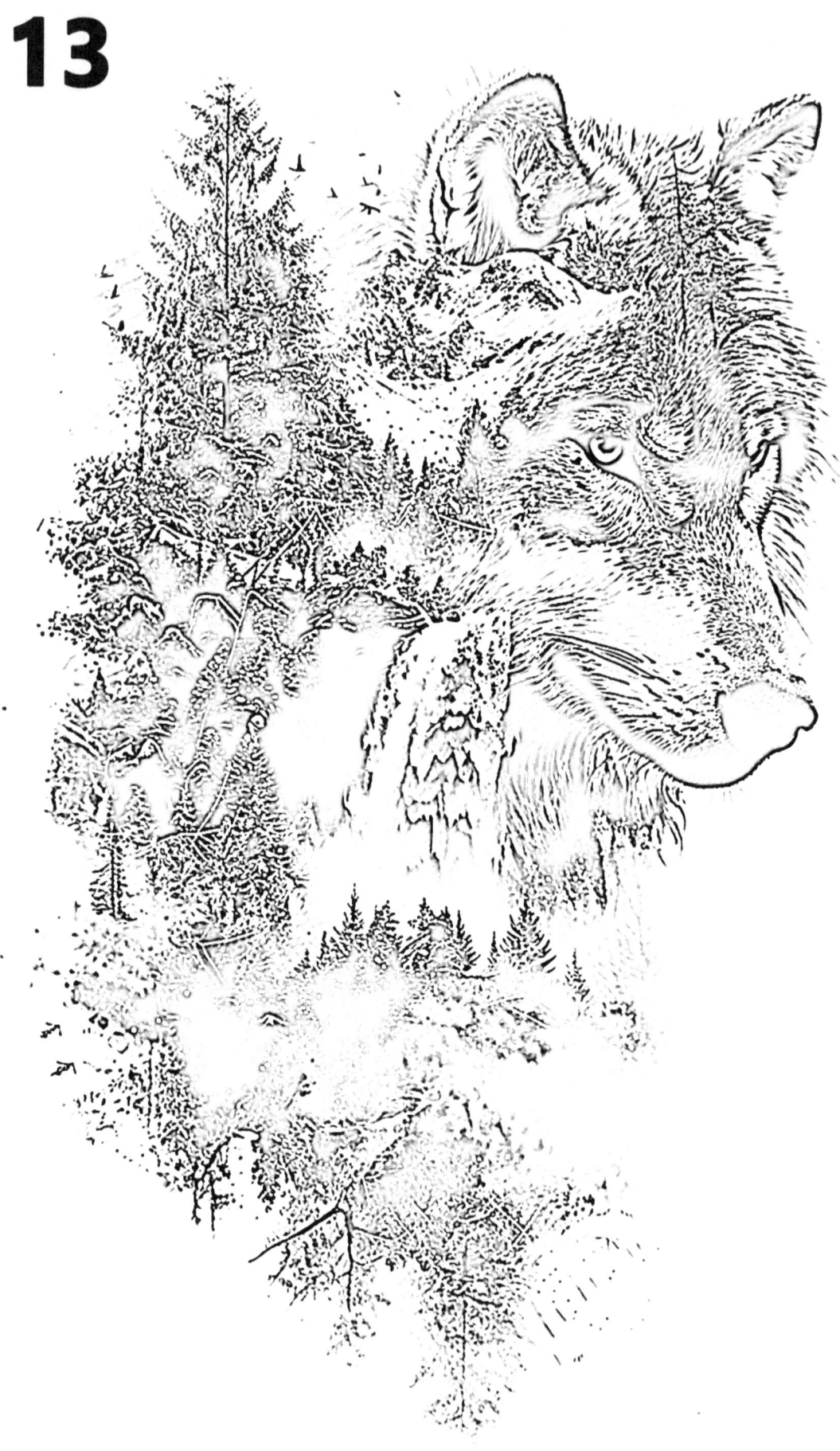

13

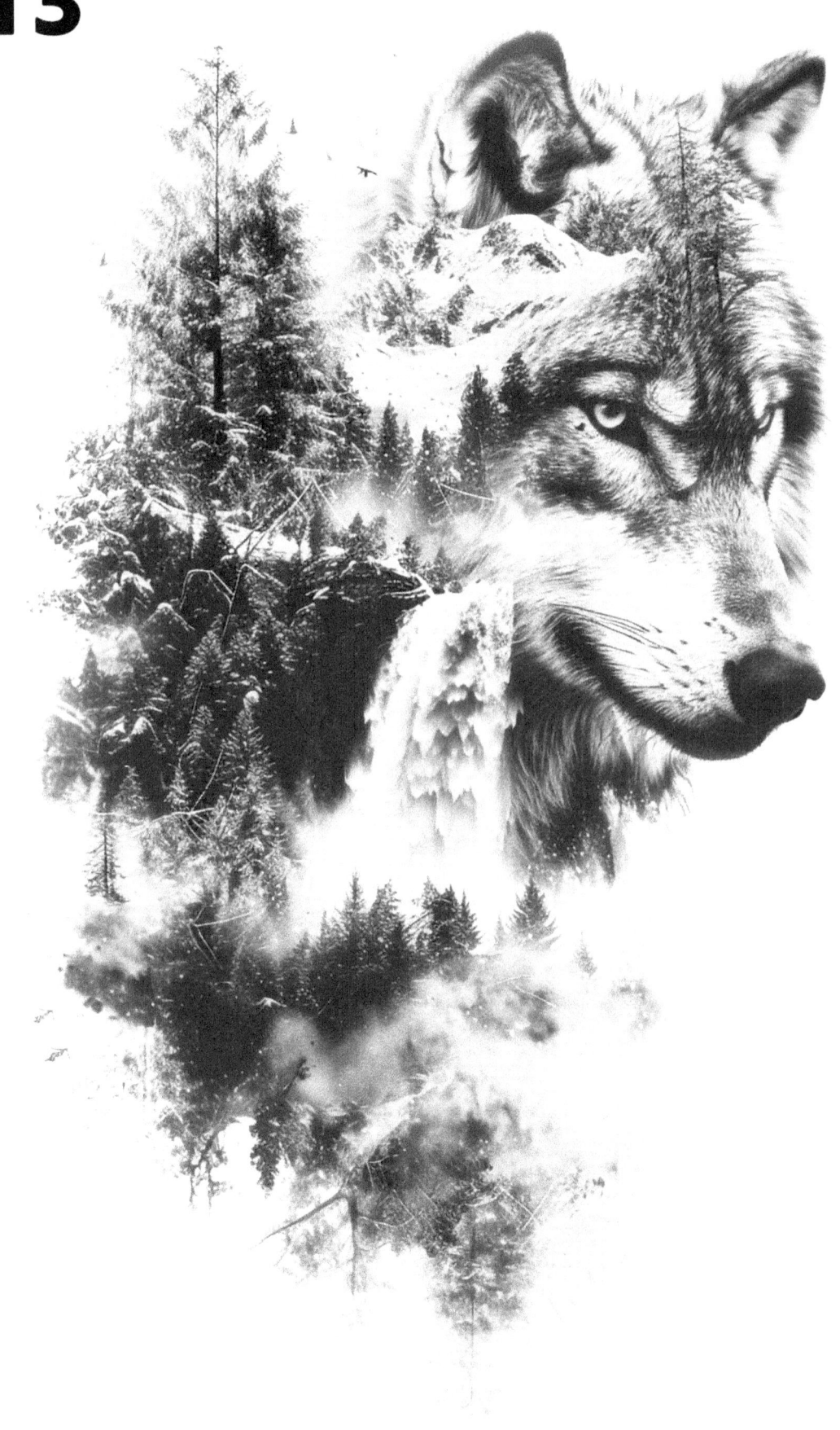

14

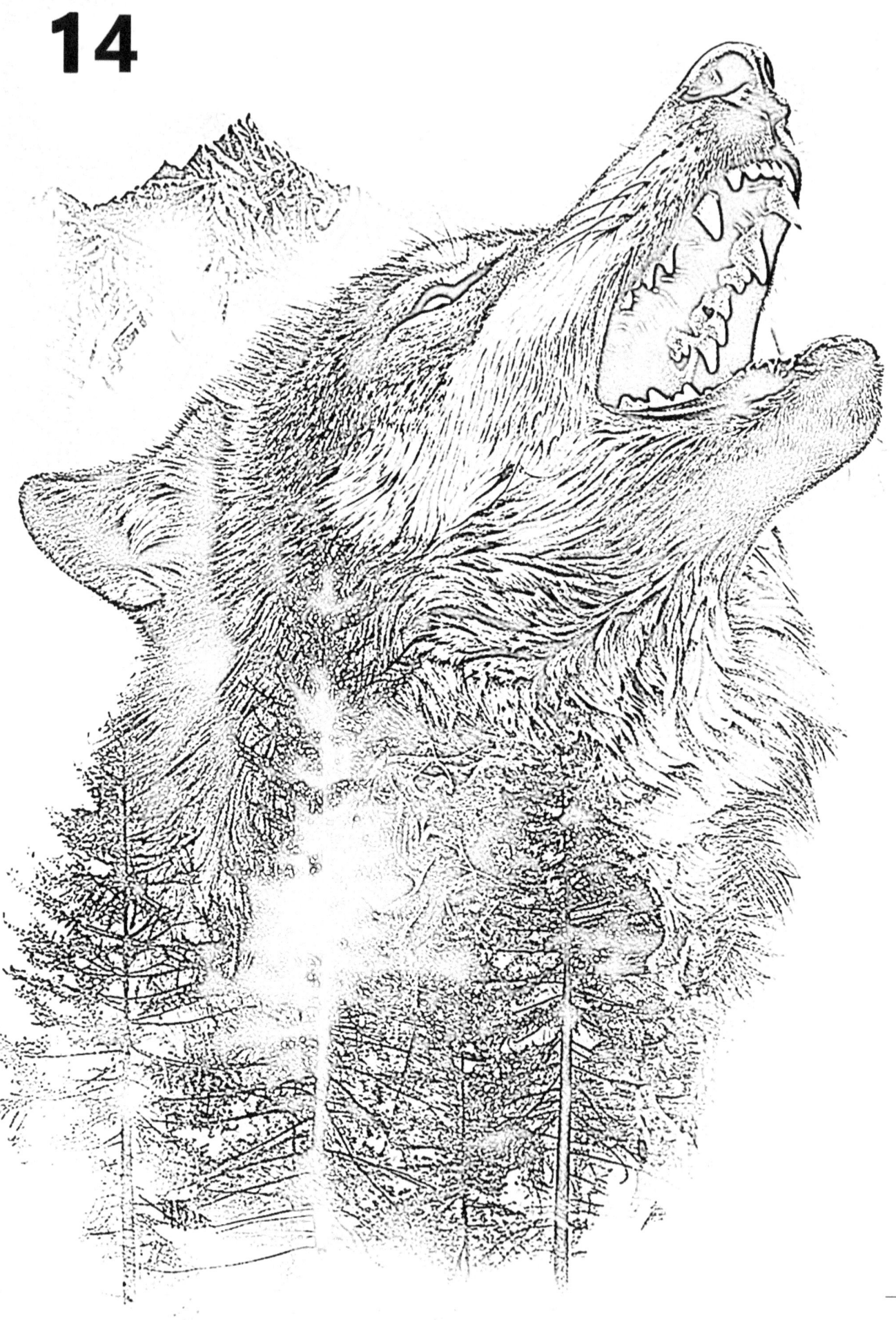

14

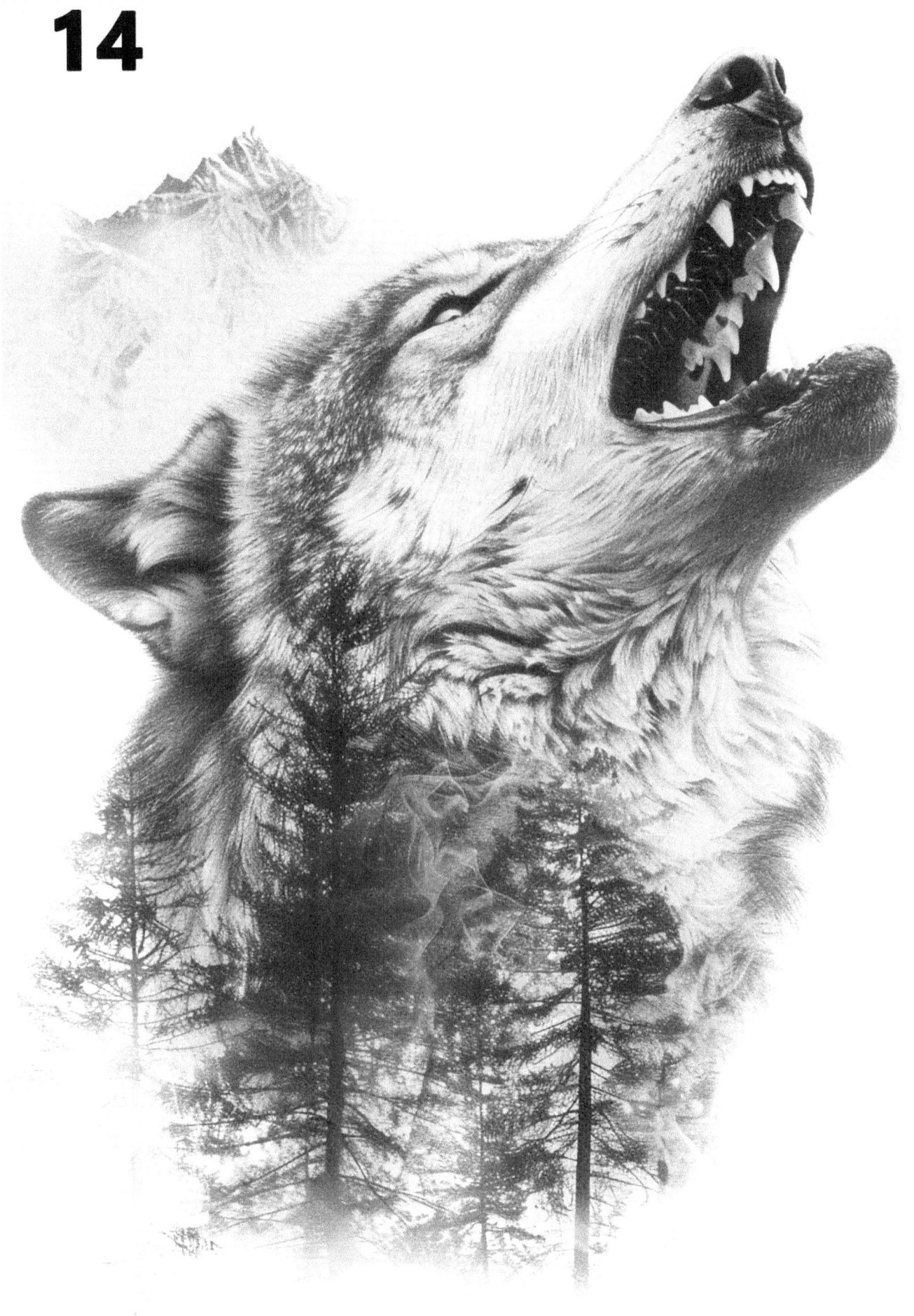

15

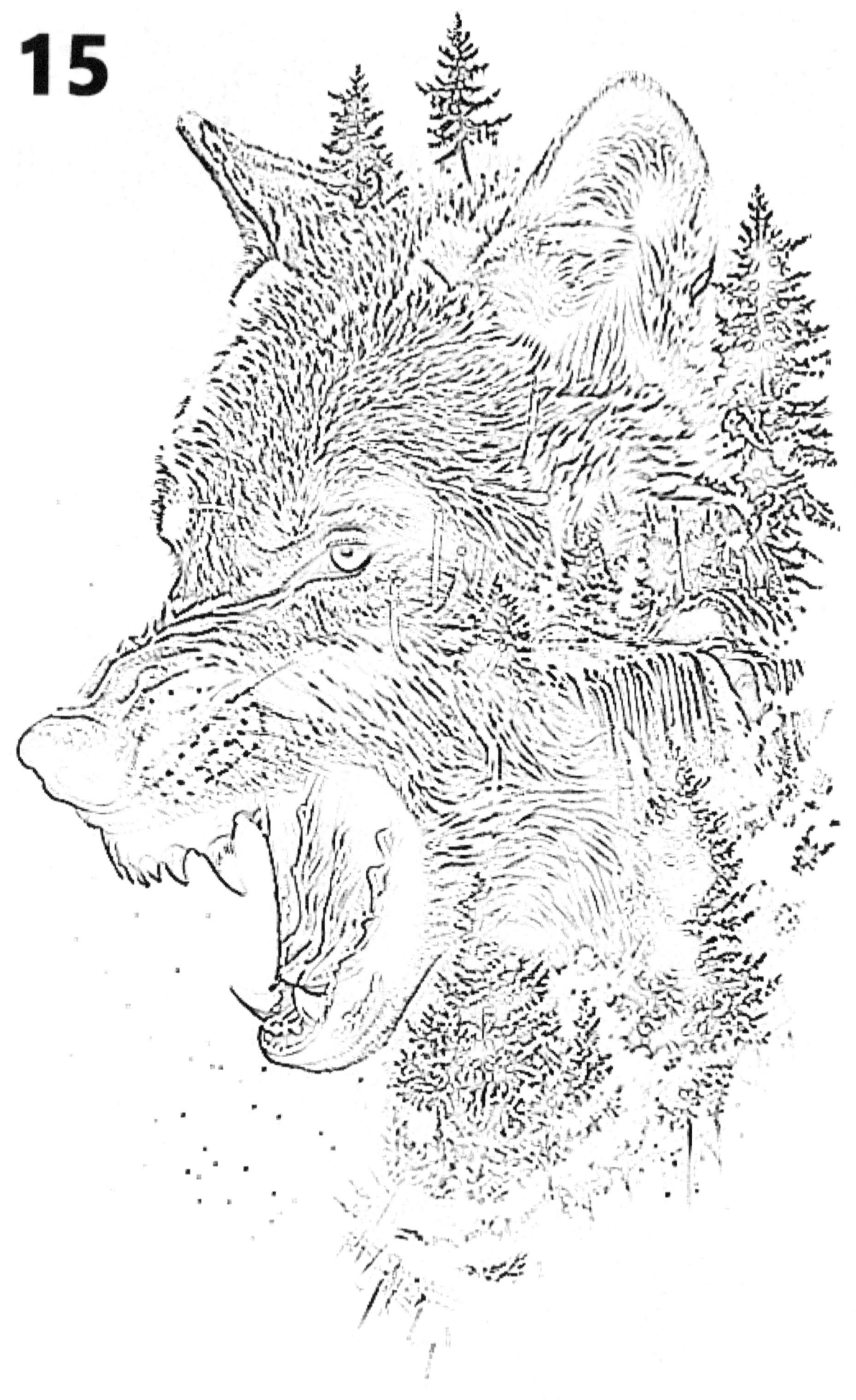

15

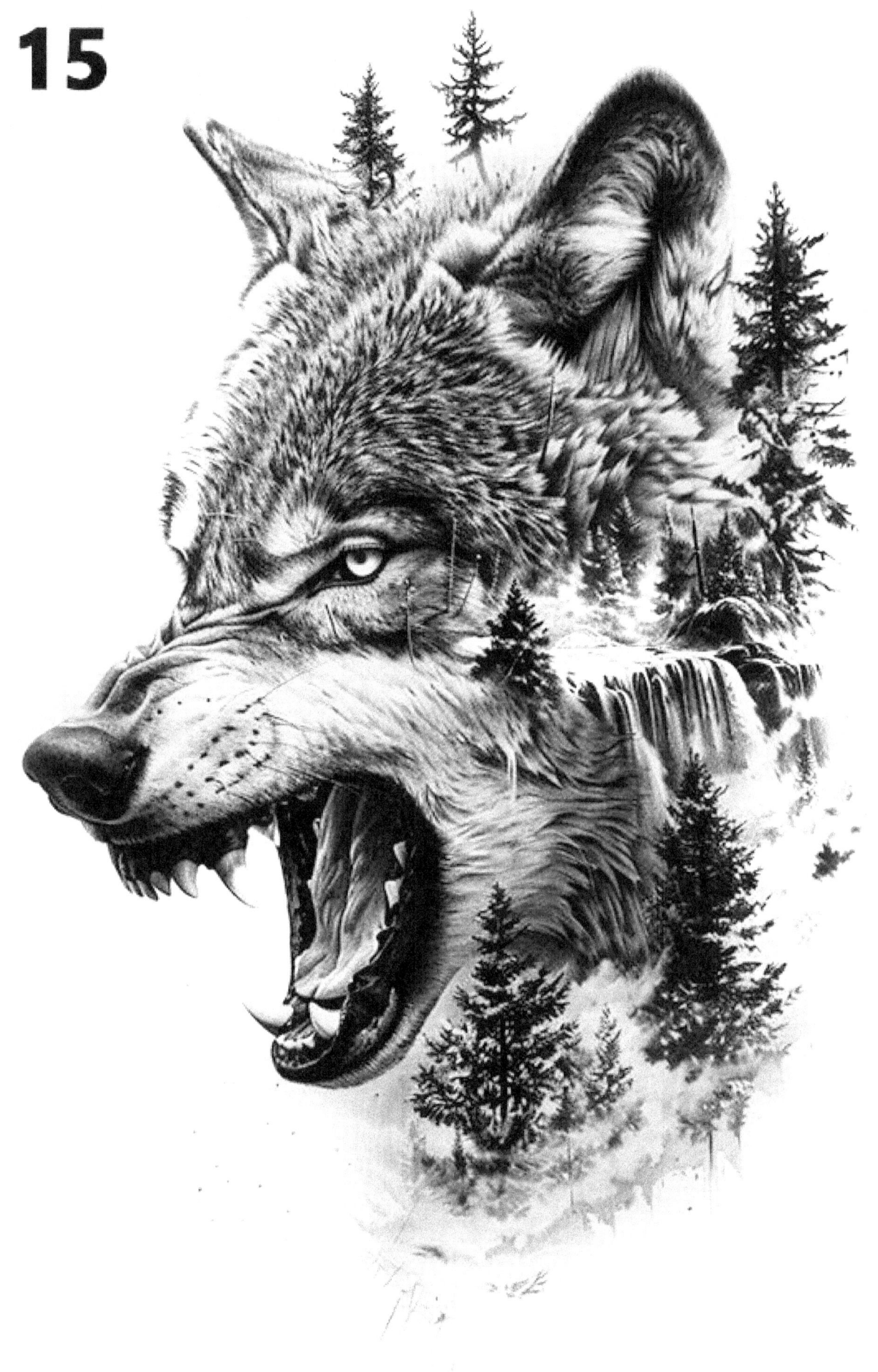

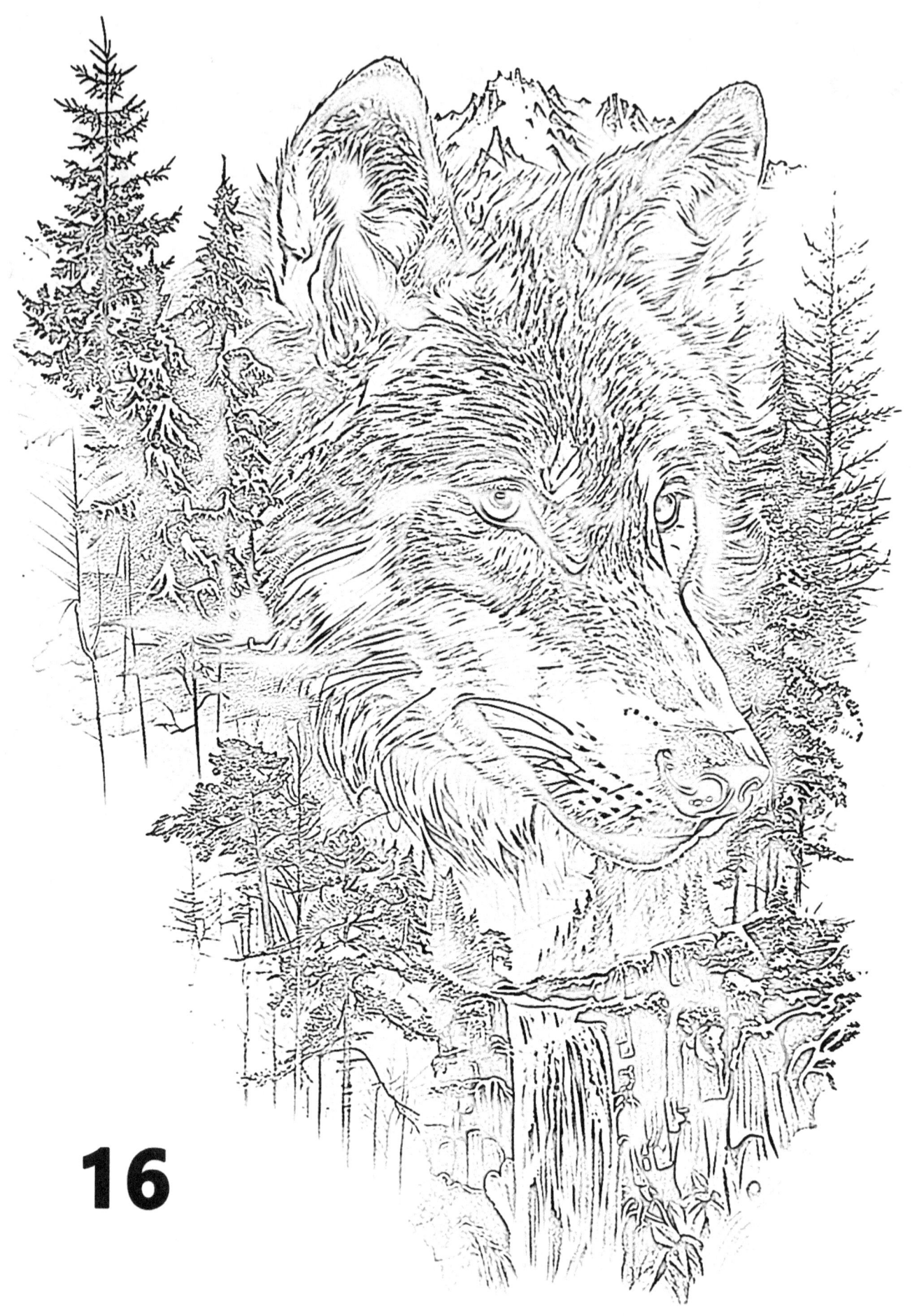

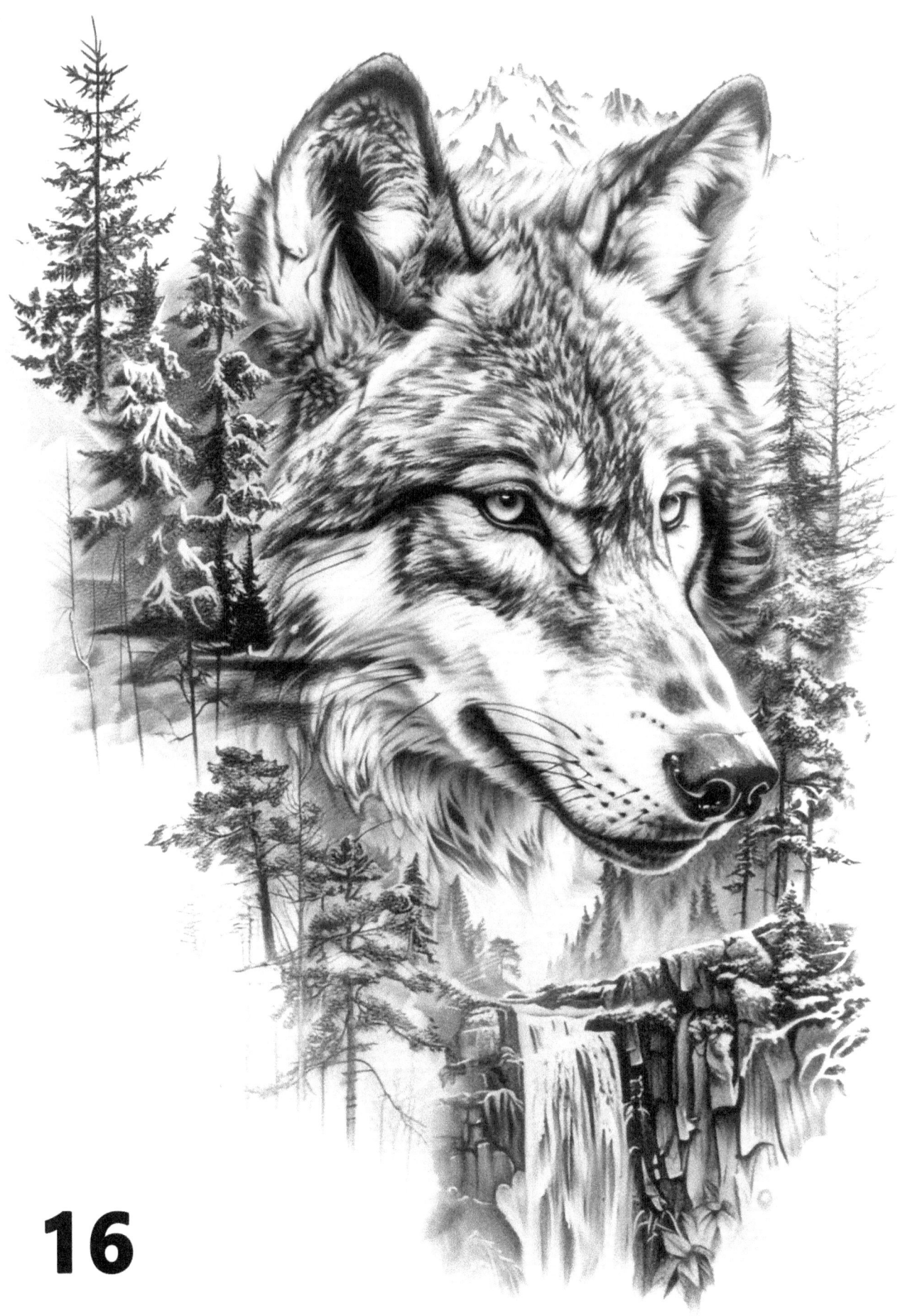

17

17

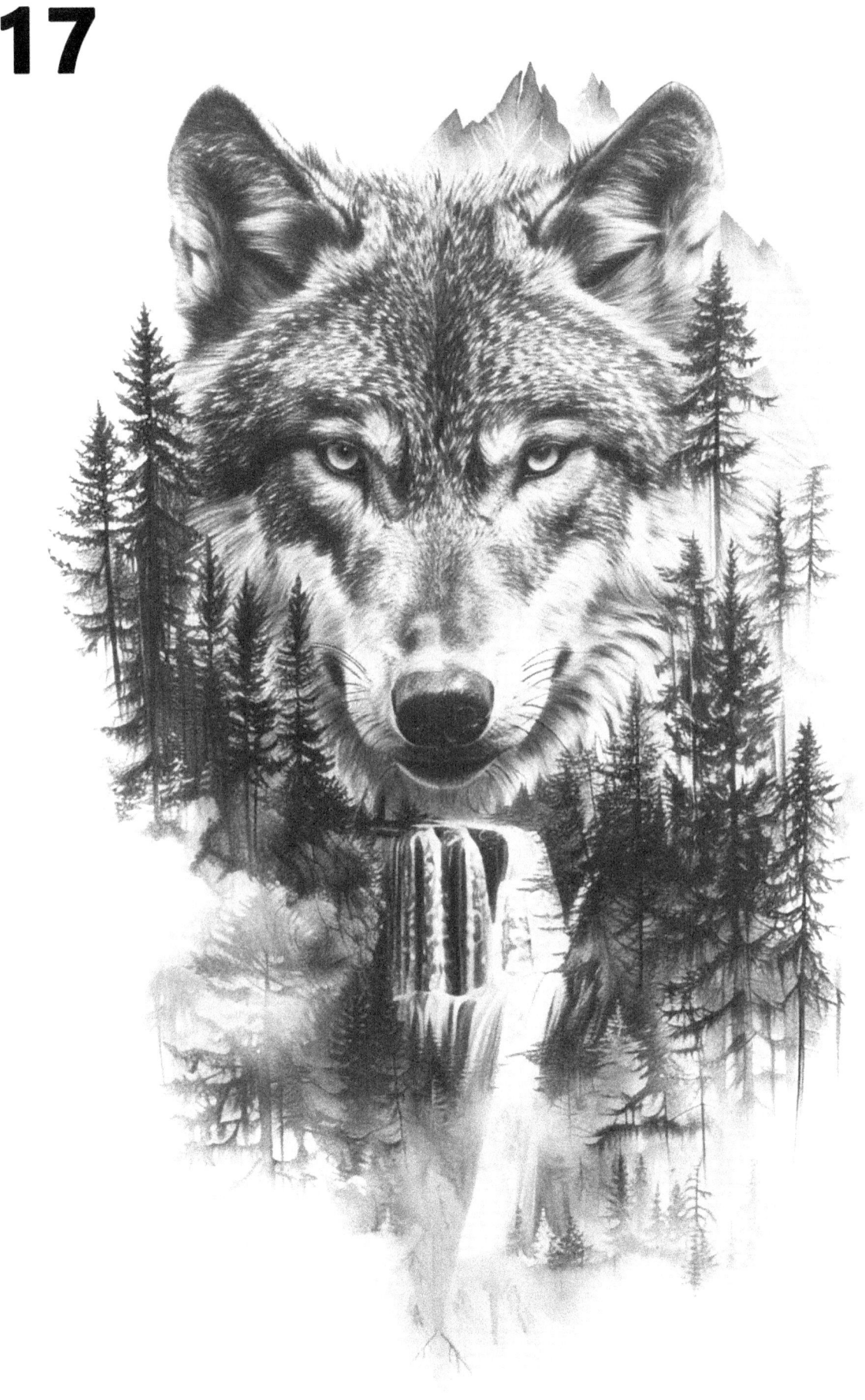

18

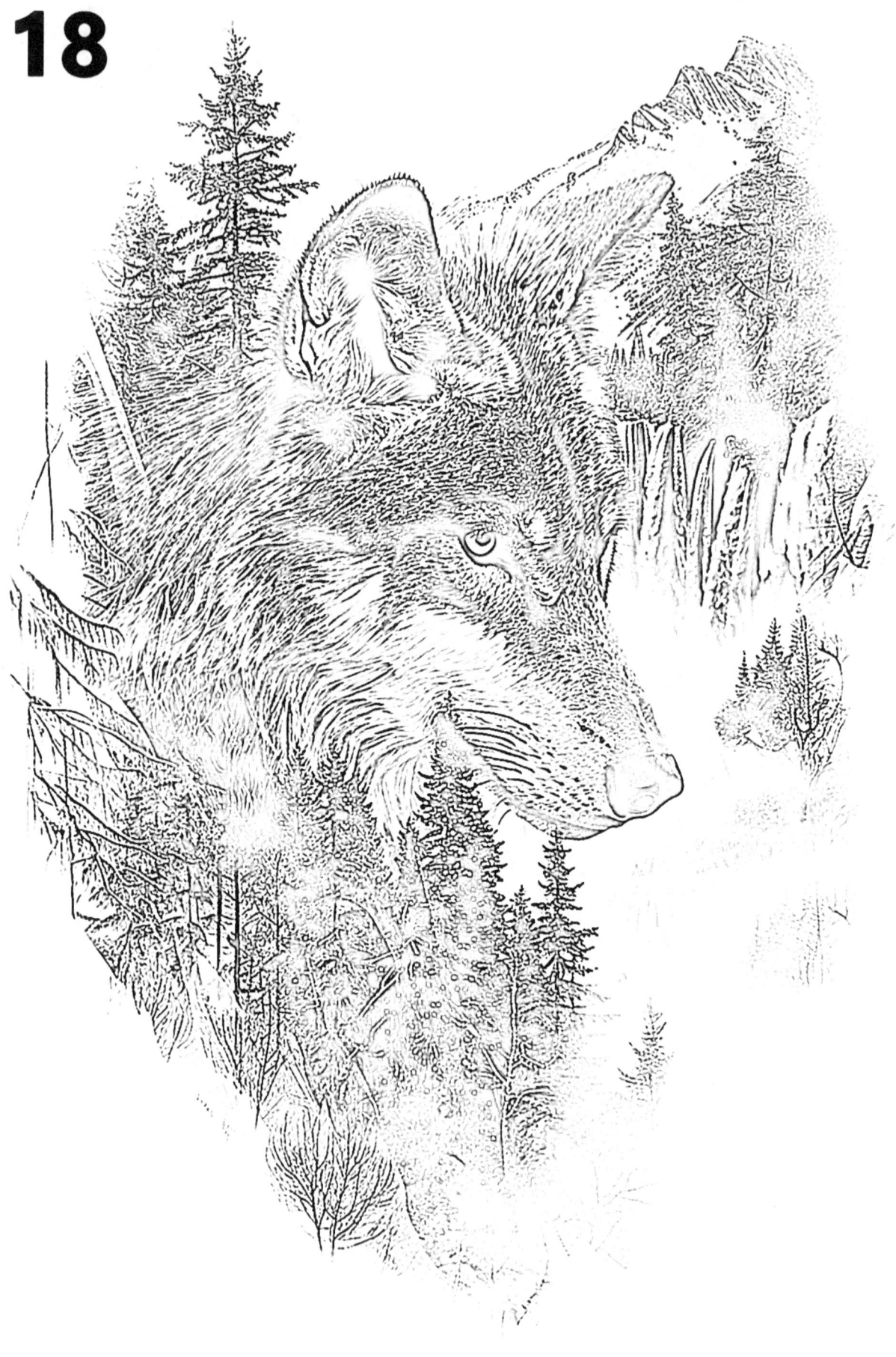

18

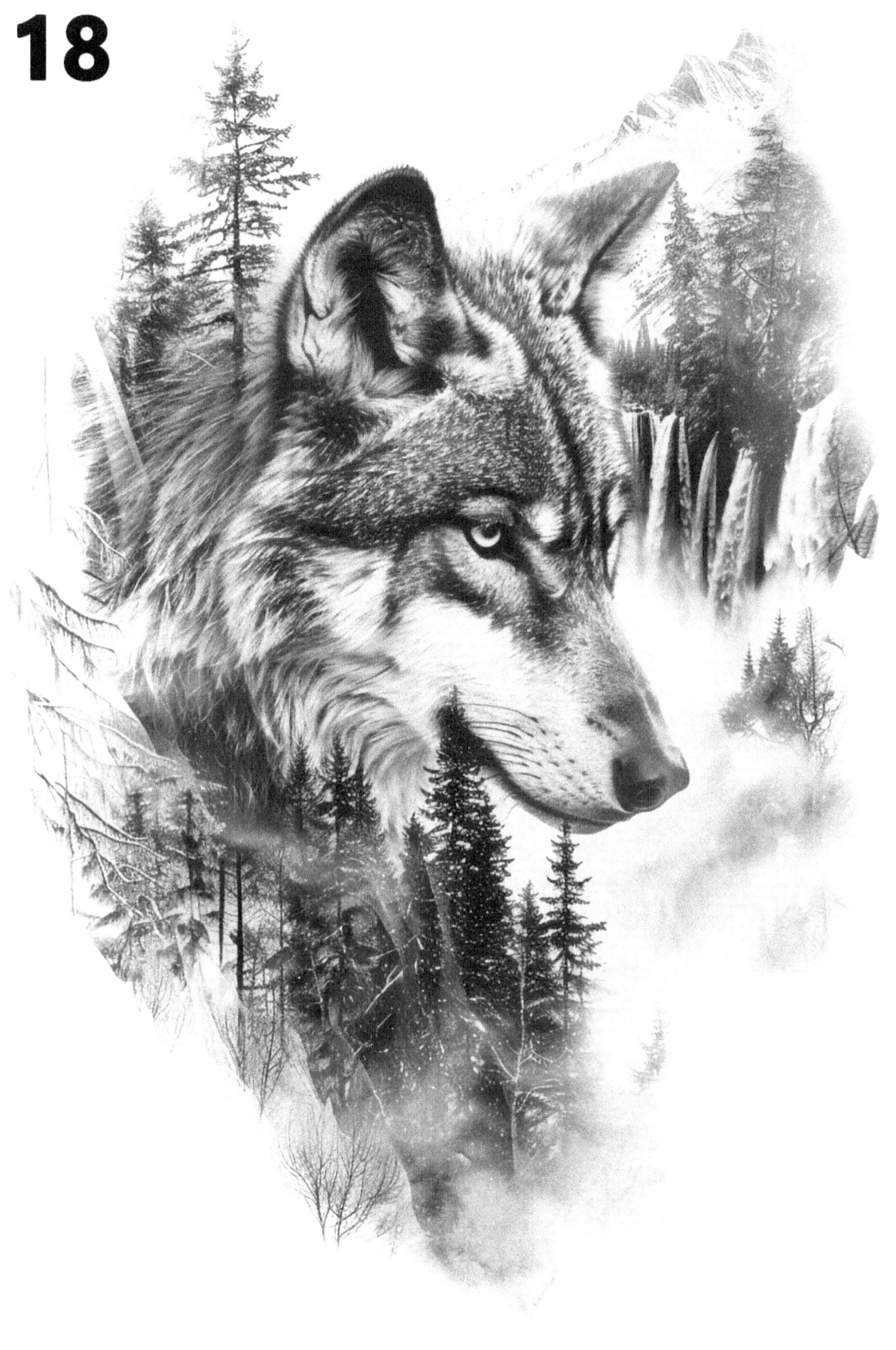

19

19

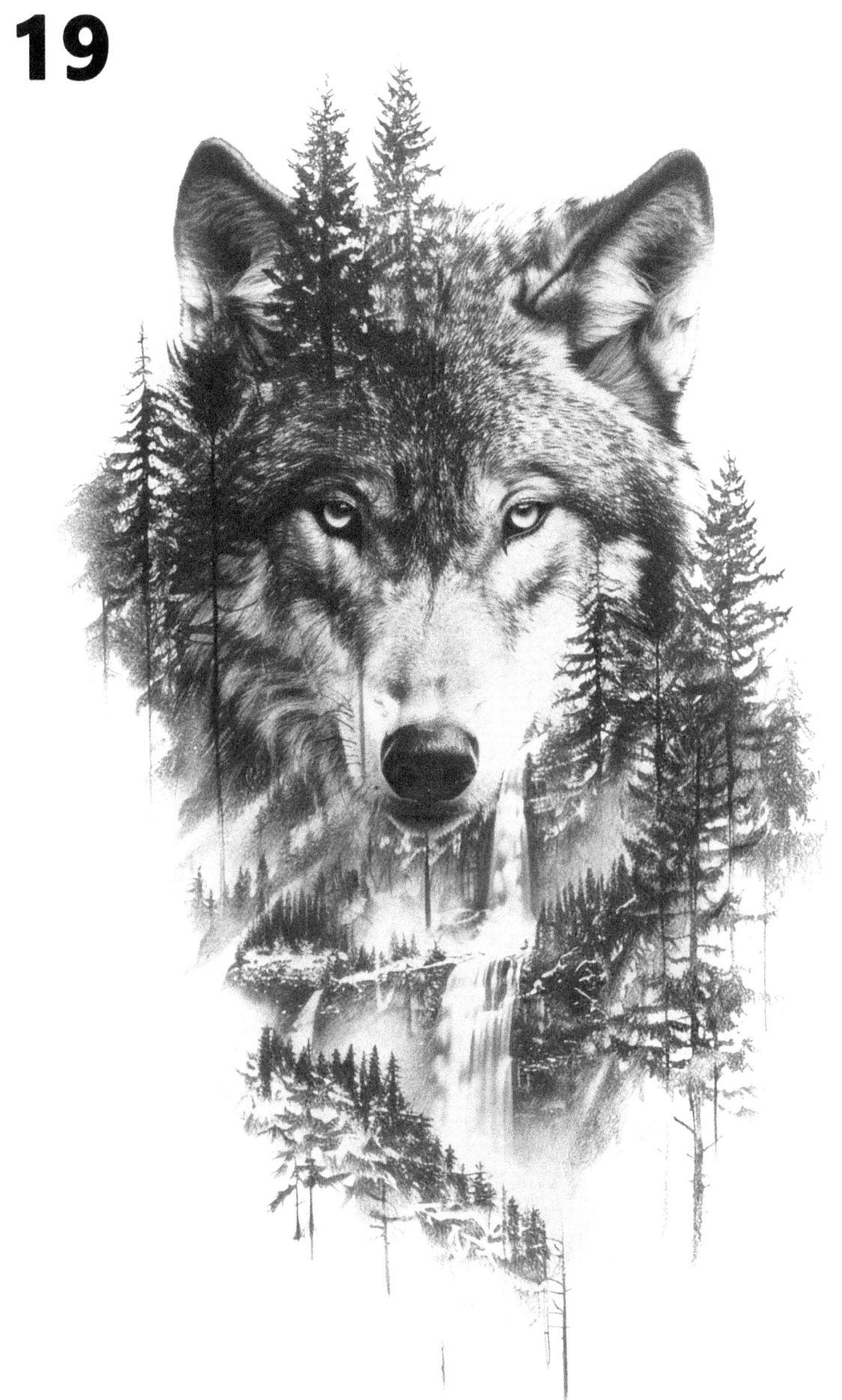

20

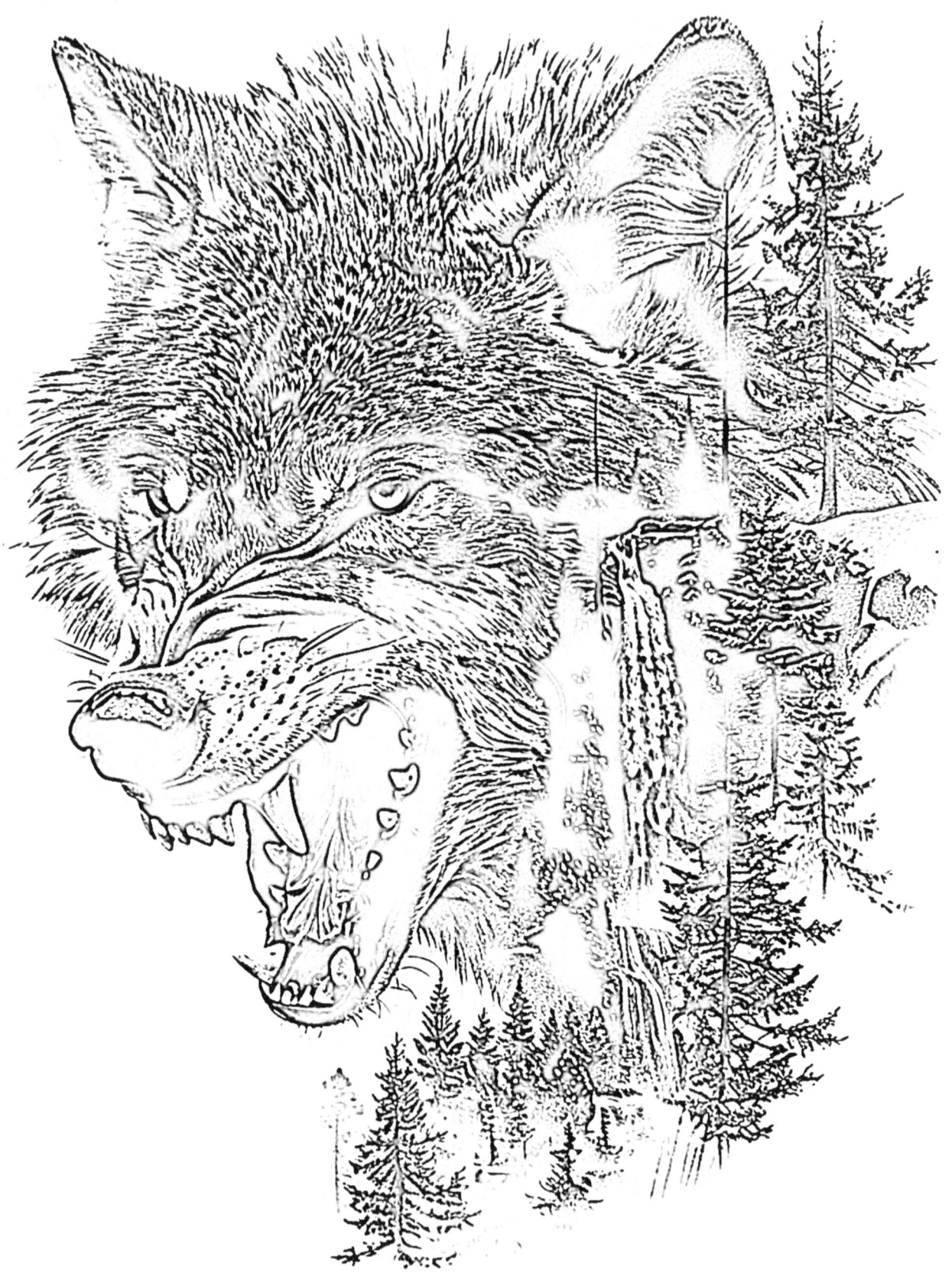

20

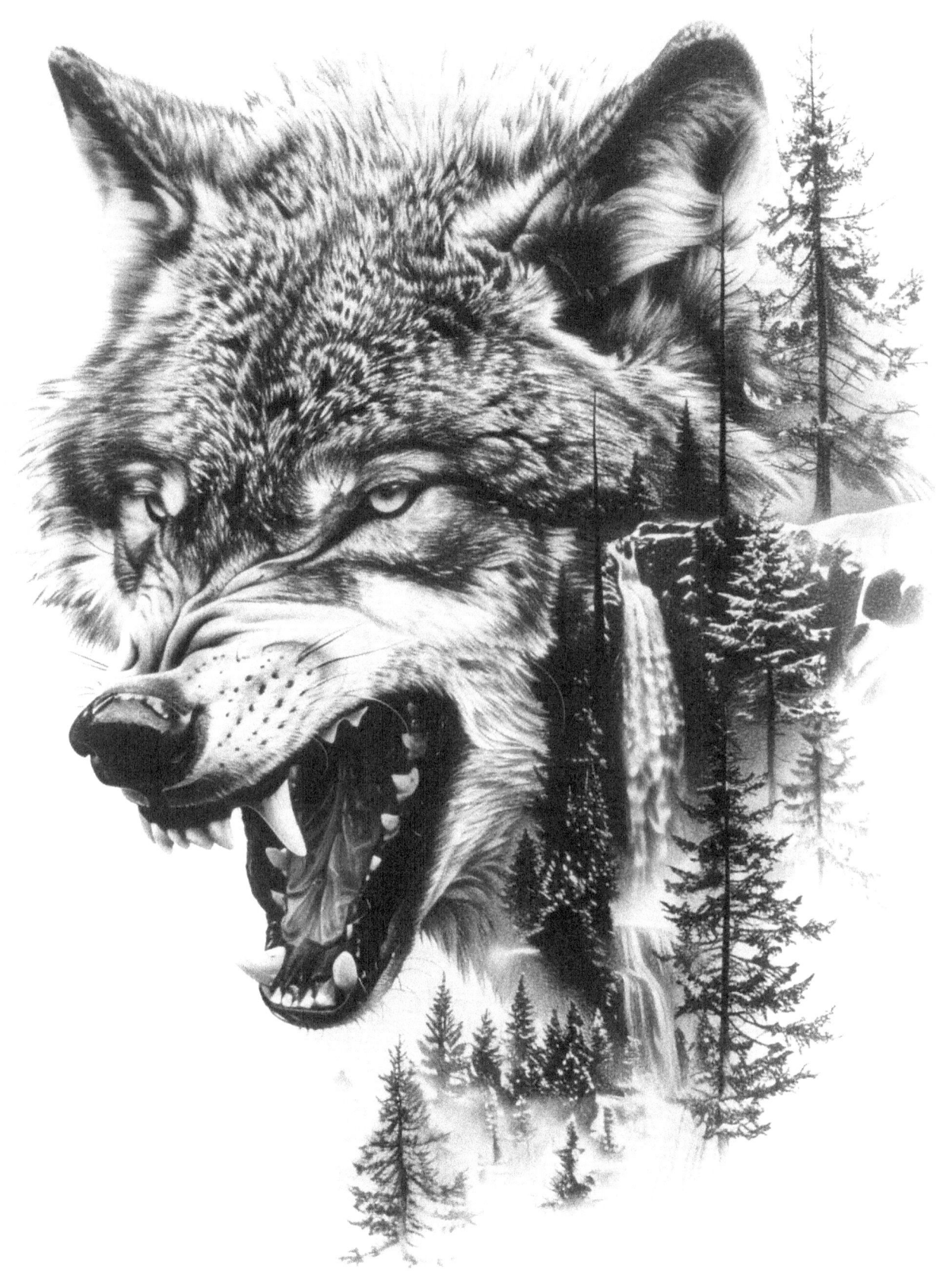

21

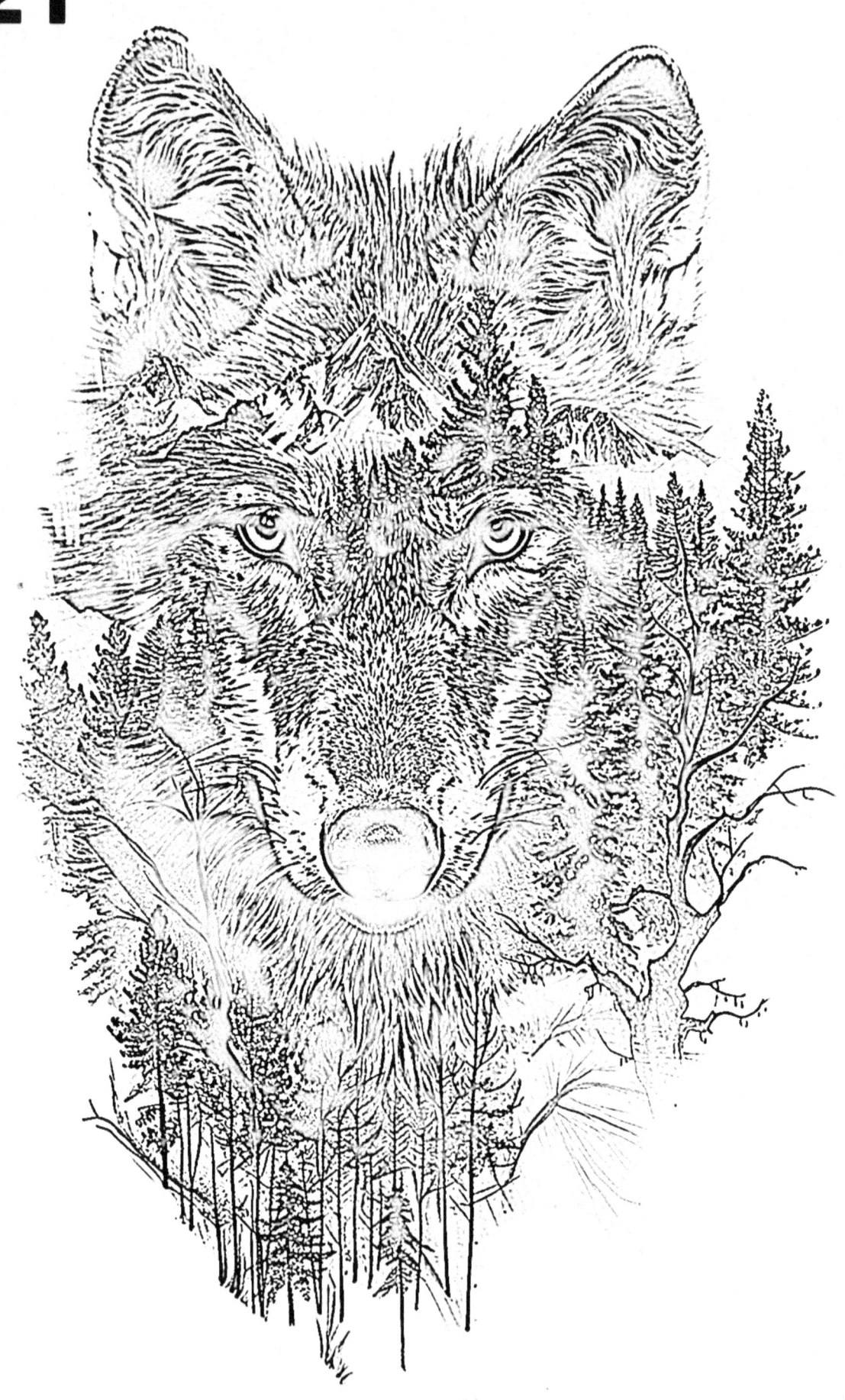

21

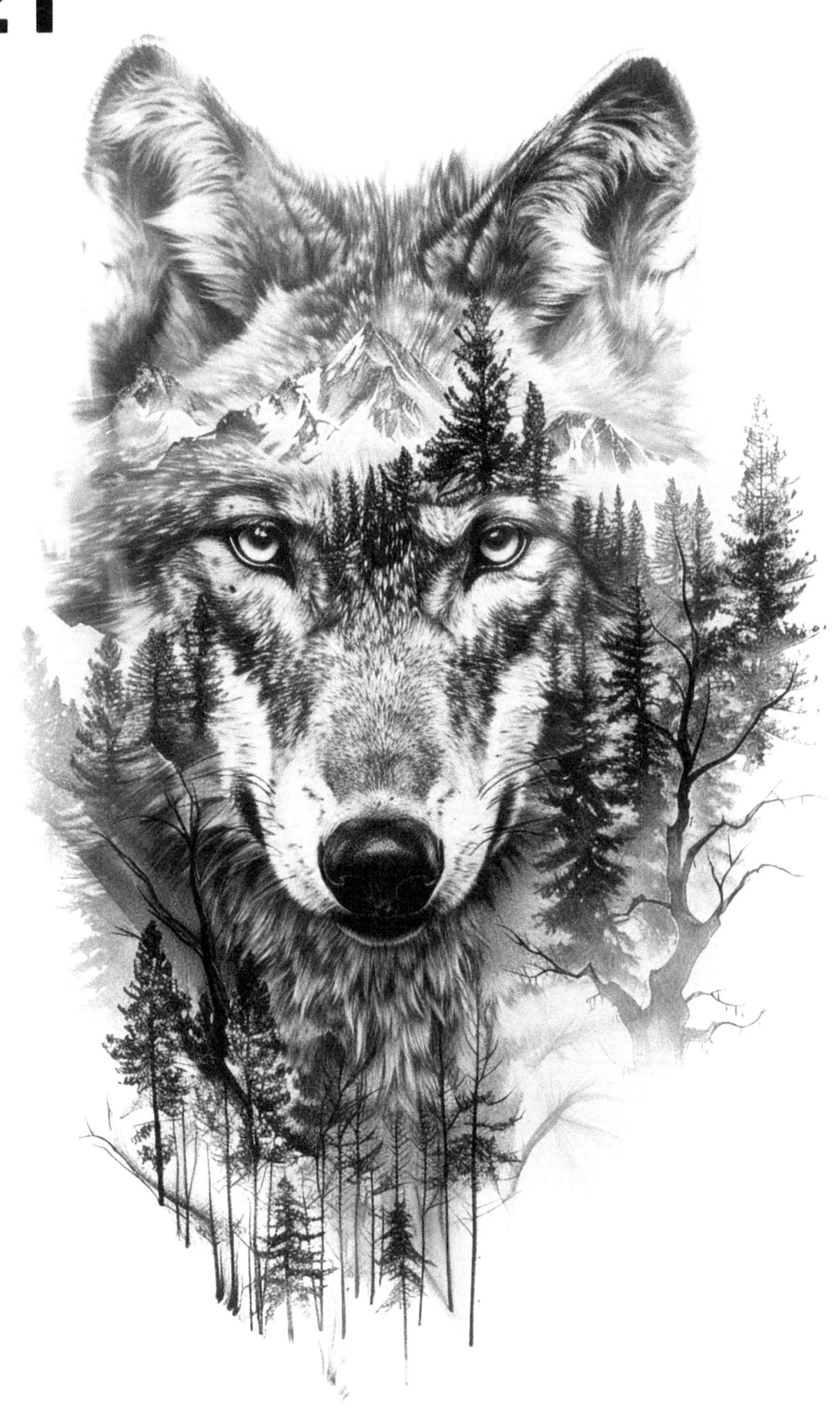

22

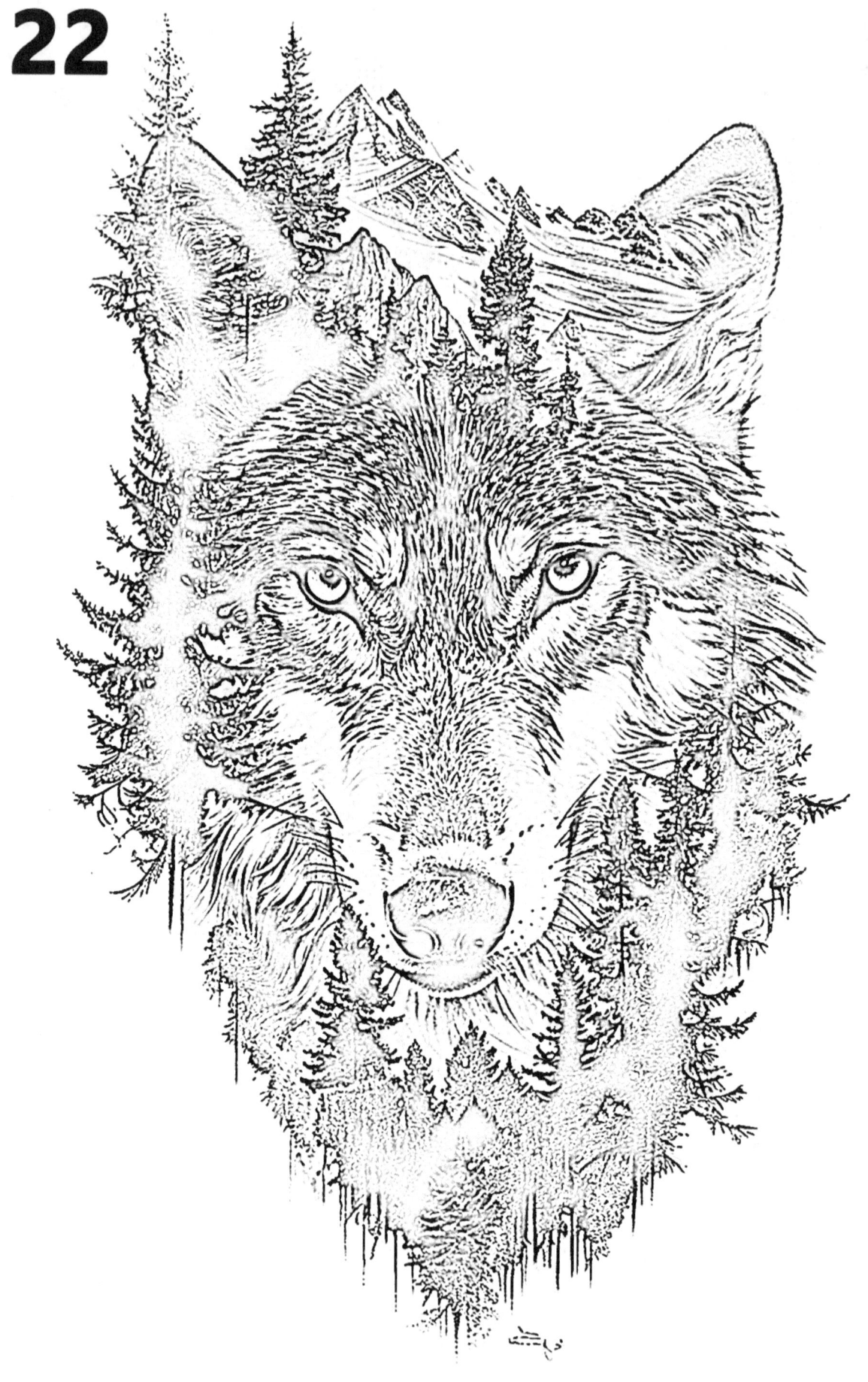

22

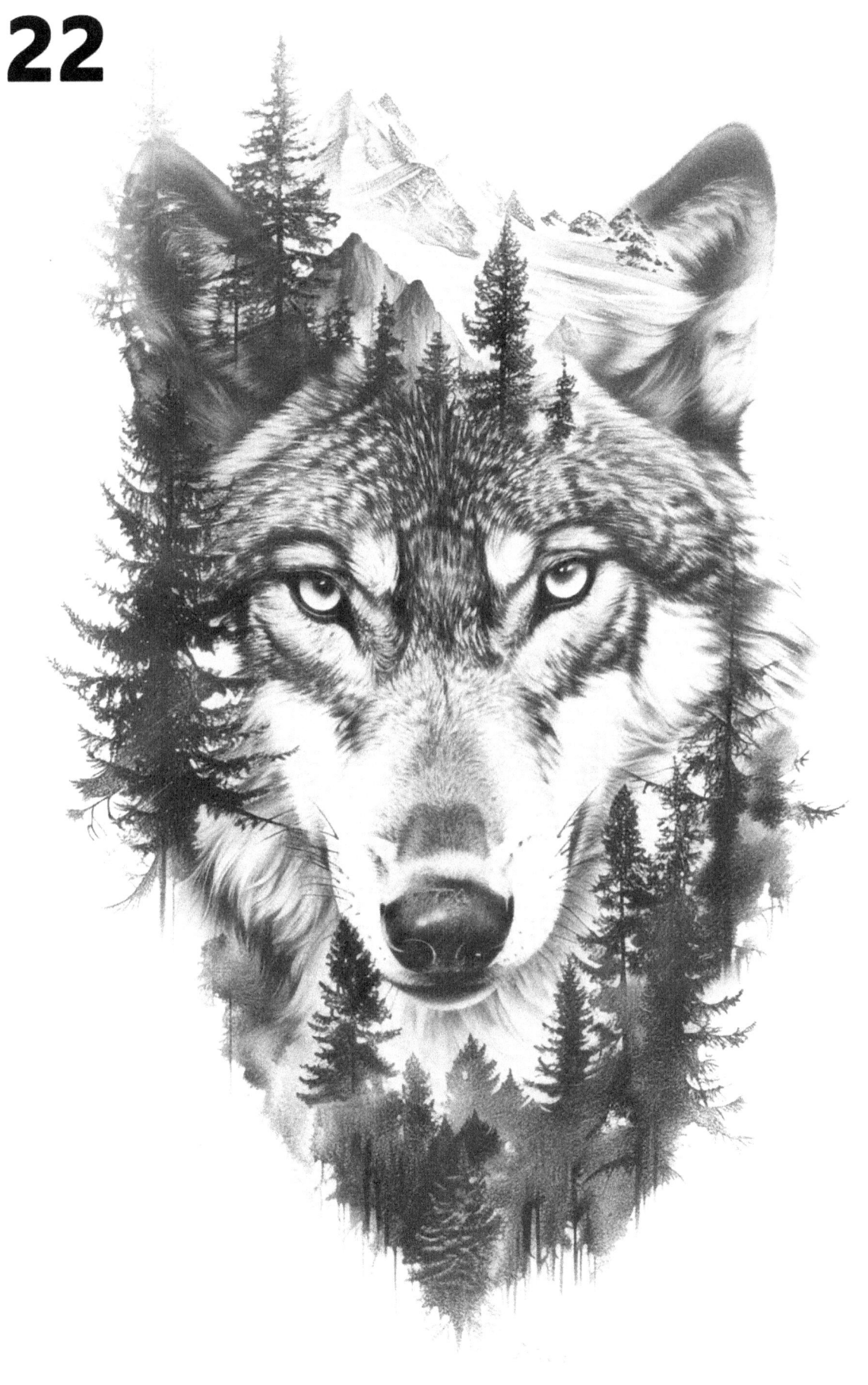

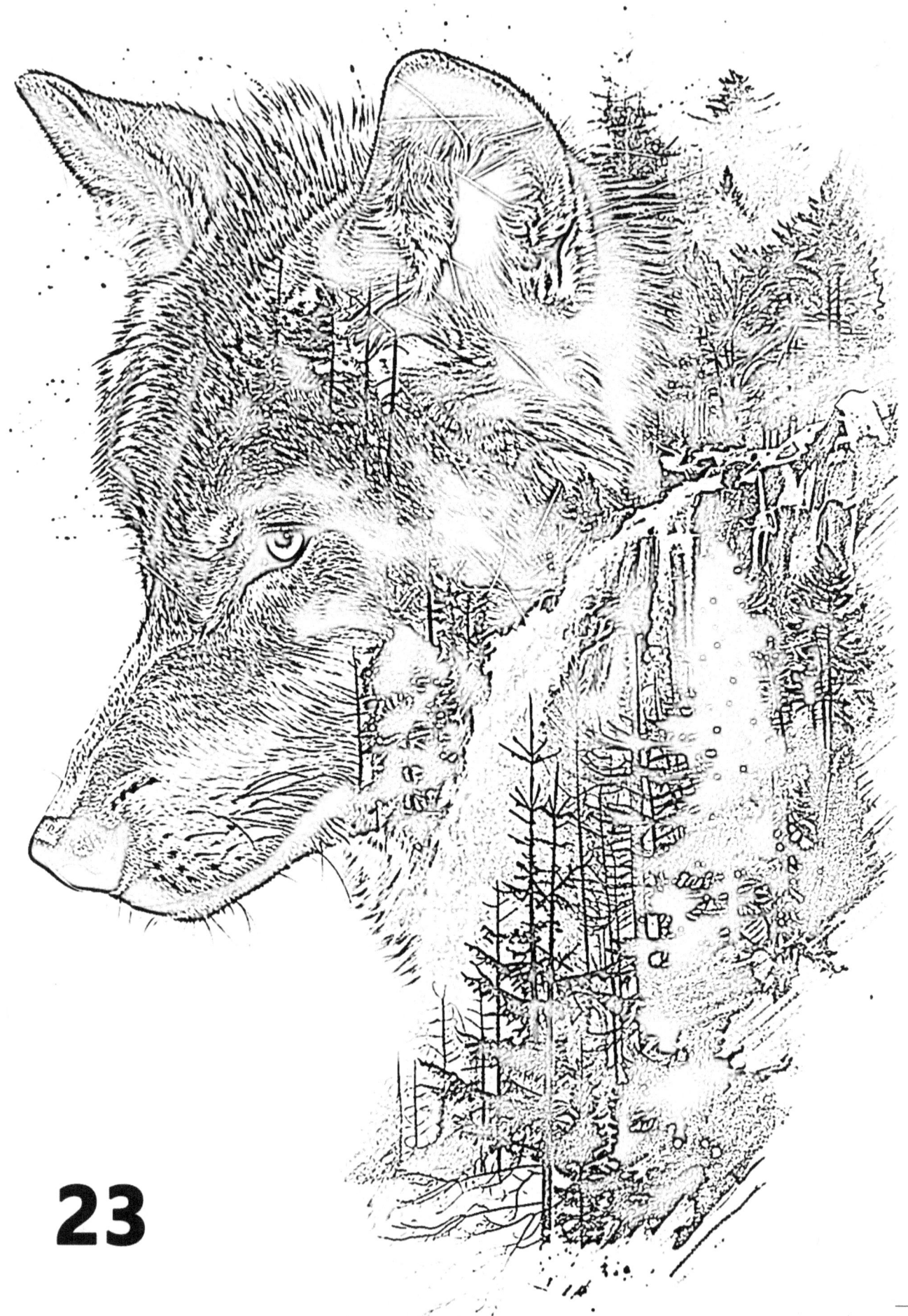

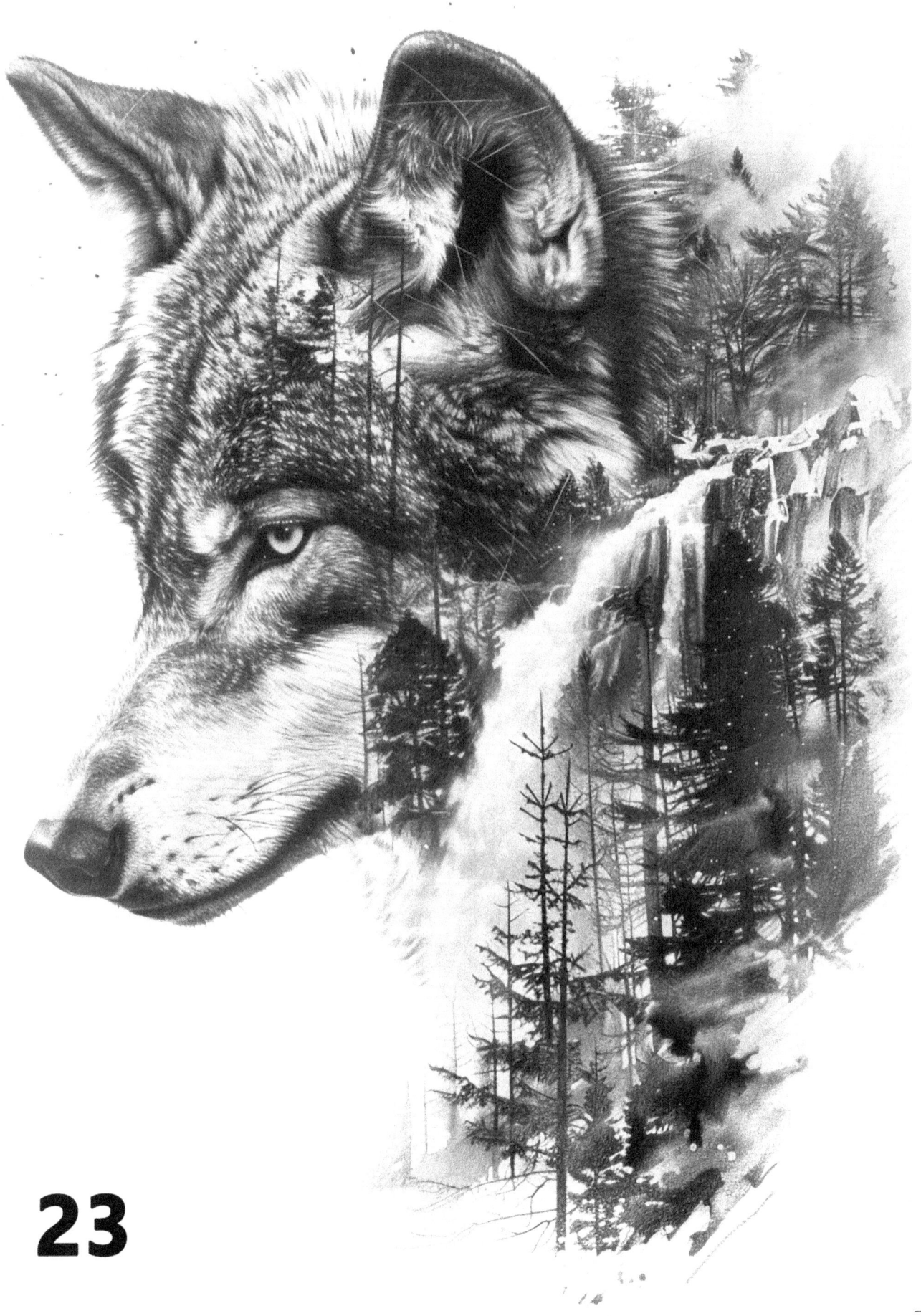

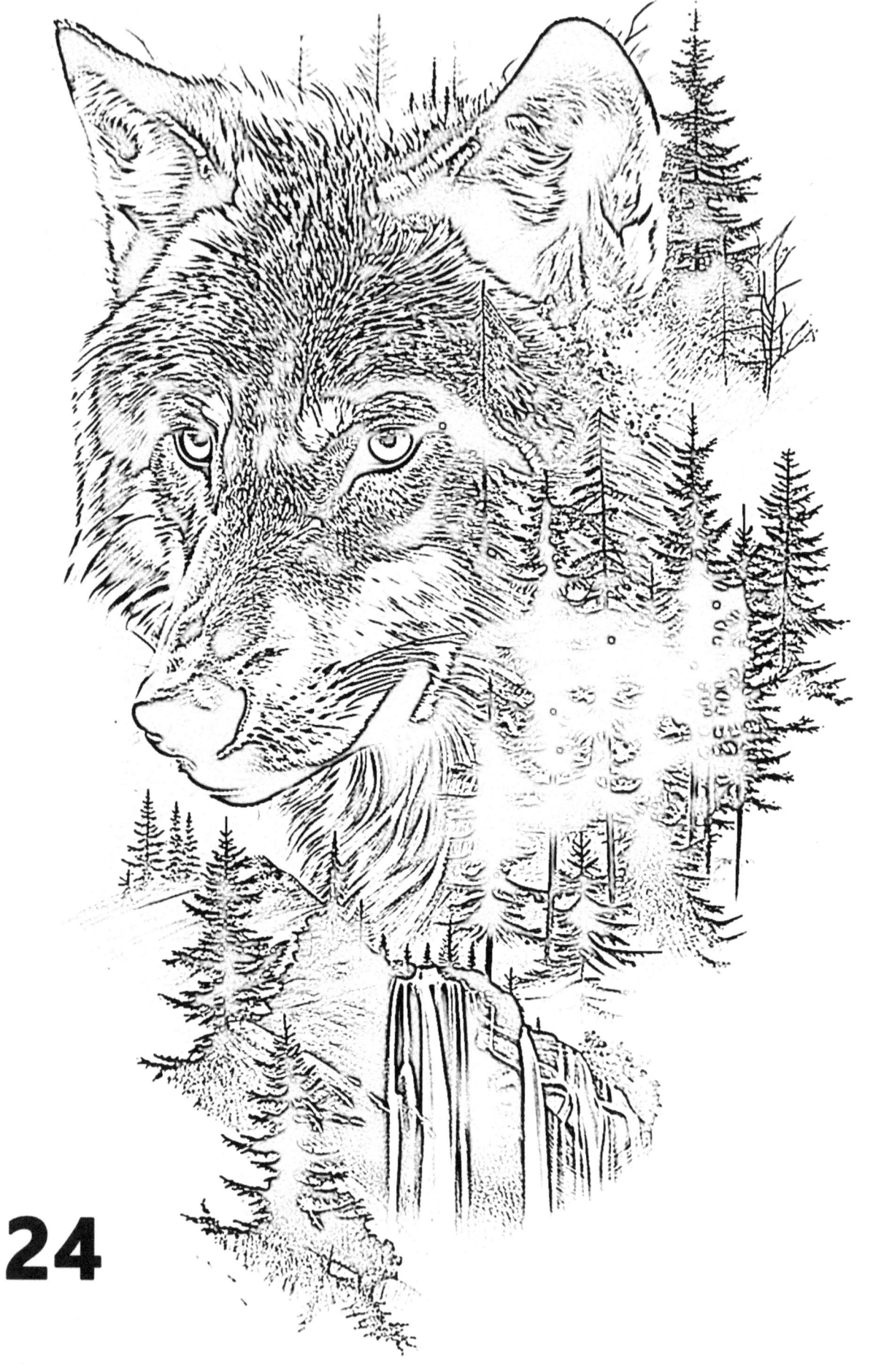
24

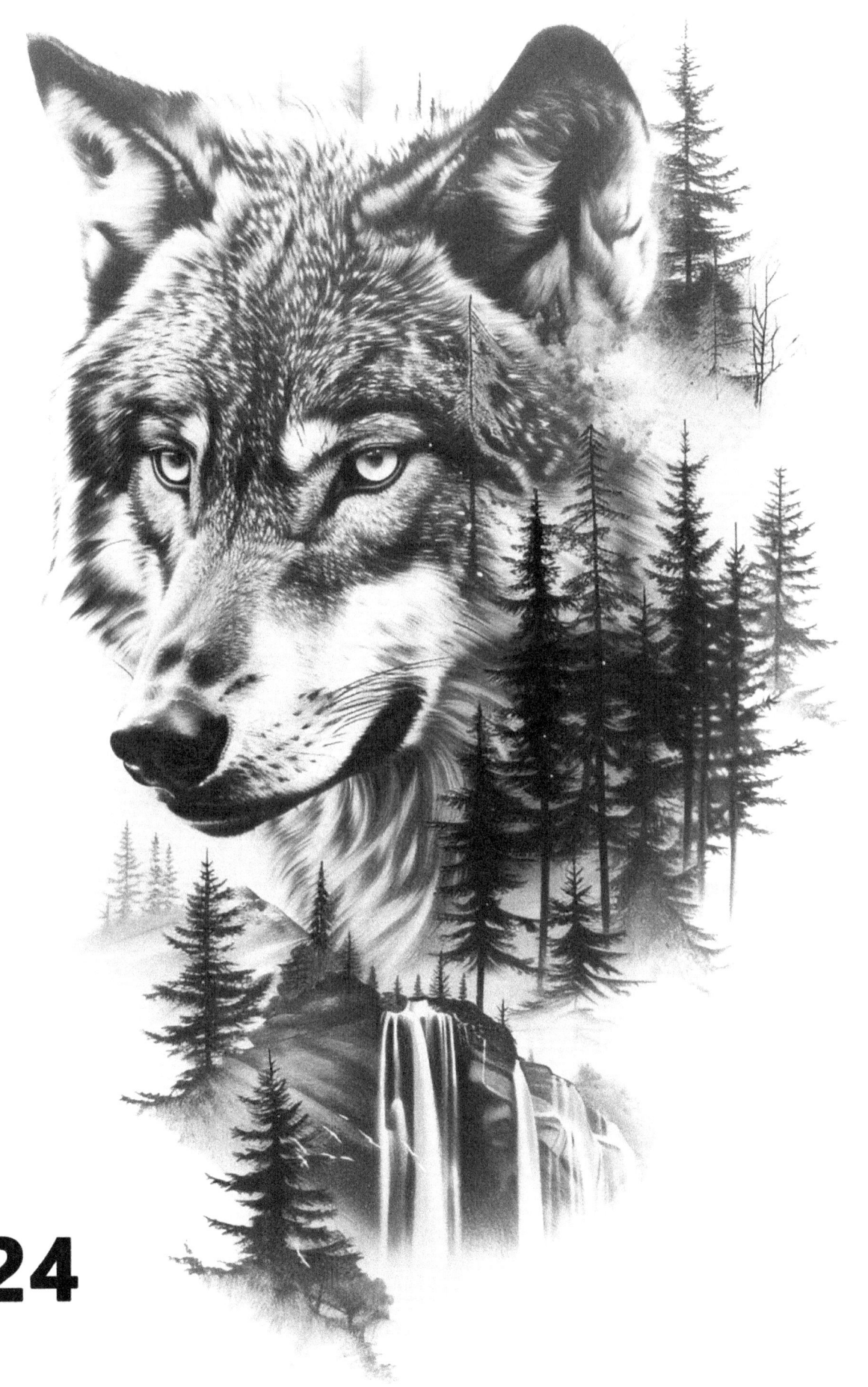

25

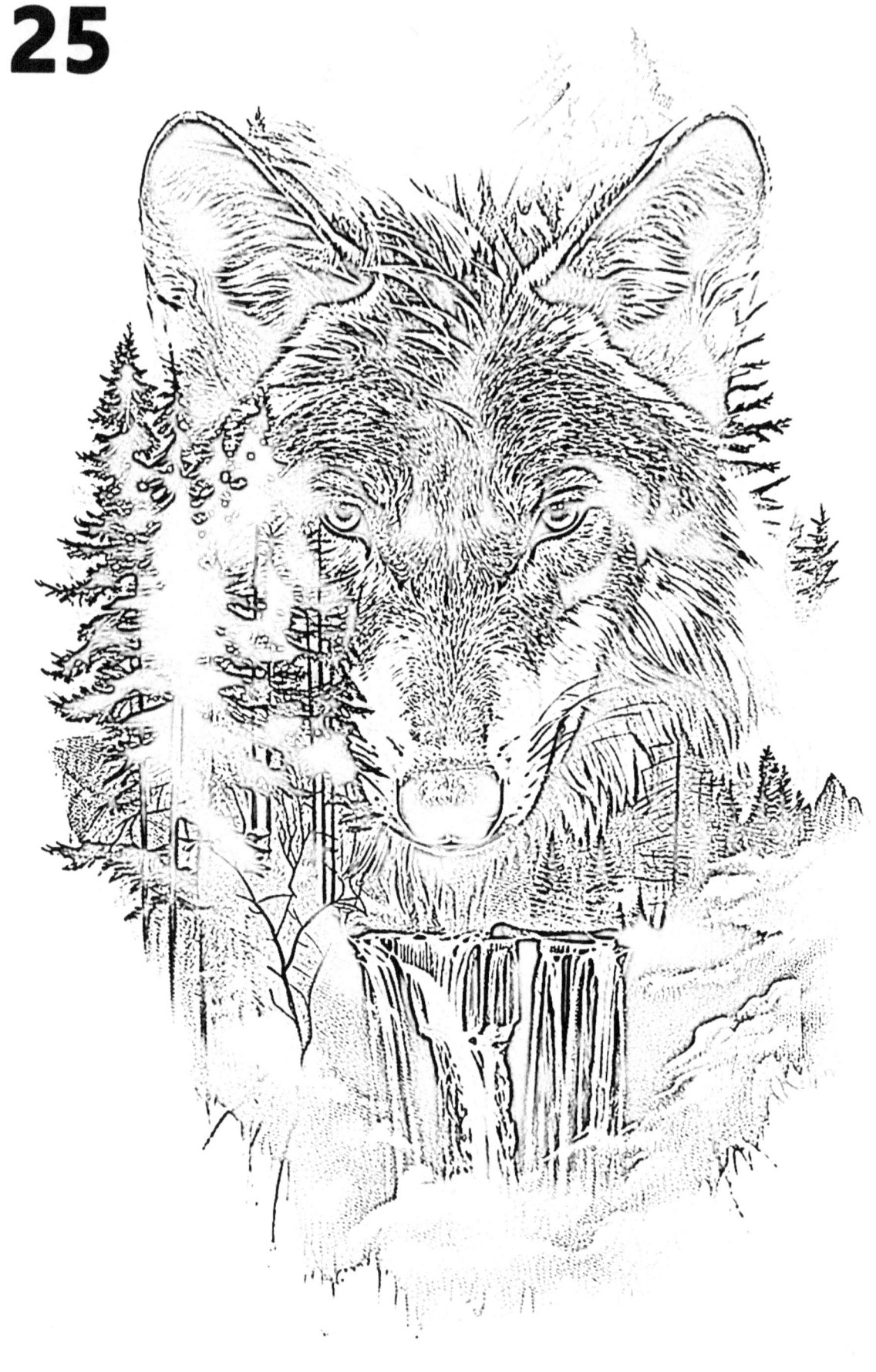

25

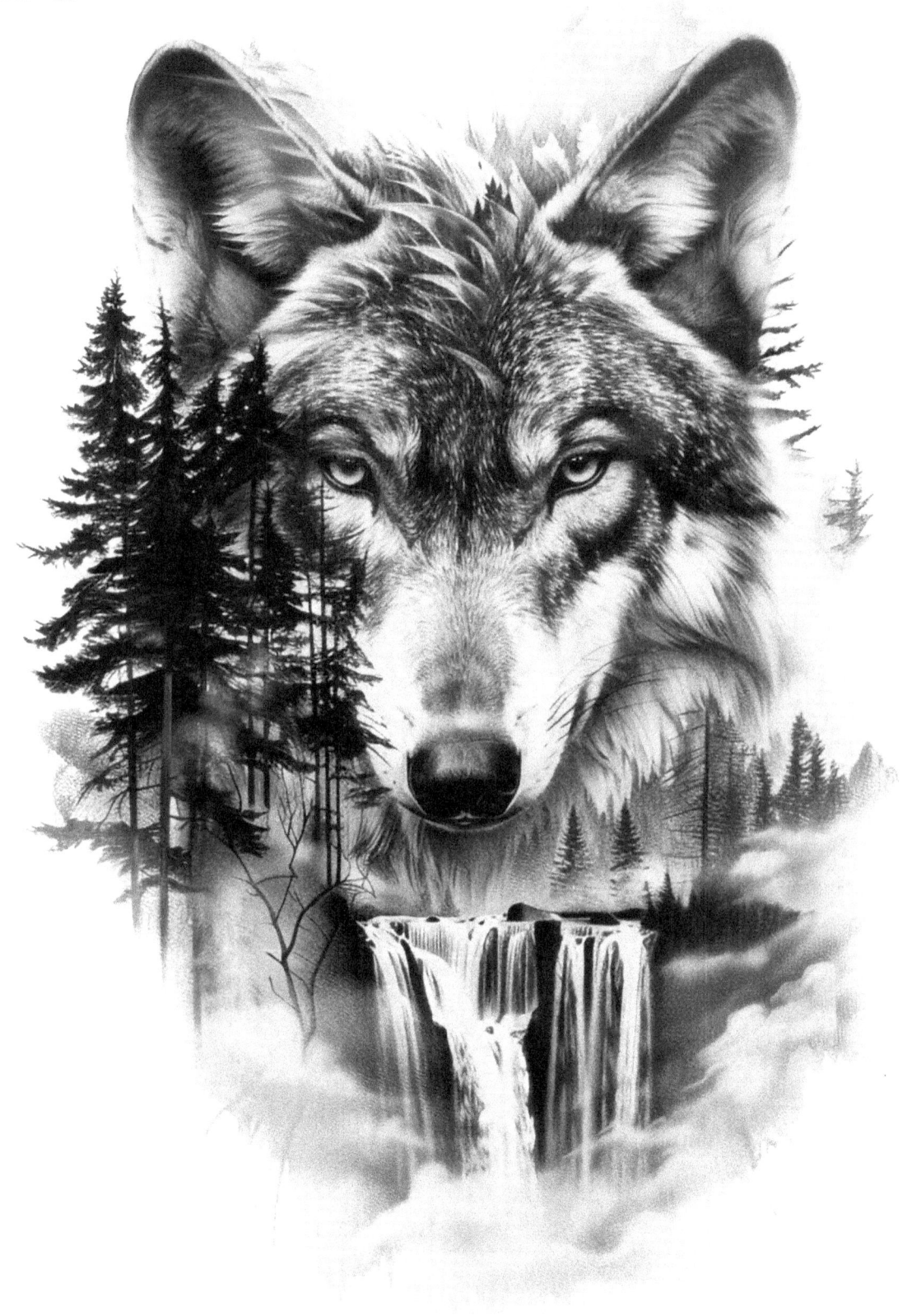

26

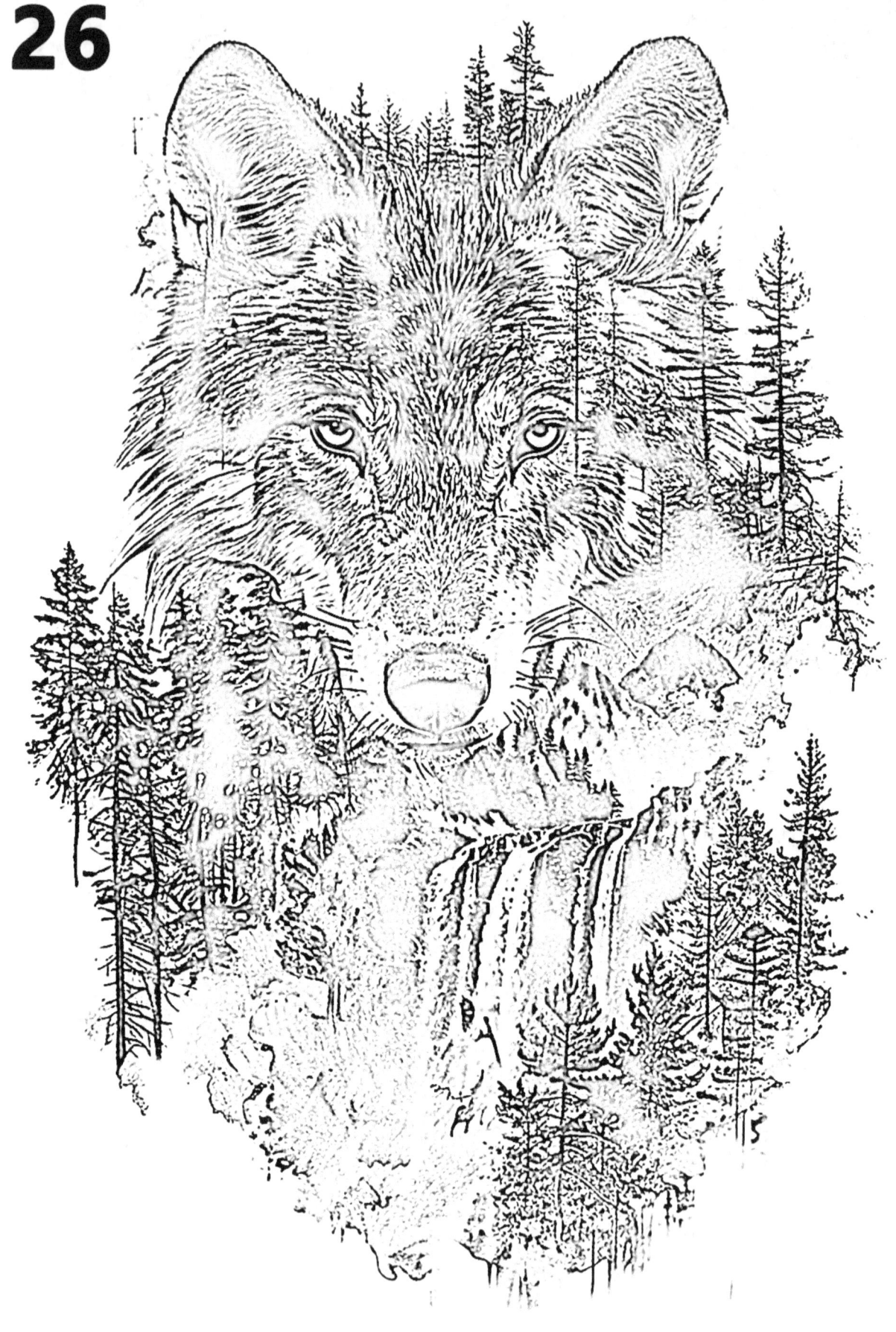

26

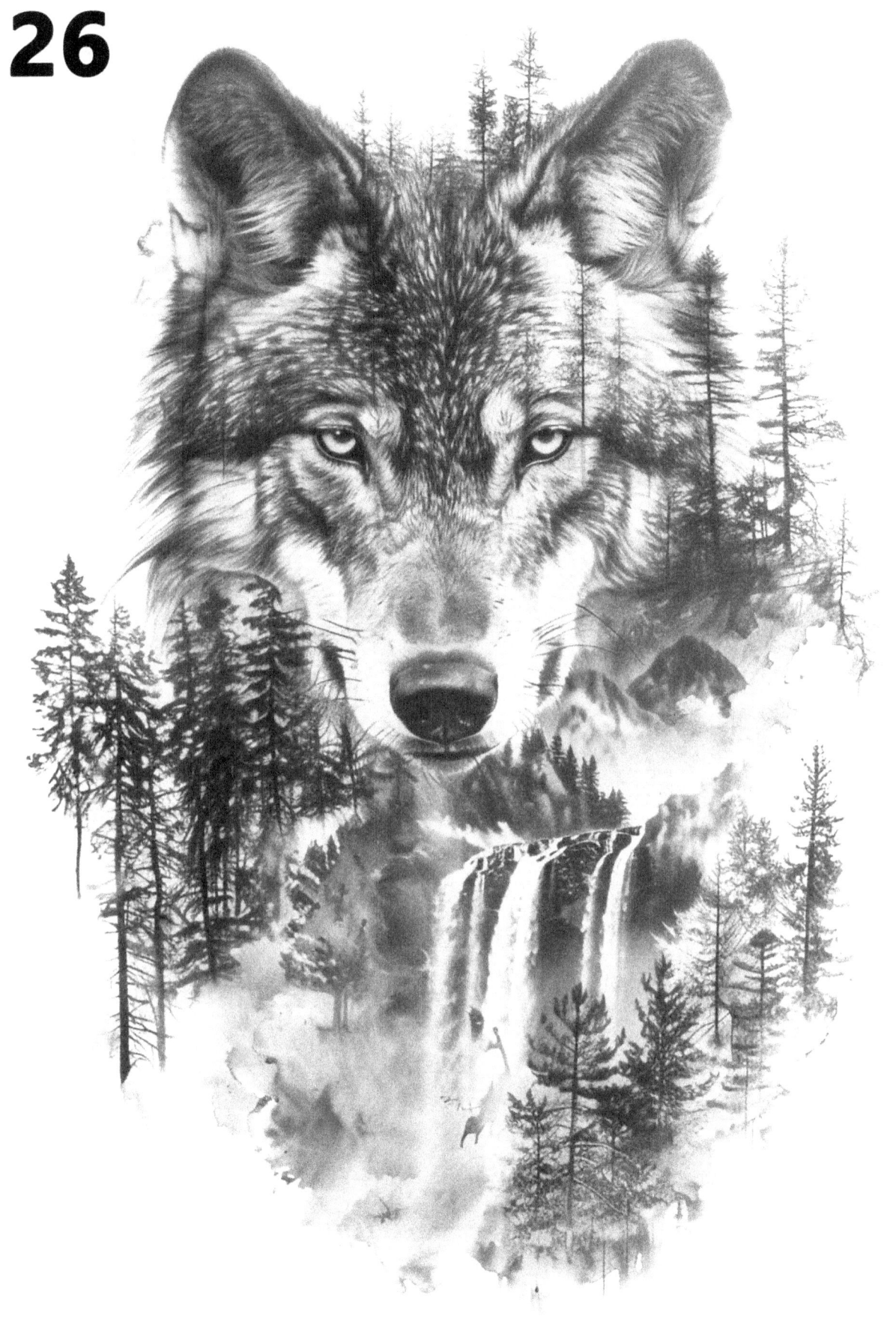

27

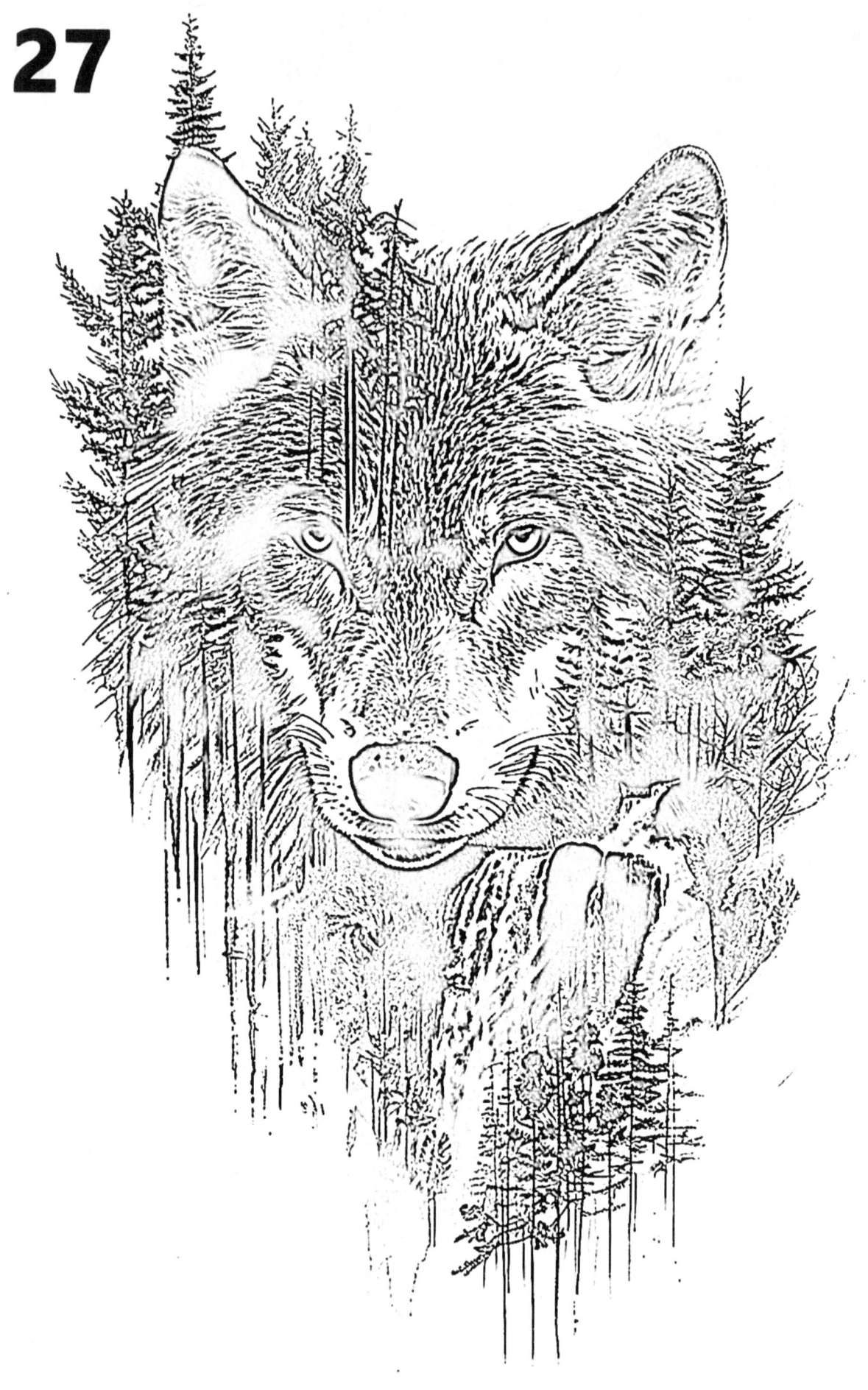

27

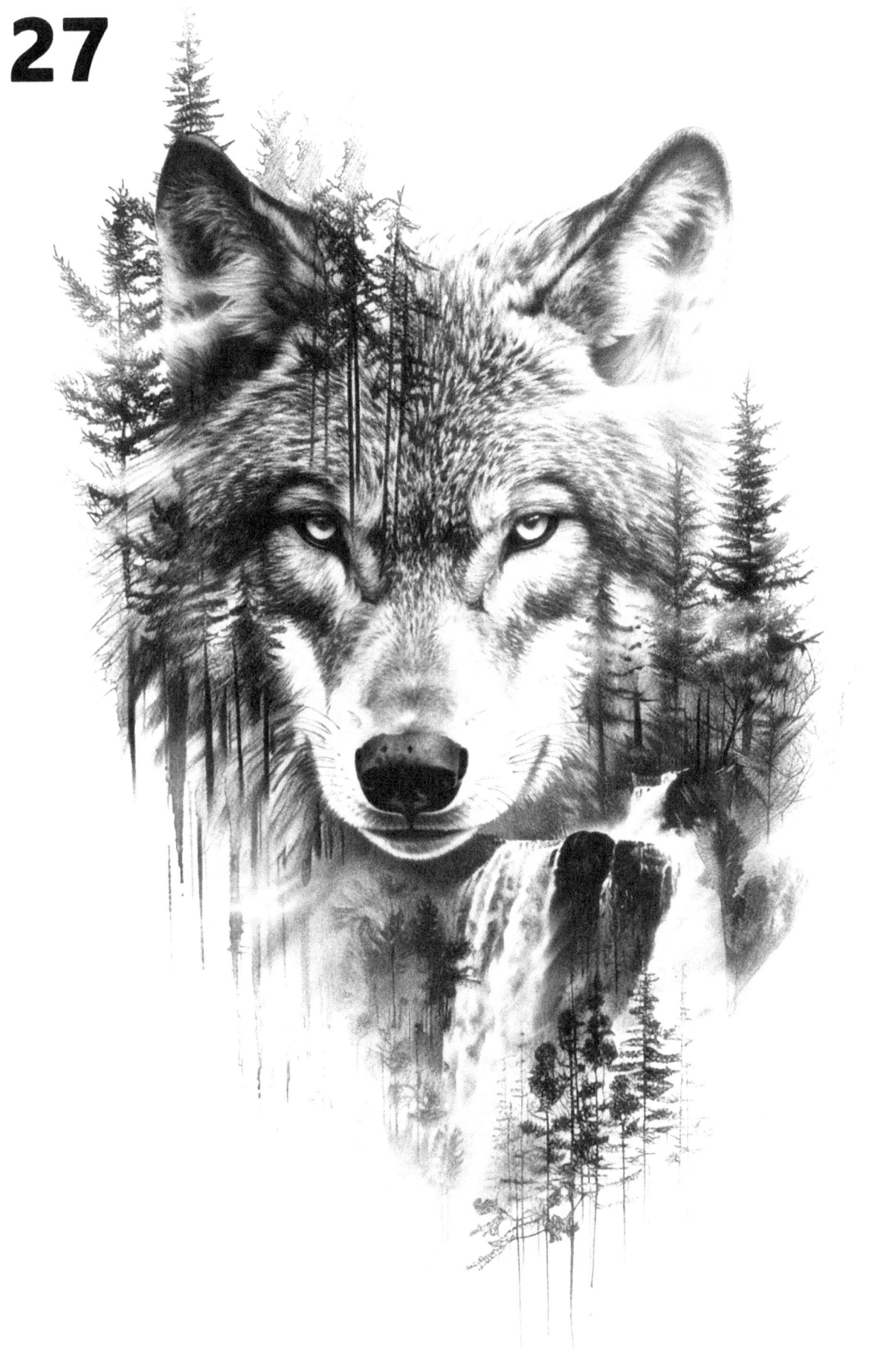

28

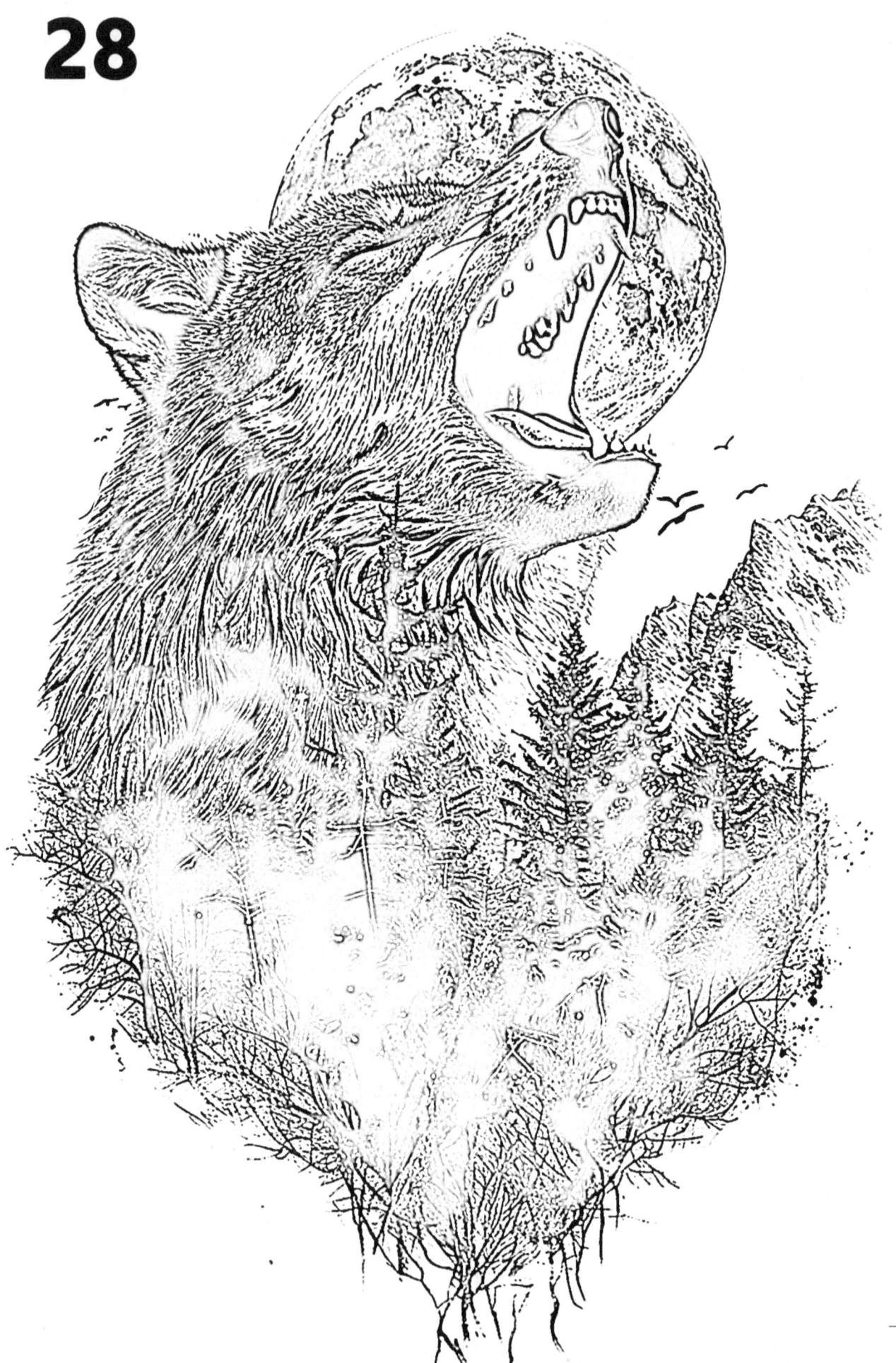

28

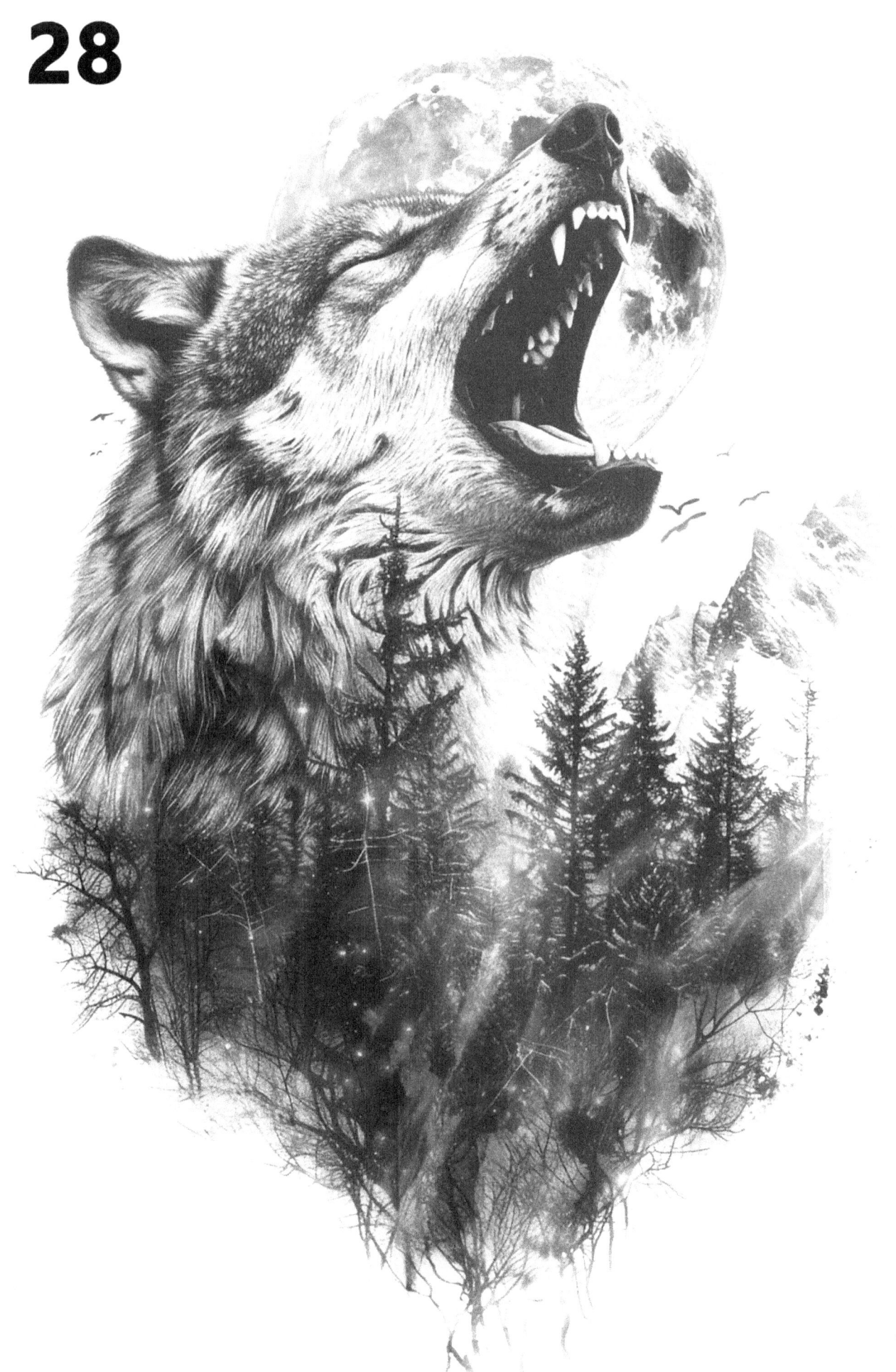

29

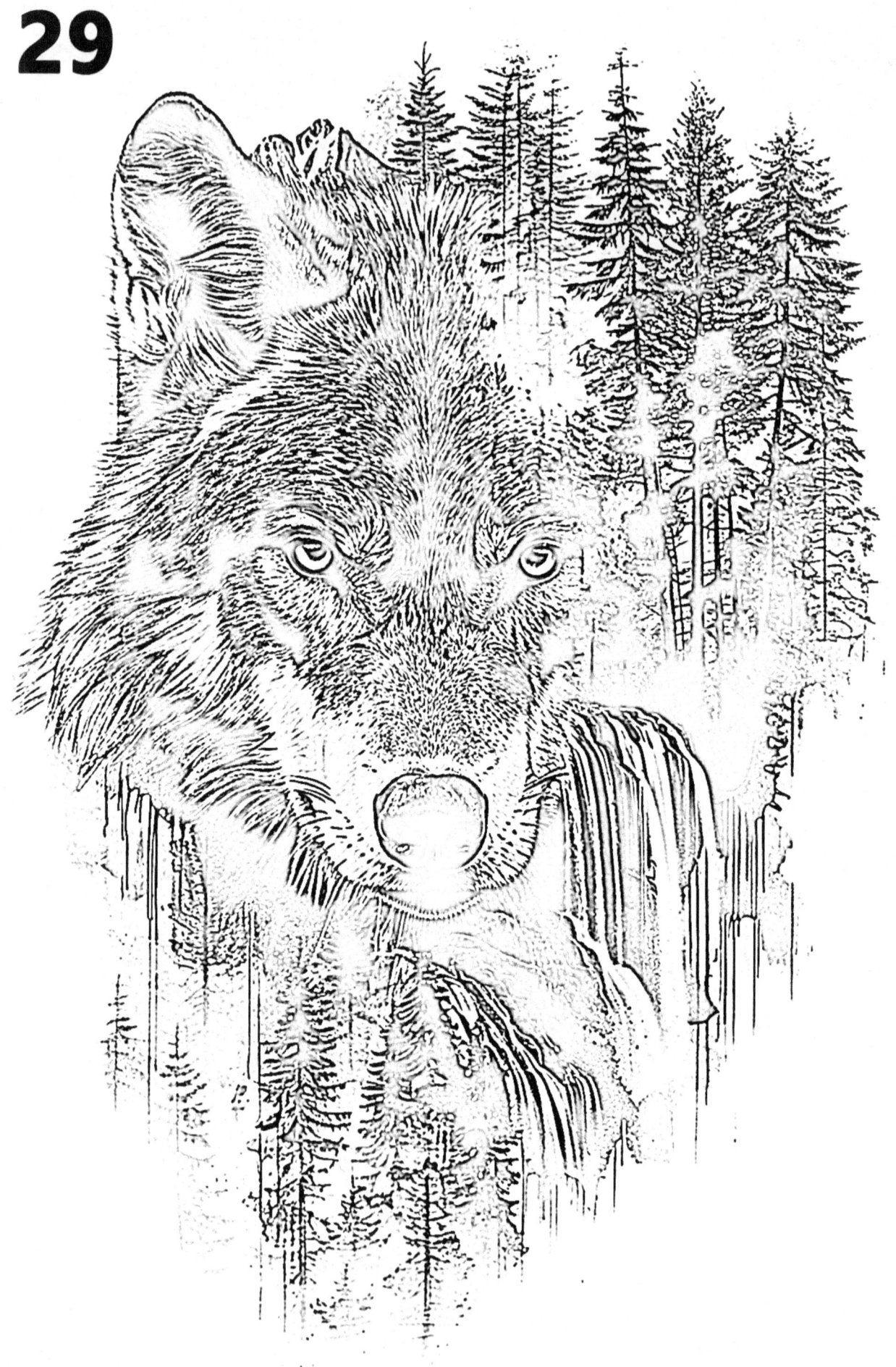

29

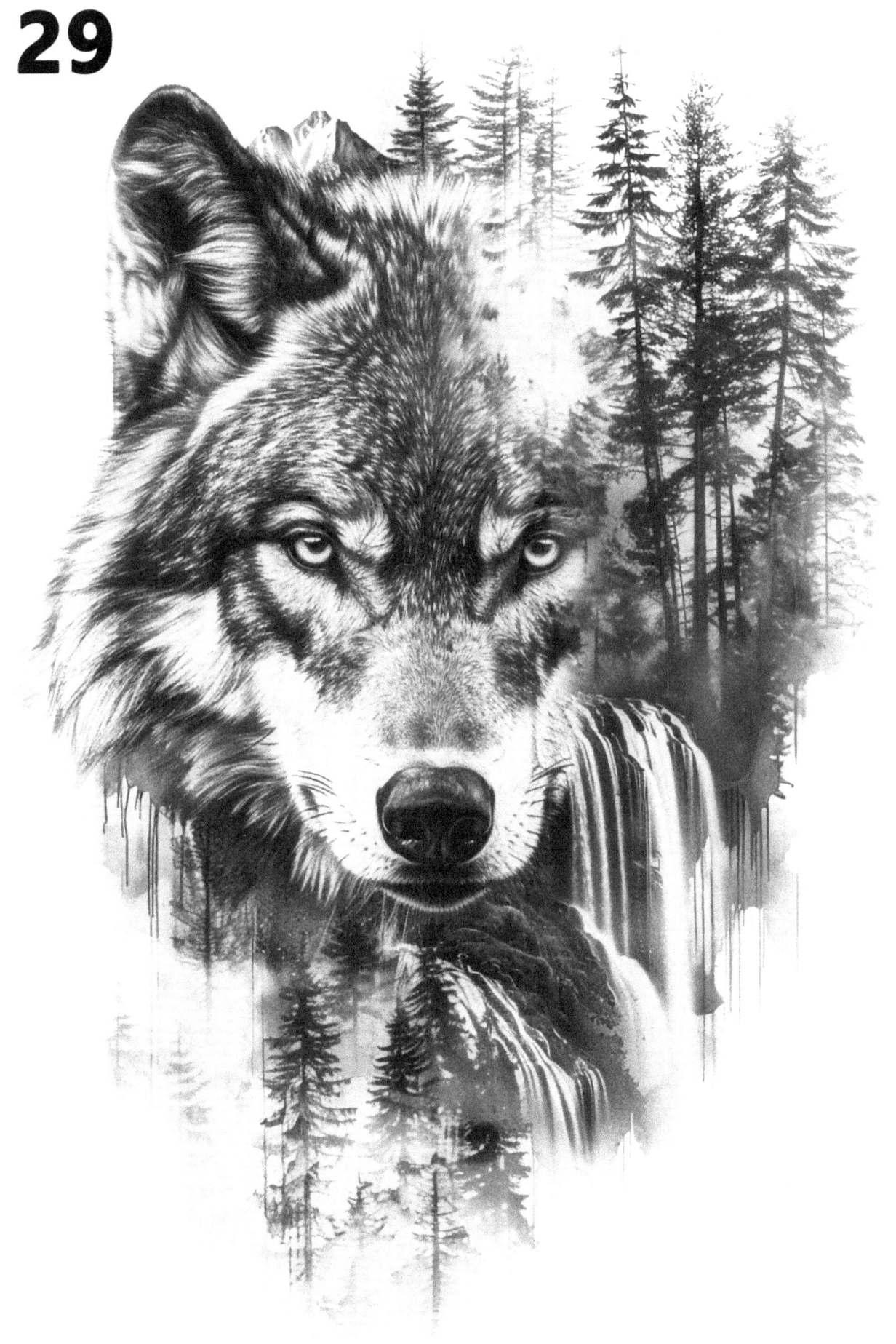

30

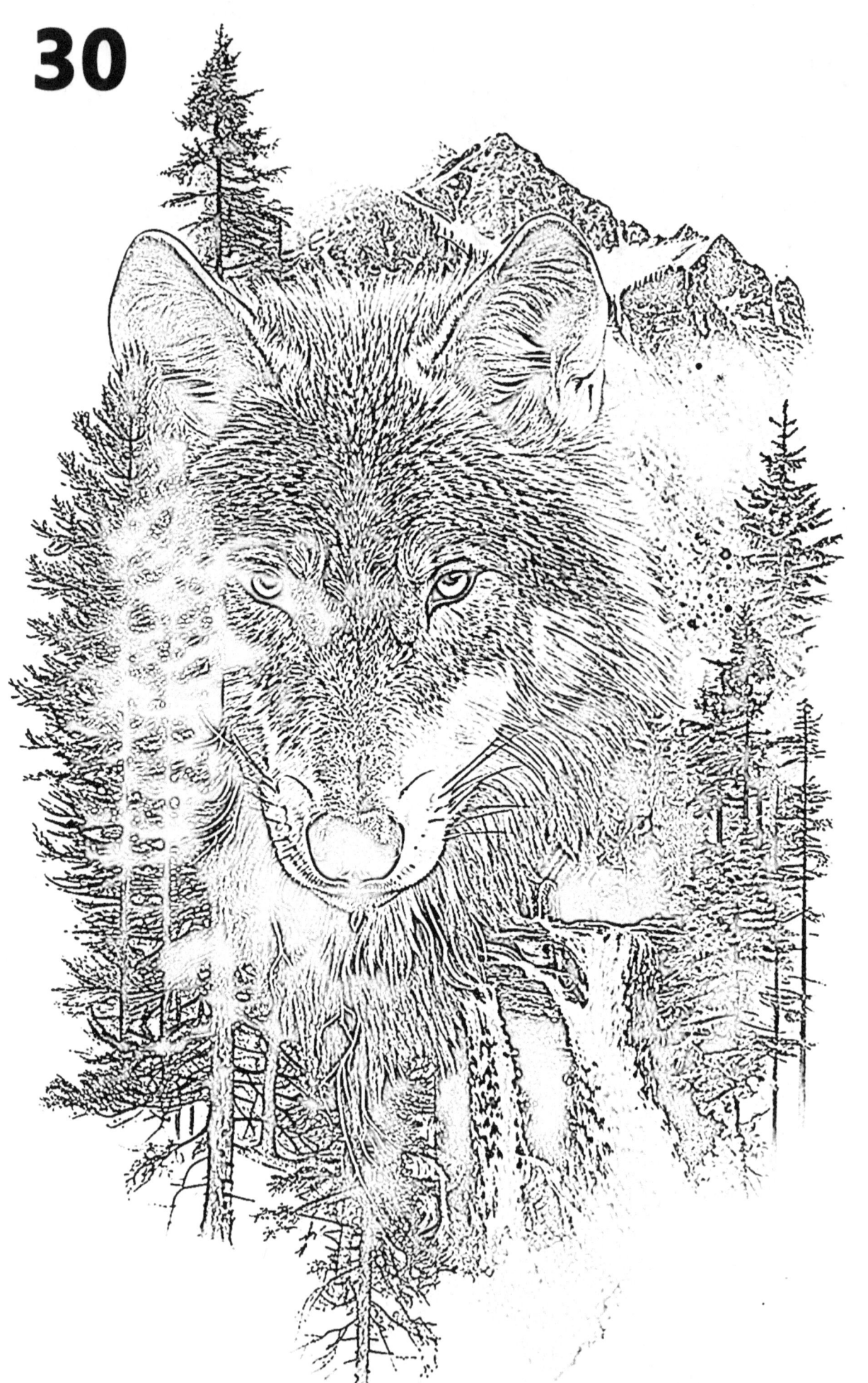

30

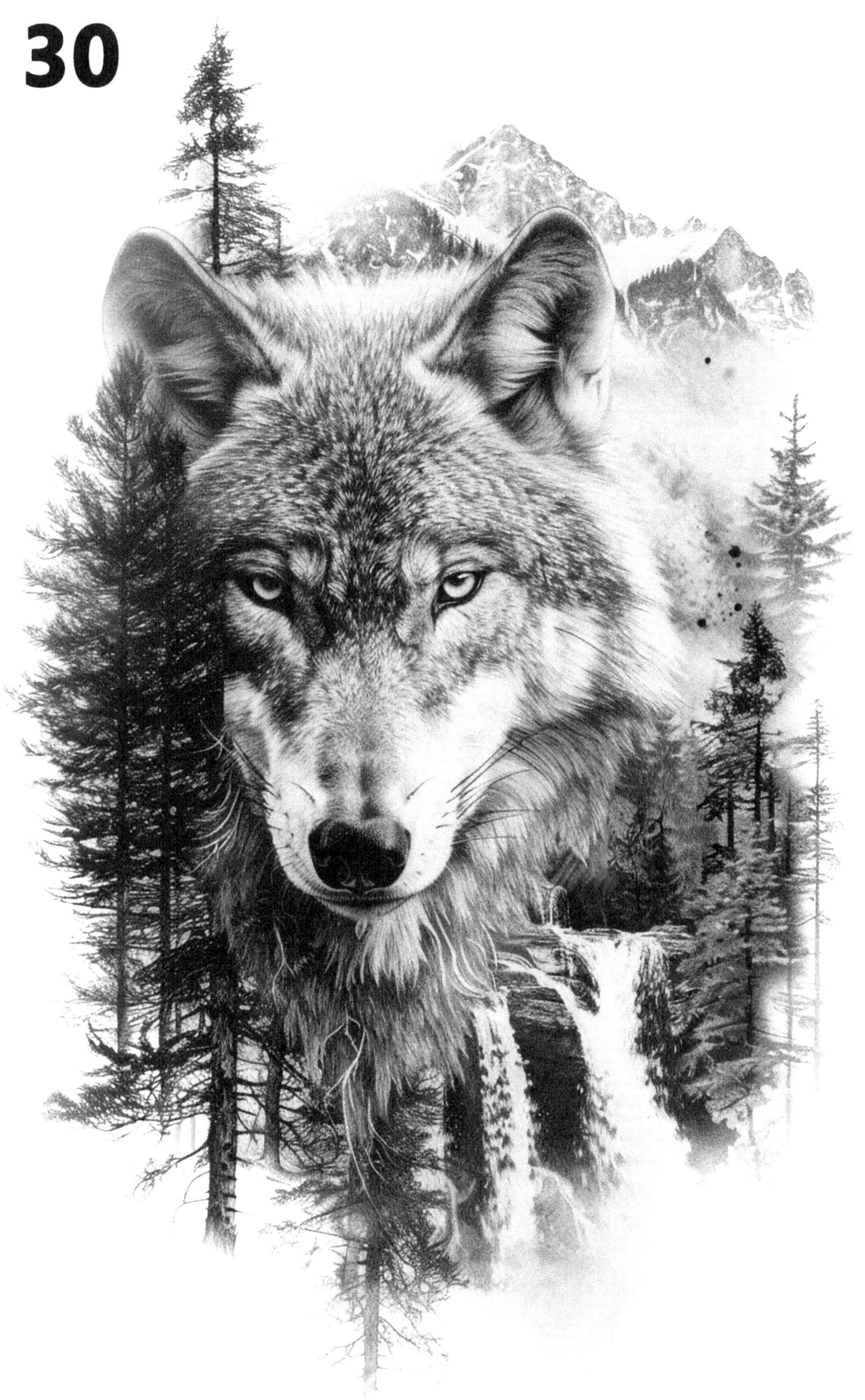

31

31

32

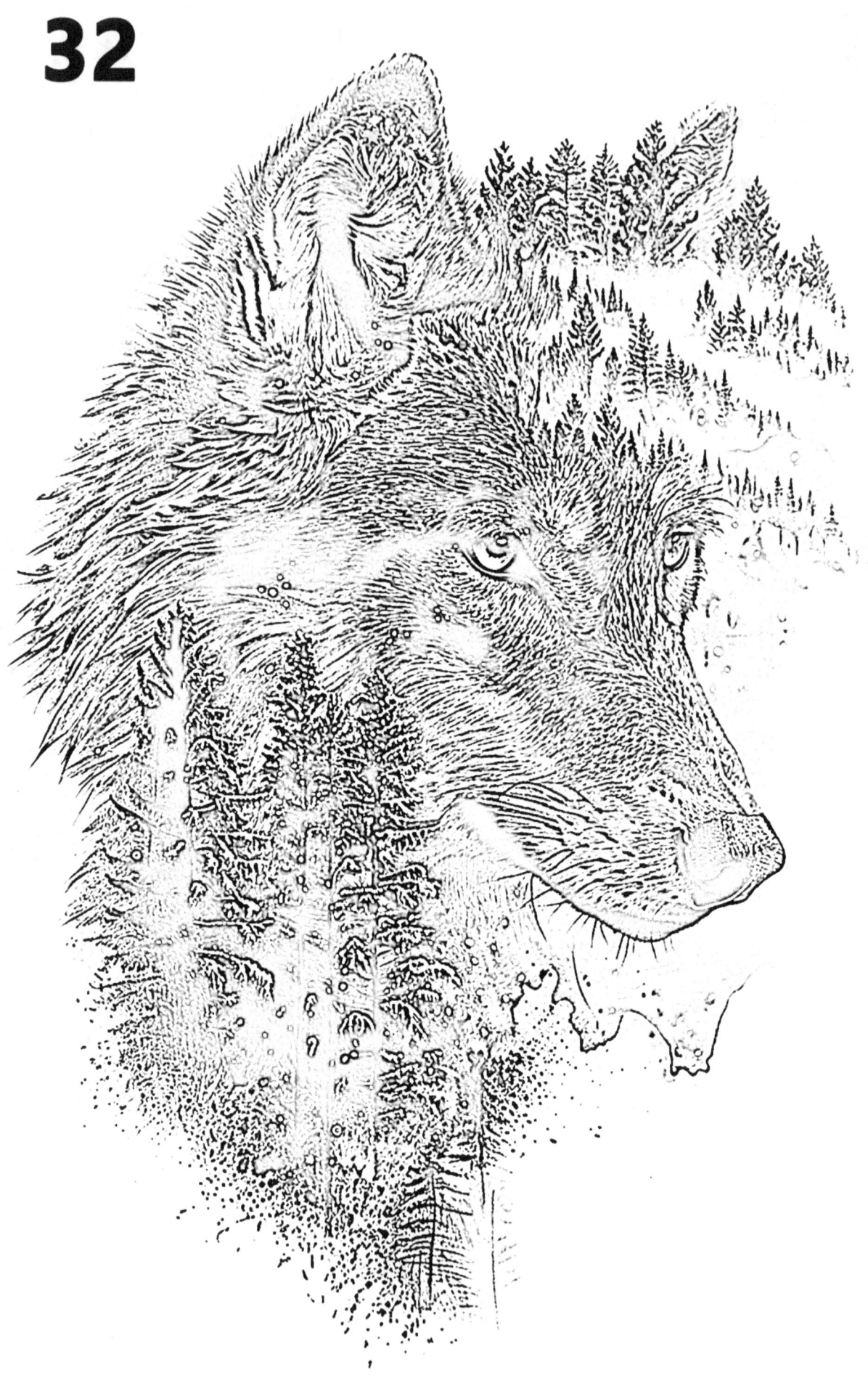

32

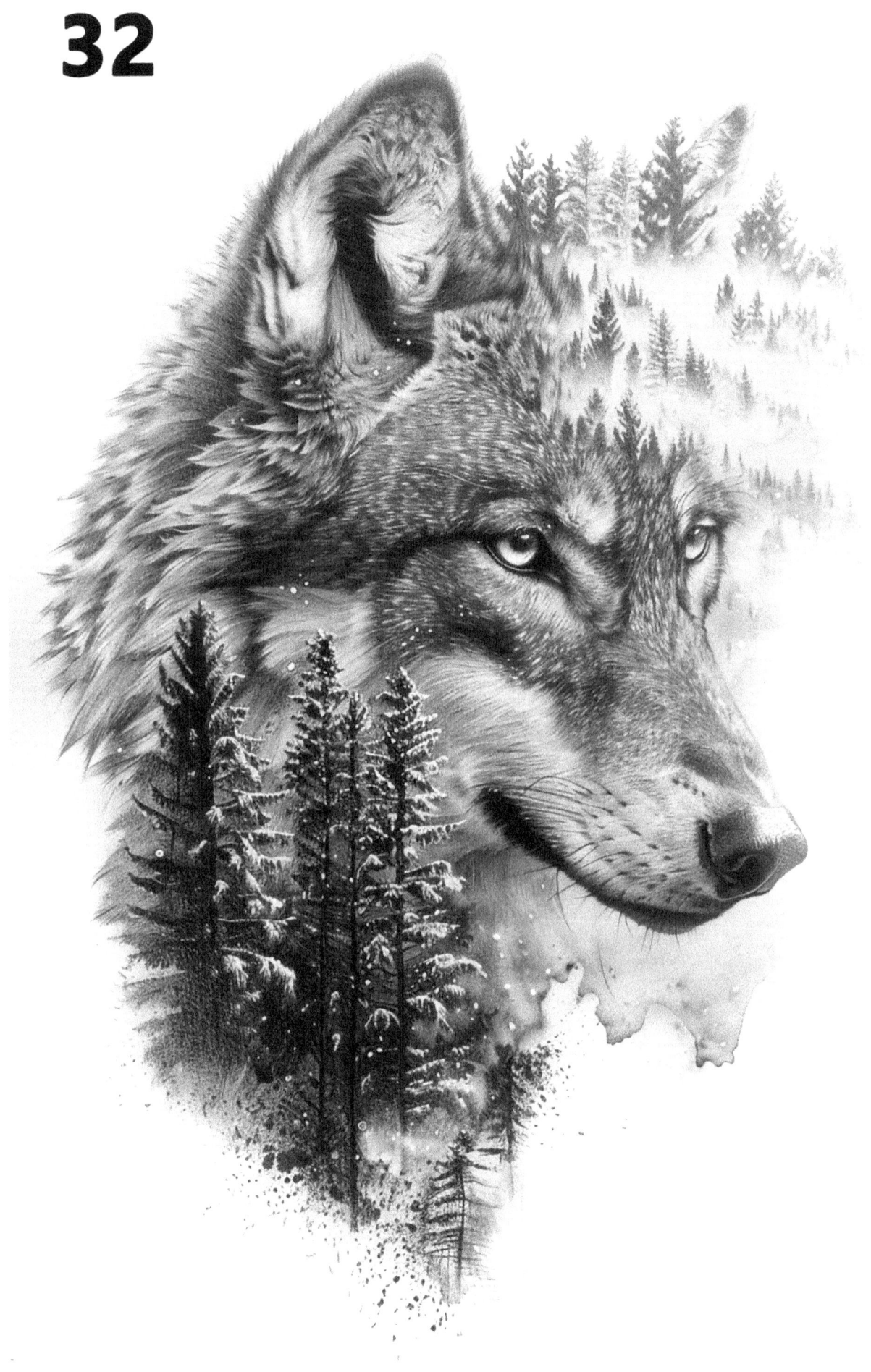

33

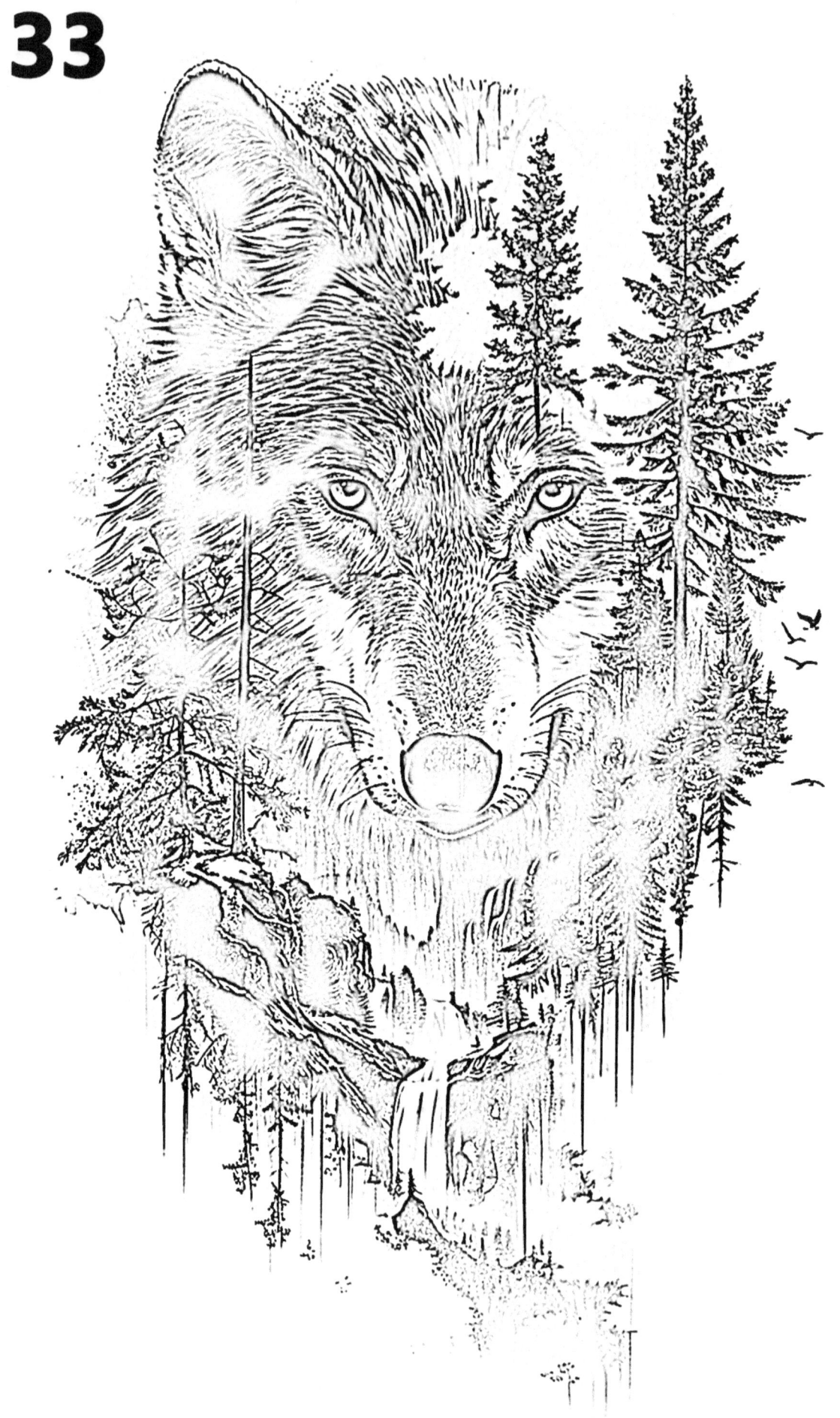

33

34

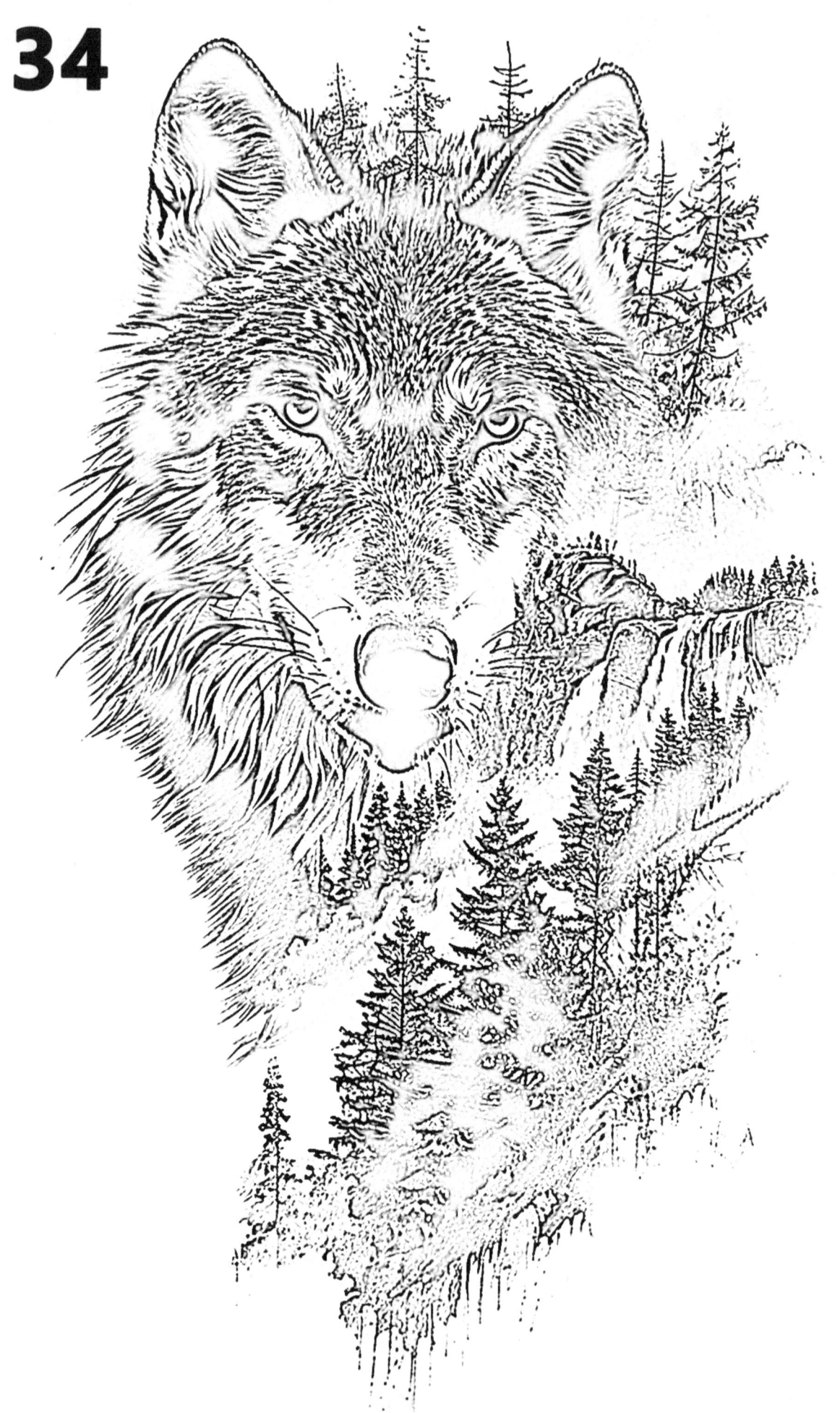

34

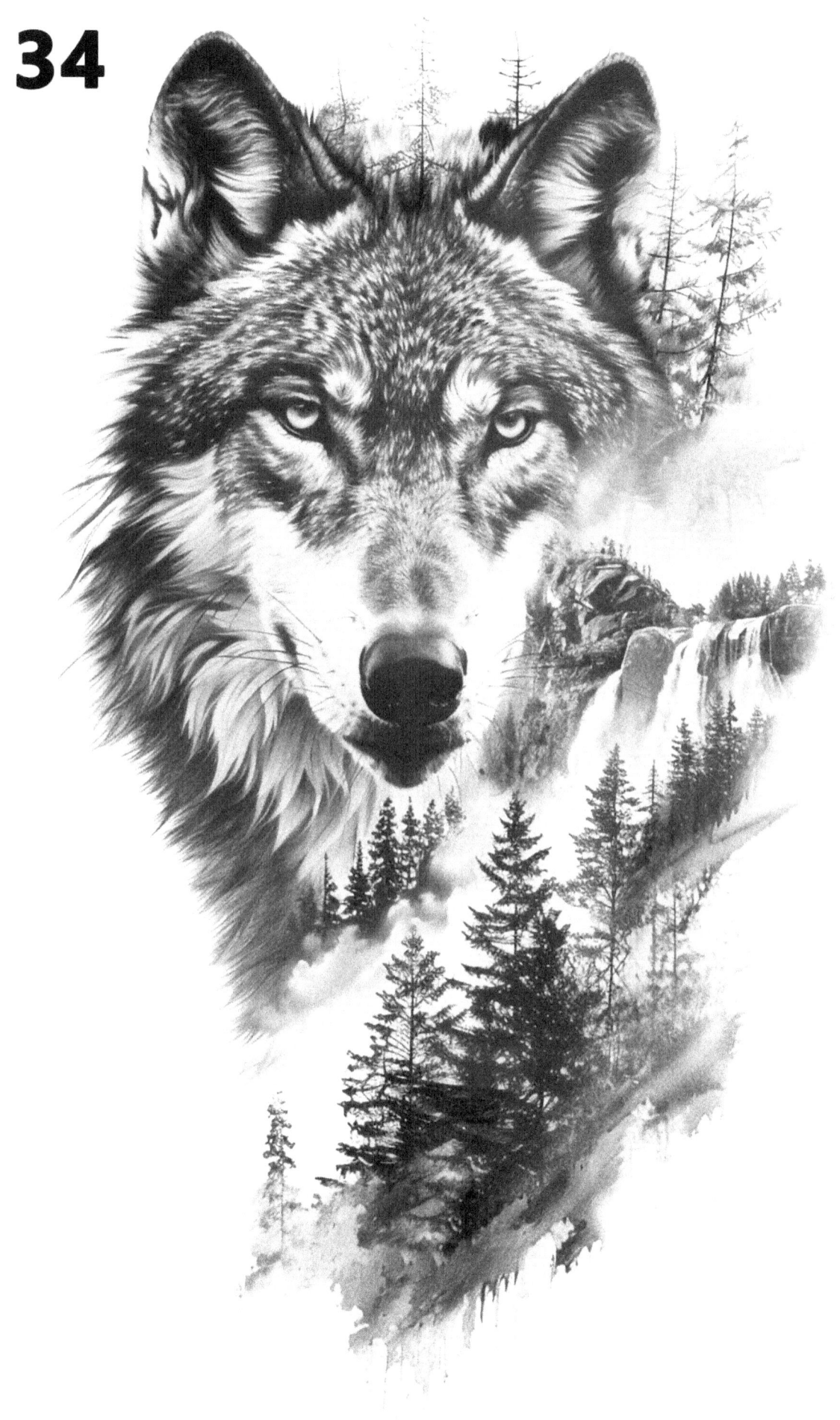

35

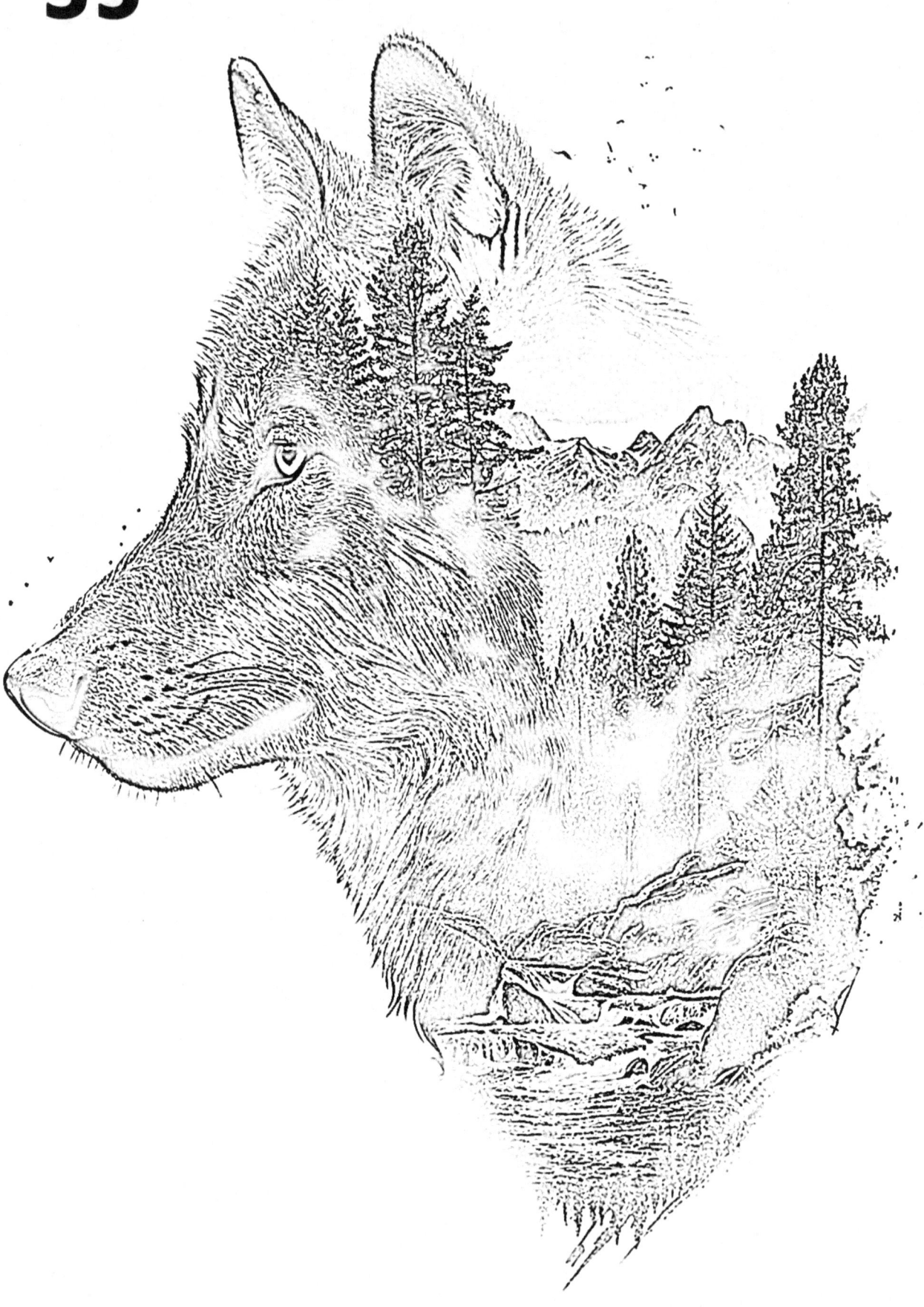

35

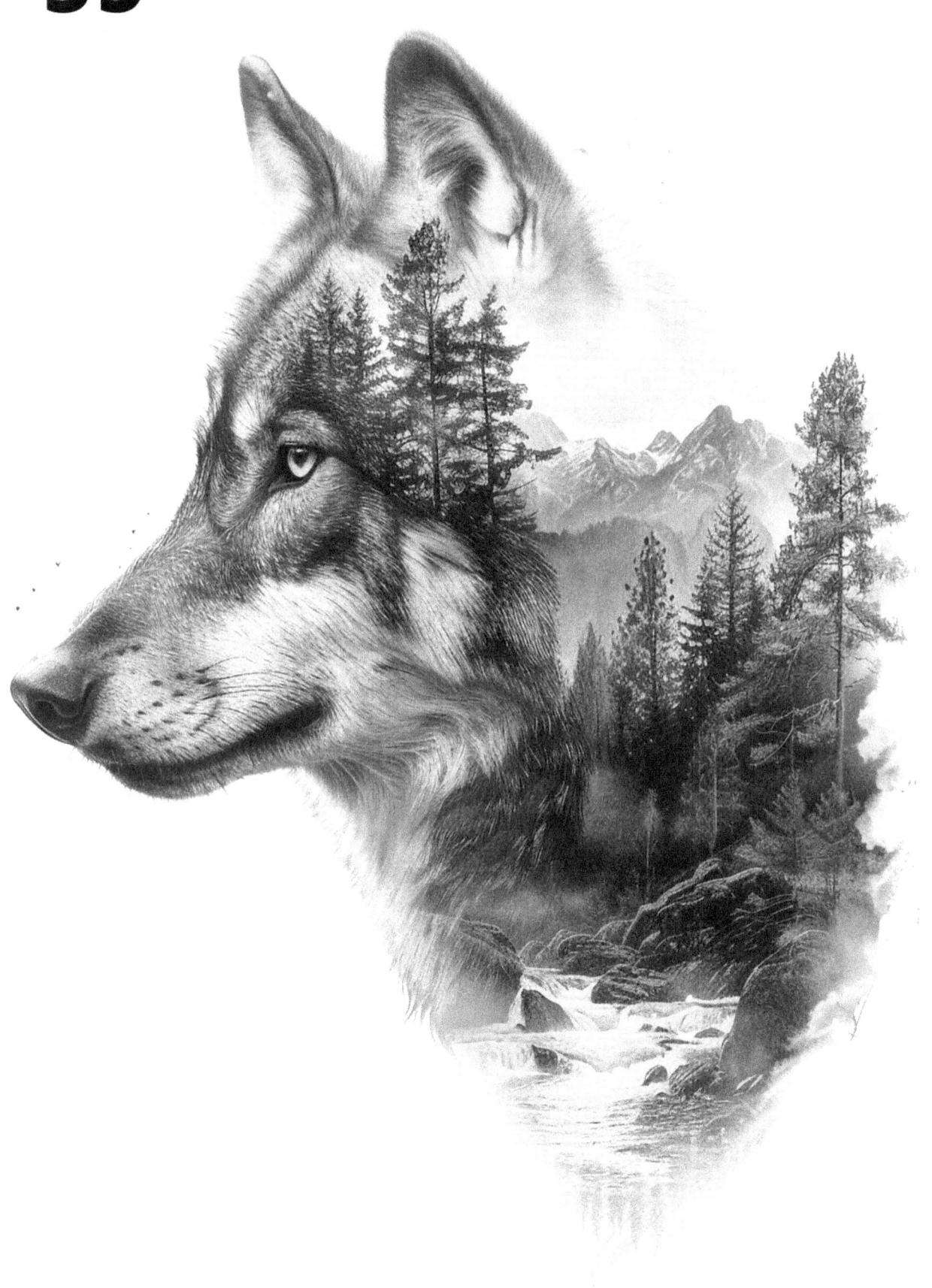

36

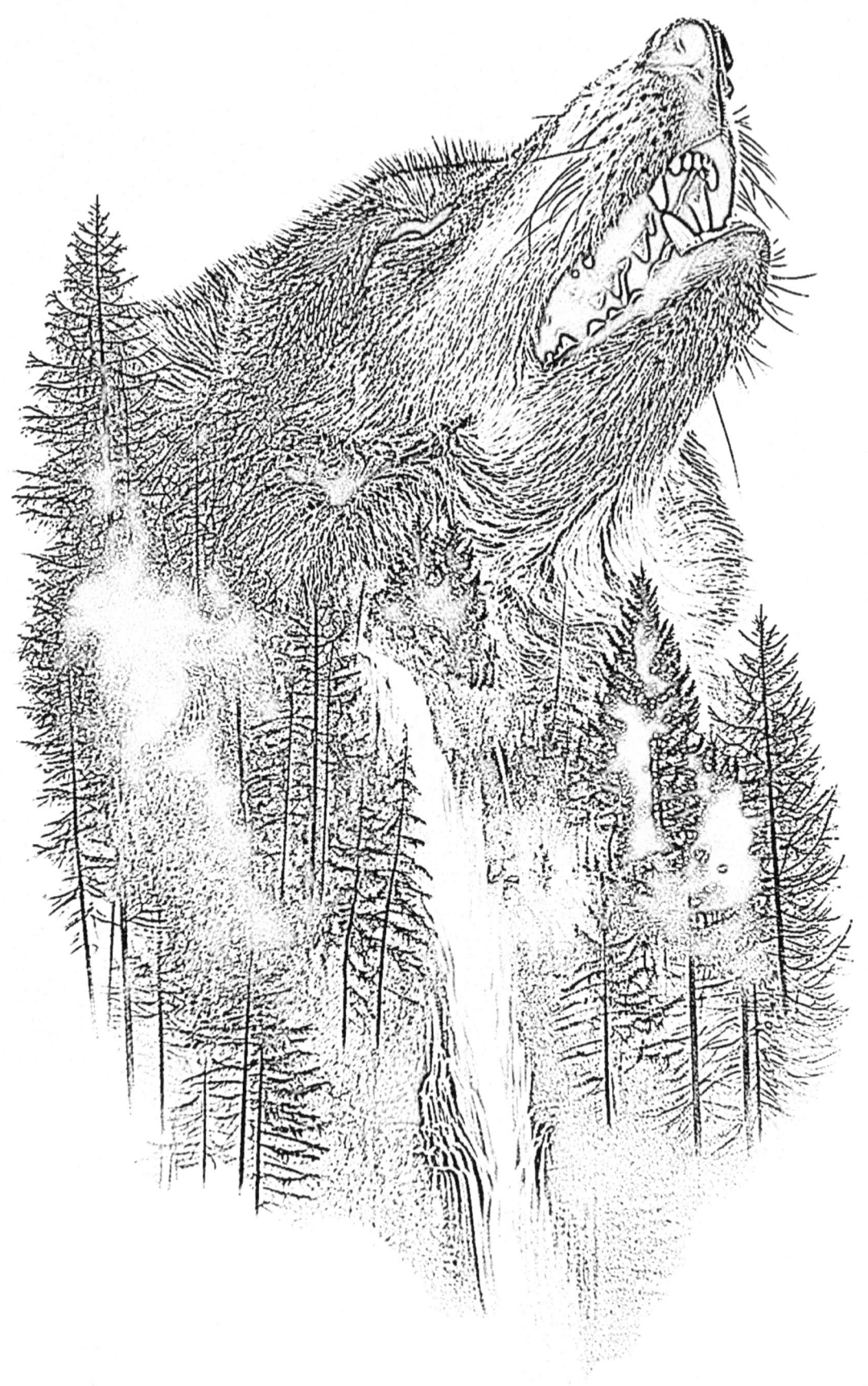

36

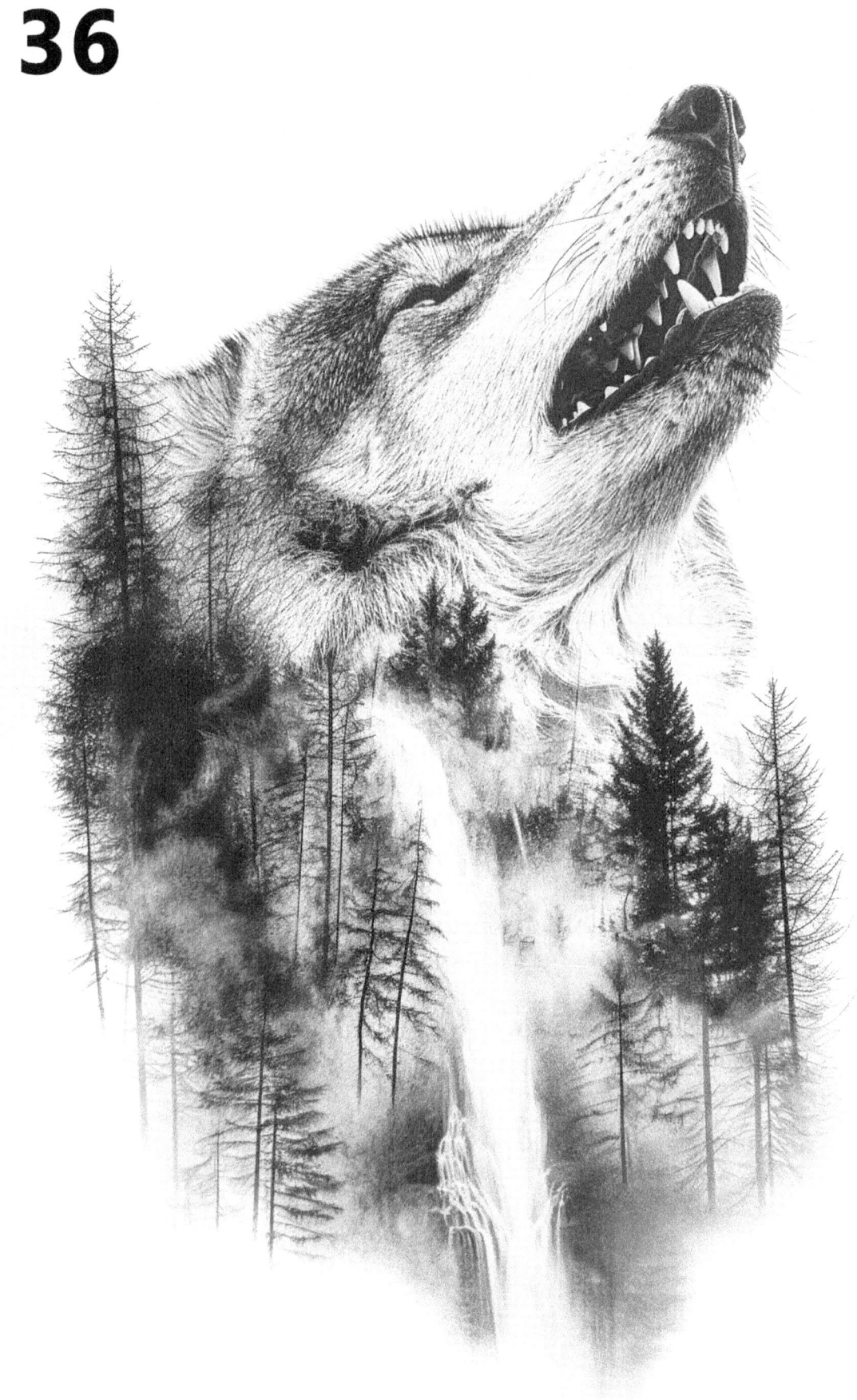

ABOUT THE AUTHOR

Immerse yourself in the captivating world of art, where imagination knows no bounds. With over three decades of experience as a painter, tattoo artist, and author, I have dedicated my life to the pursuit of artistic excellence.
Through countless hours of dedication, I have honed my skills in charcoal, pencils, and acrylic colors, specializing in the realms of realism, photorealism, and impressionism. My unique style blends elements of fantasy and impressionism, resulting in mesmerizing works of art that evoke deep emotions and leave a lasting impact.

In the realm of tattoo artistry, I have emerged as a trailblazer, revolutionizing the industry with my fresh and distinctive designs. Recognizing the need for innovation, I have created a new age of tattoo art that seamlessly combines my preferred style with eye-catching aesthetics. My designs not only captivate the eye but also empower individuals to express their individuality and uniqueness.

Expanding my creative horizons, I have delved into the world of coloring books. Gone are the days of simplistic designs with thick lines. I am on a mission to introduce the realms of realism and impressionism to the coloring book landscape. Each page of my coloring books offers intricate details and a chance for individuals to unleash their inner artist, resulting in remarkable and vibrant creations.

But my artistic endeavors don't stop there. I am currently engrossed in the creation of photo reference books that showcase wildlife and nature in unprecedented ways. These books will transport you to a world of vivid colors, breathtaking imagery, and seemingly impossible poses.

Prepare to be captivated by the untamed beauty of the natural world, brought to life through my keen eye for detail and my passion for pushing artistic boundaries.

Join me on an awe-inspiring journey where creativity knows no limits. Together, let's explore new dimensions of artistry, where fresh perspectives, remarkable designs, and boundless inspiration await.

Welcome to my world of art, where dreams become reality, and the extraordinary is transformed into tangible beauty

Scan the QR code below in order to download the PDF.

You will need WINRAR (or equivelant program) to open the archive. Enter the password :
   WolfUntamedSpirit!2

If download does not work please contact us at our Facebook page
Or email at divinetattoodesign@gmail.com

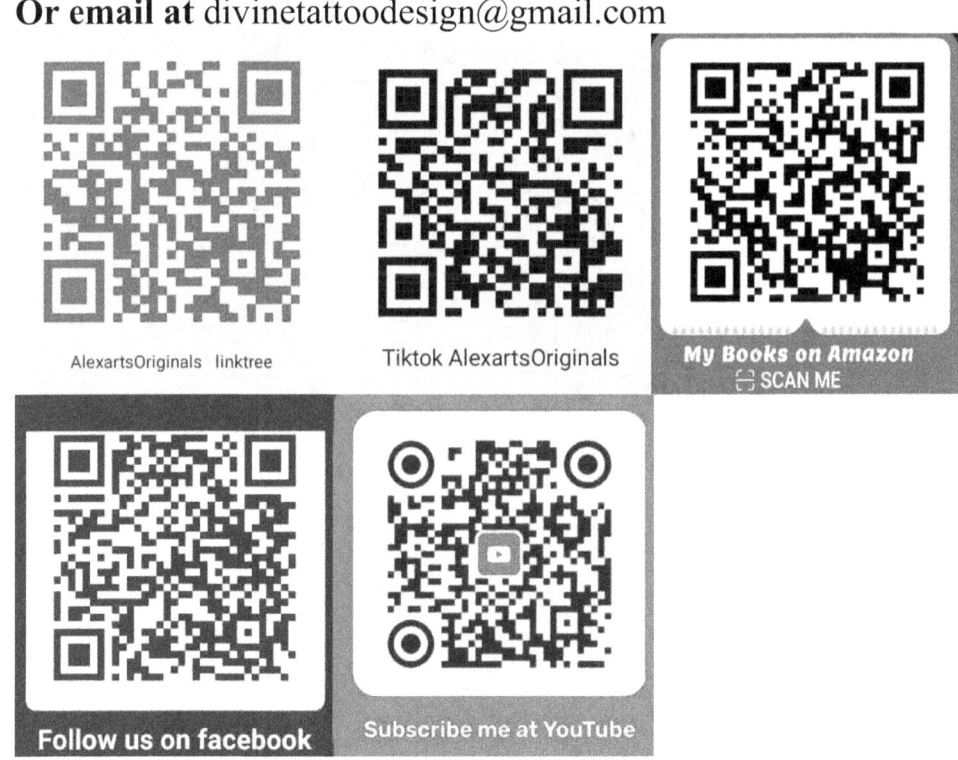

37

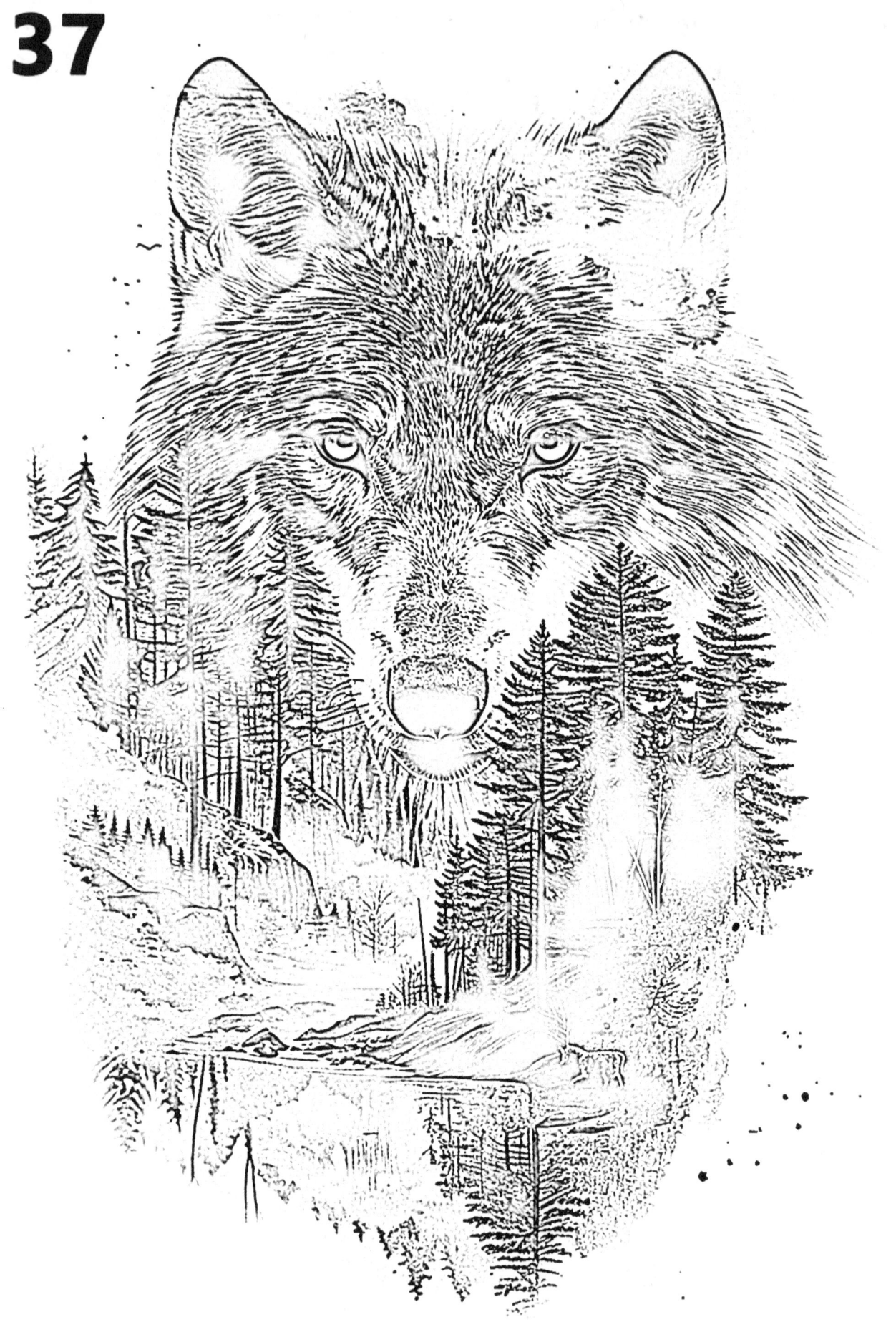

37

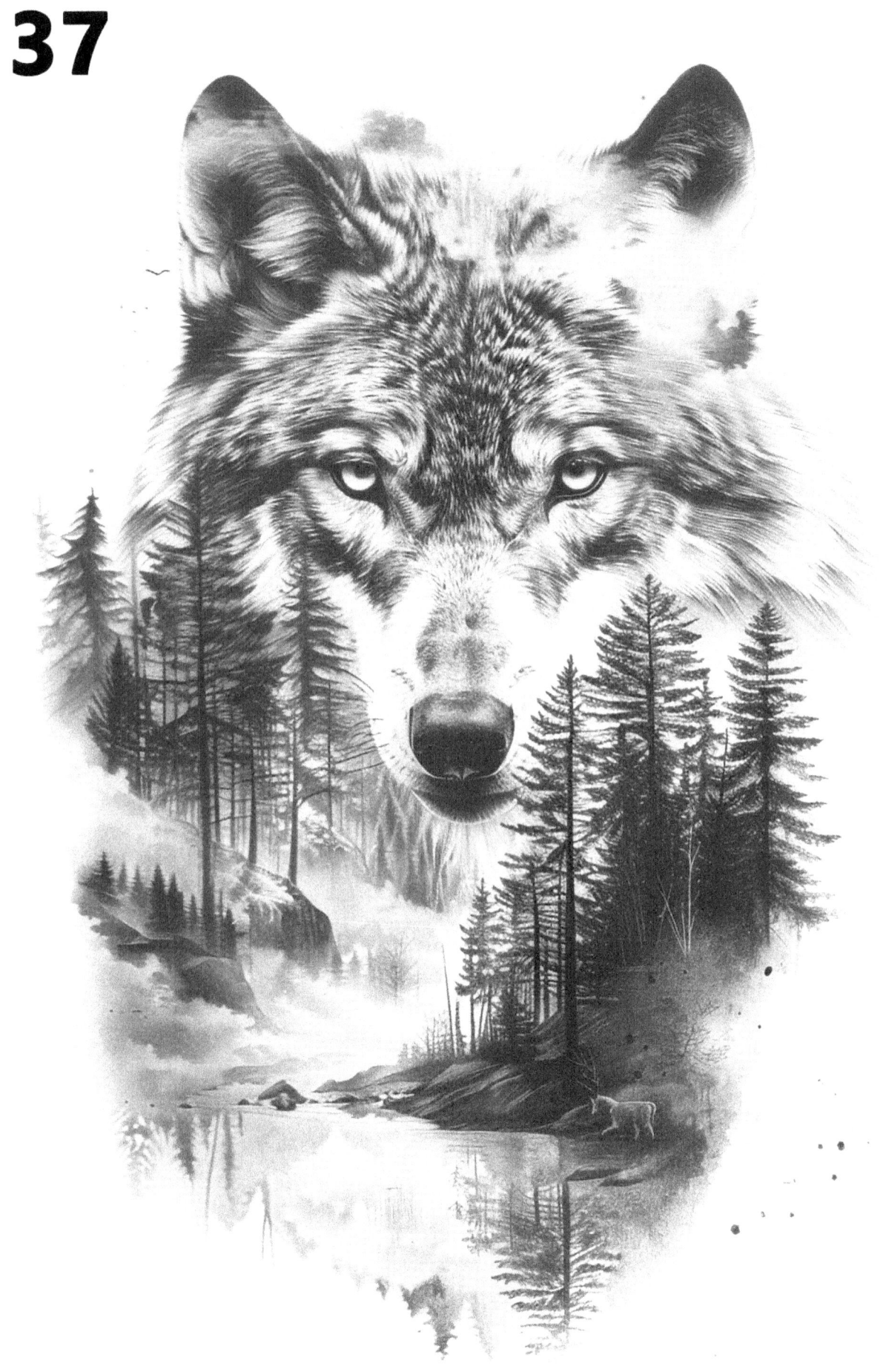

38

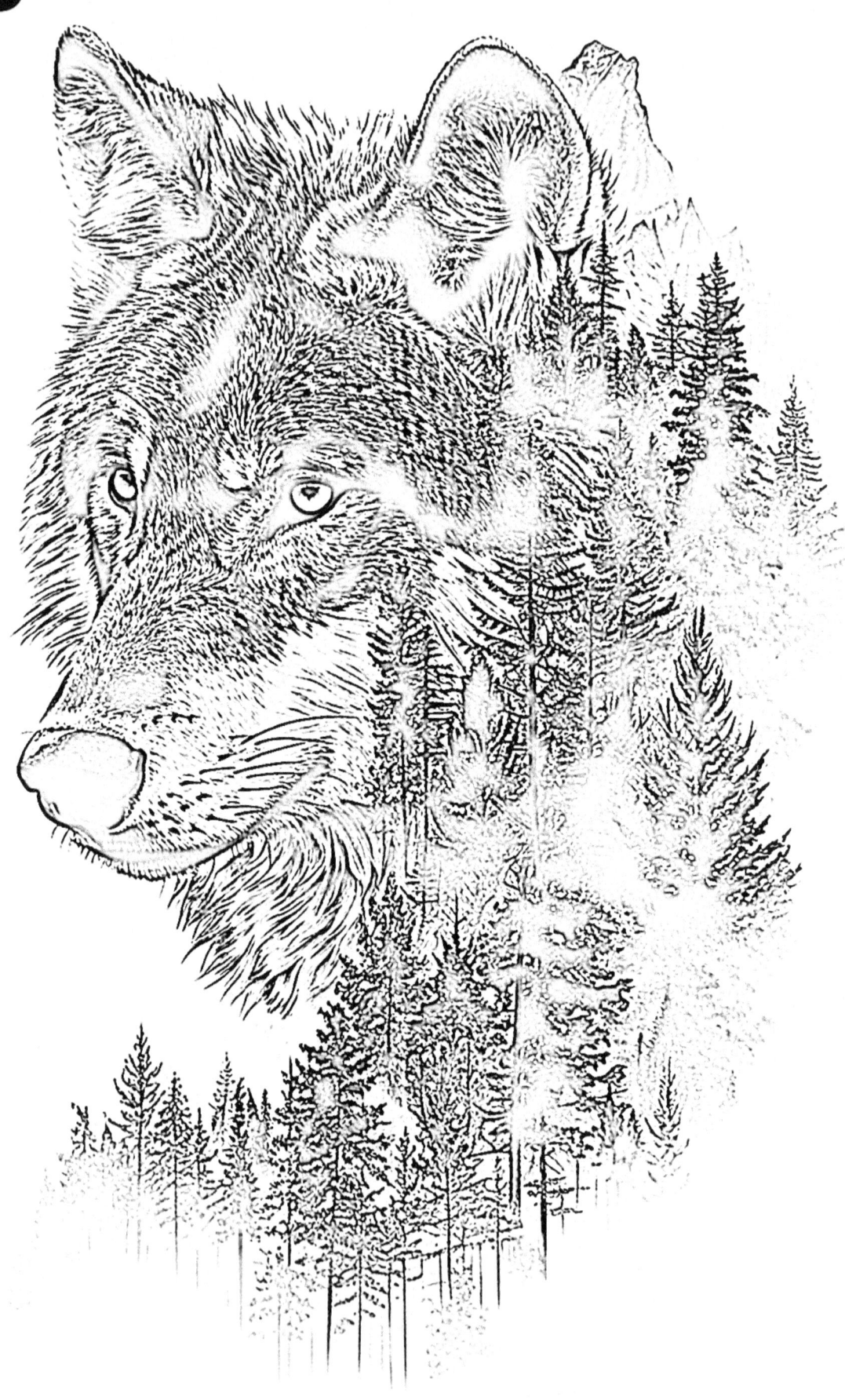

38

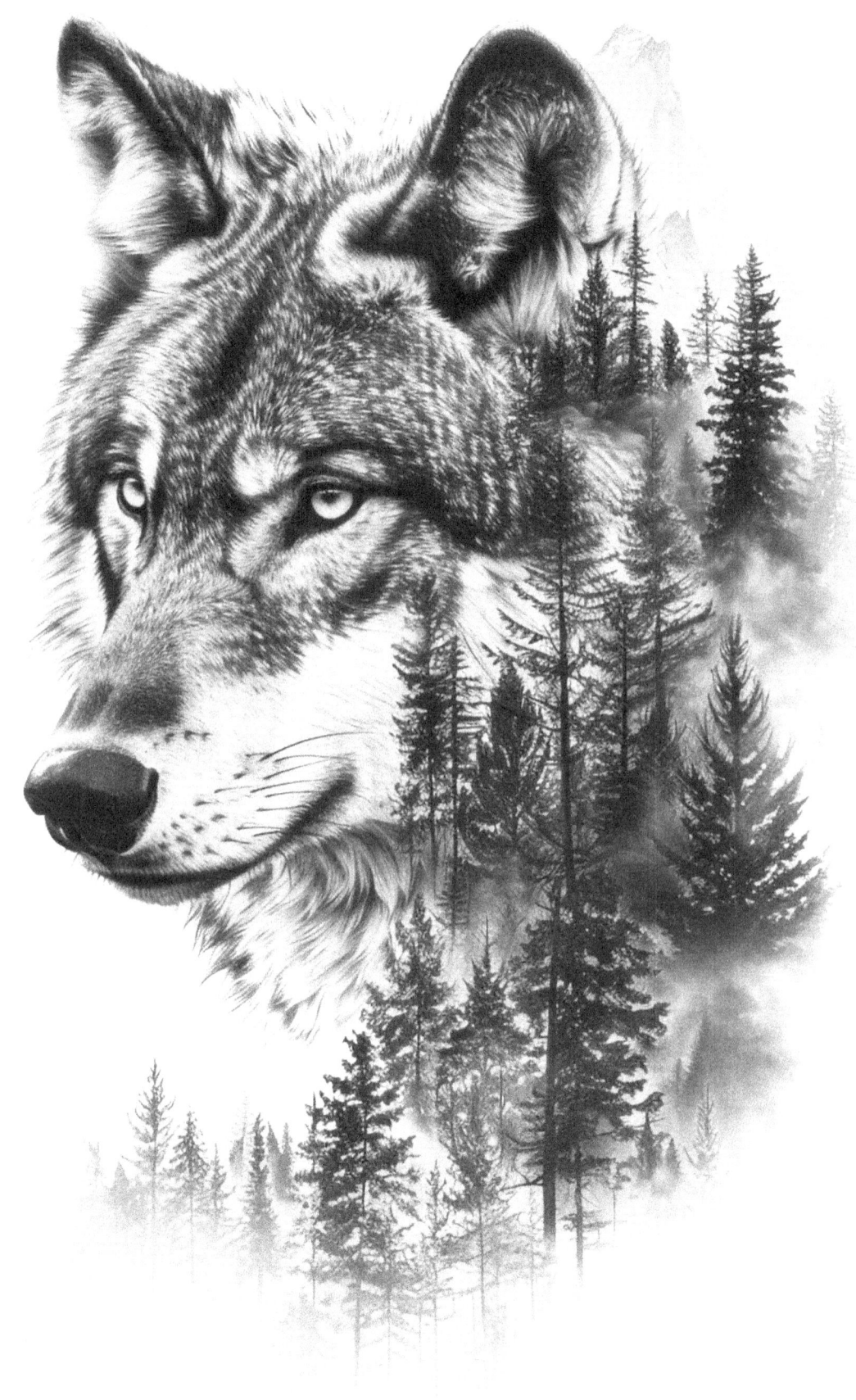

39

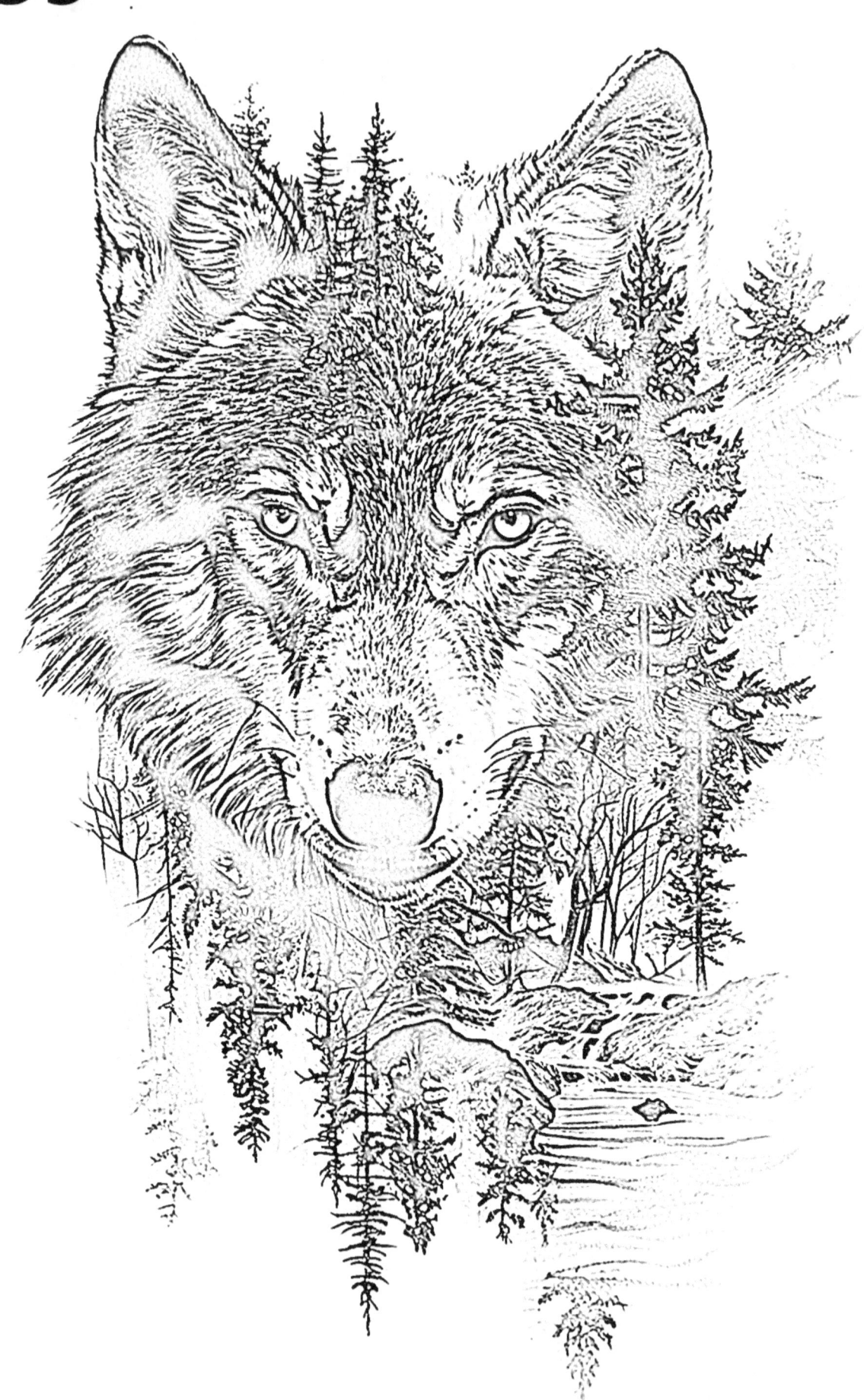

39

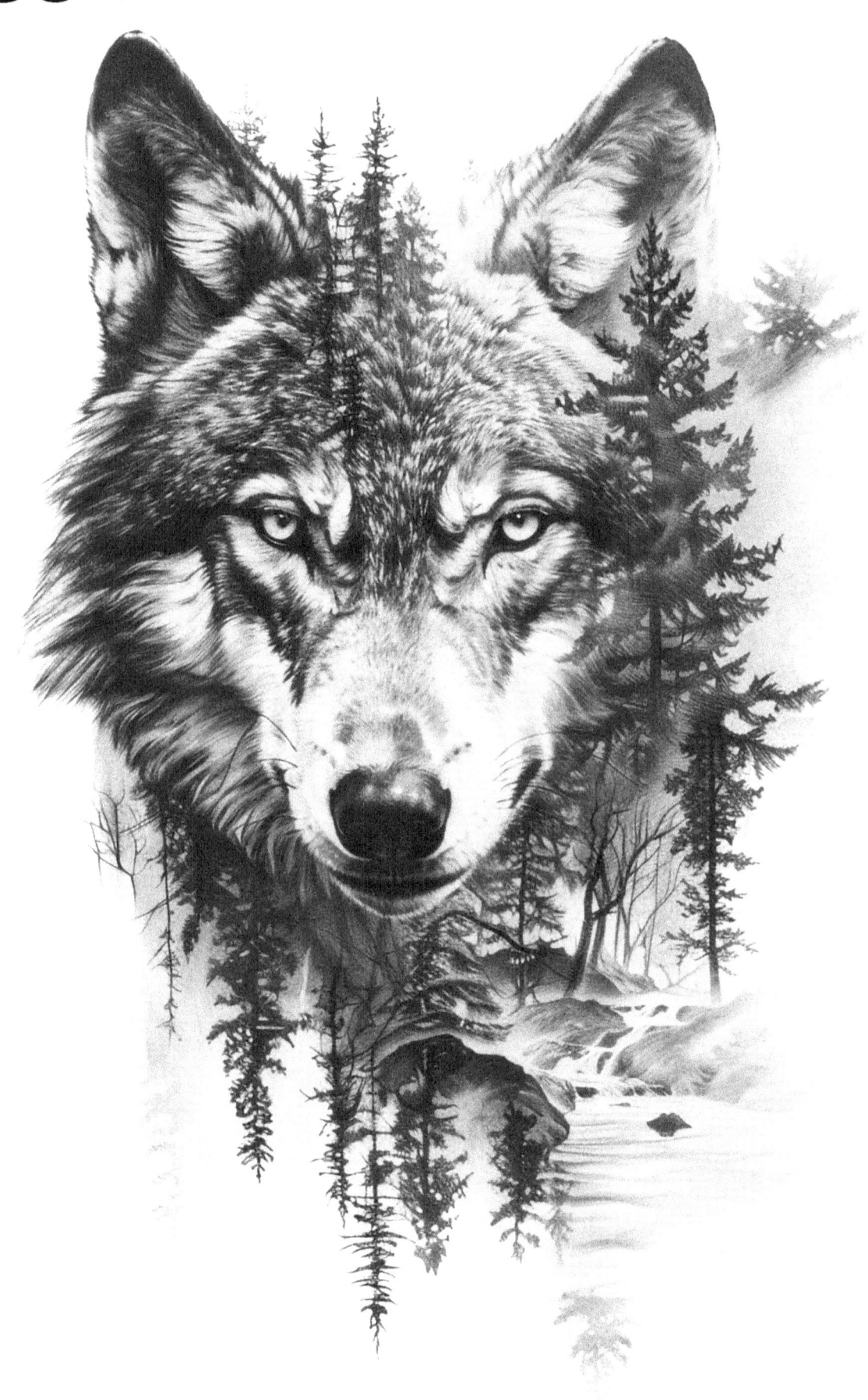

40

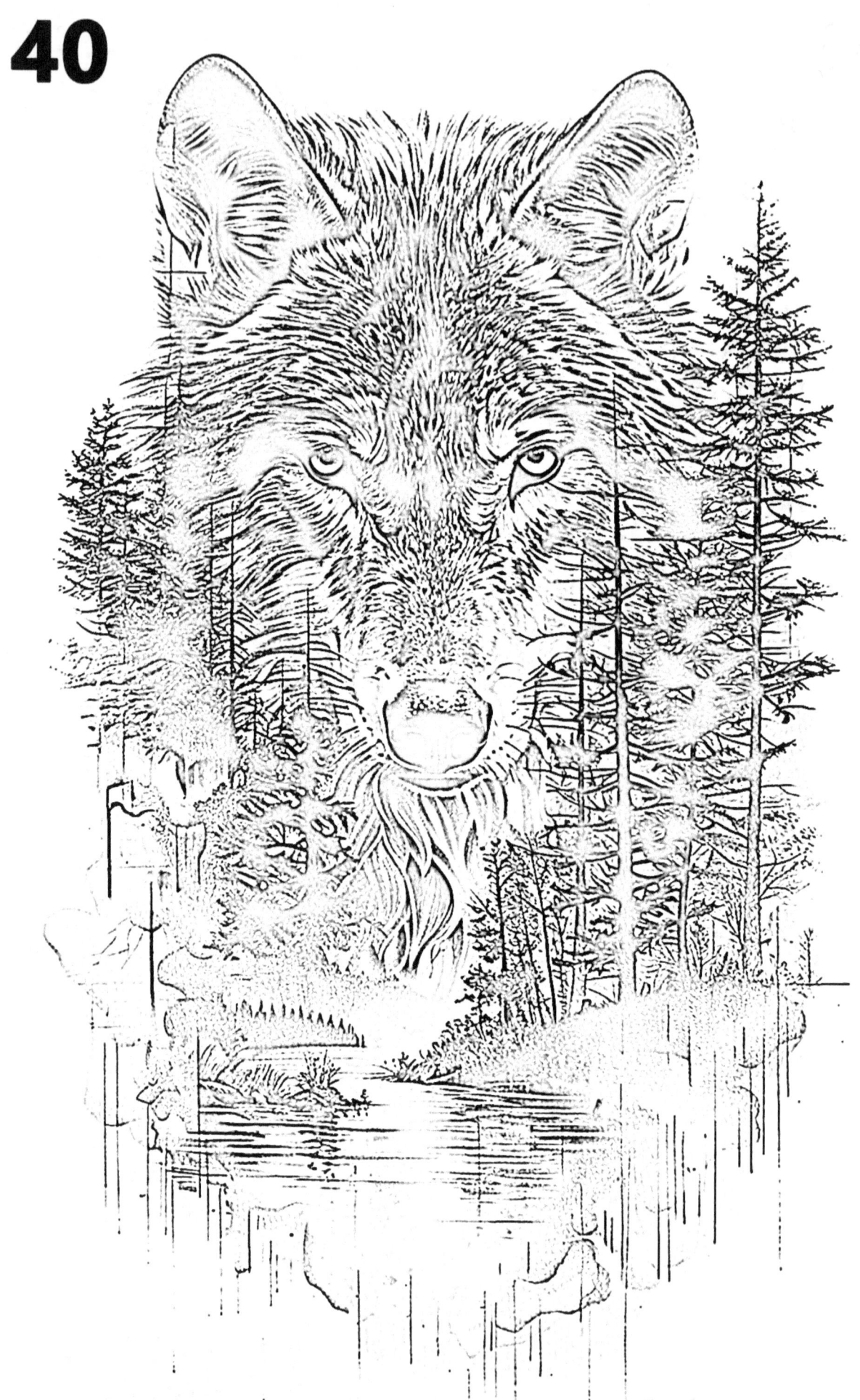

40

41

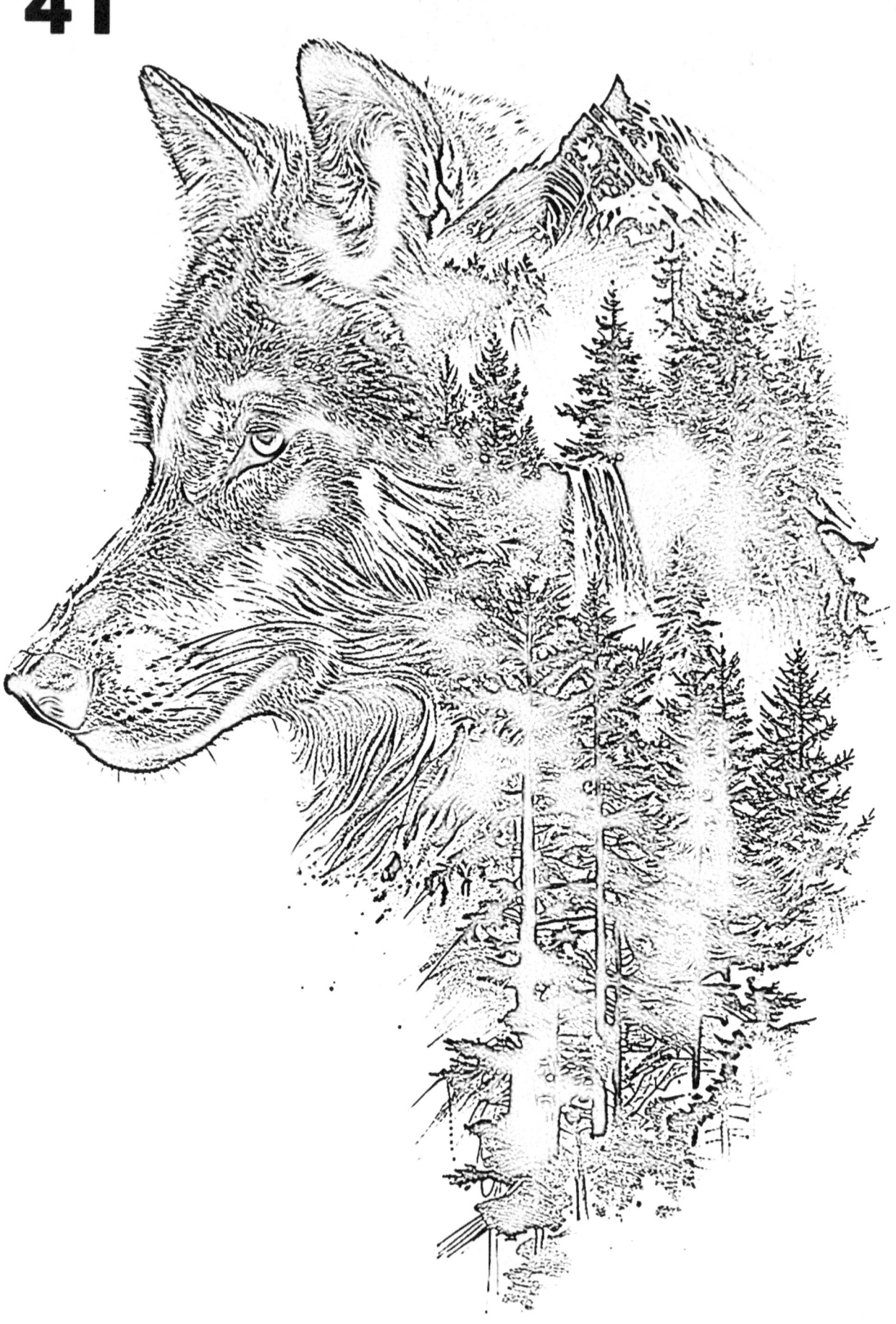

41

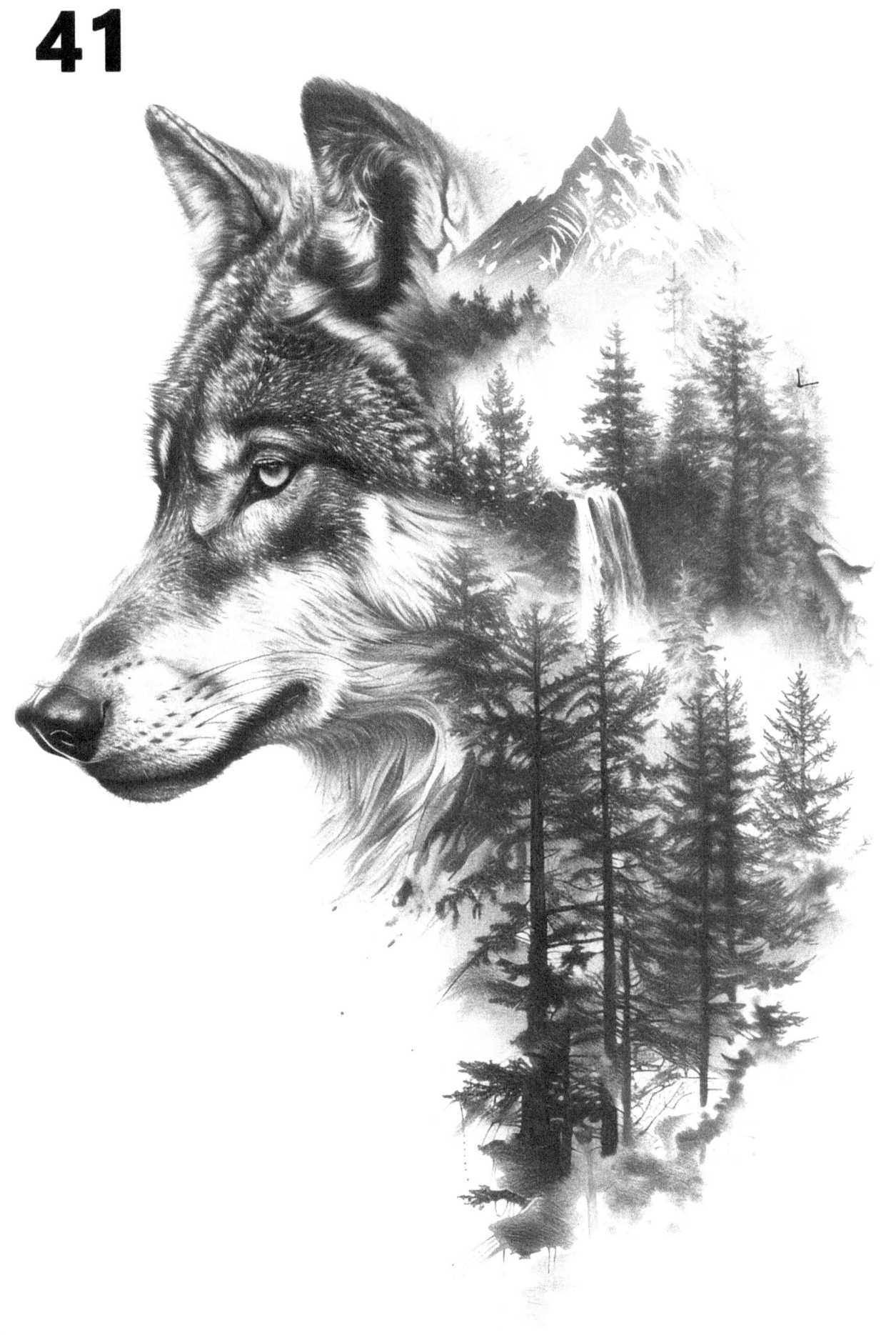

42

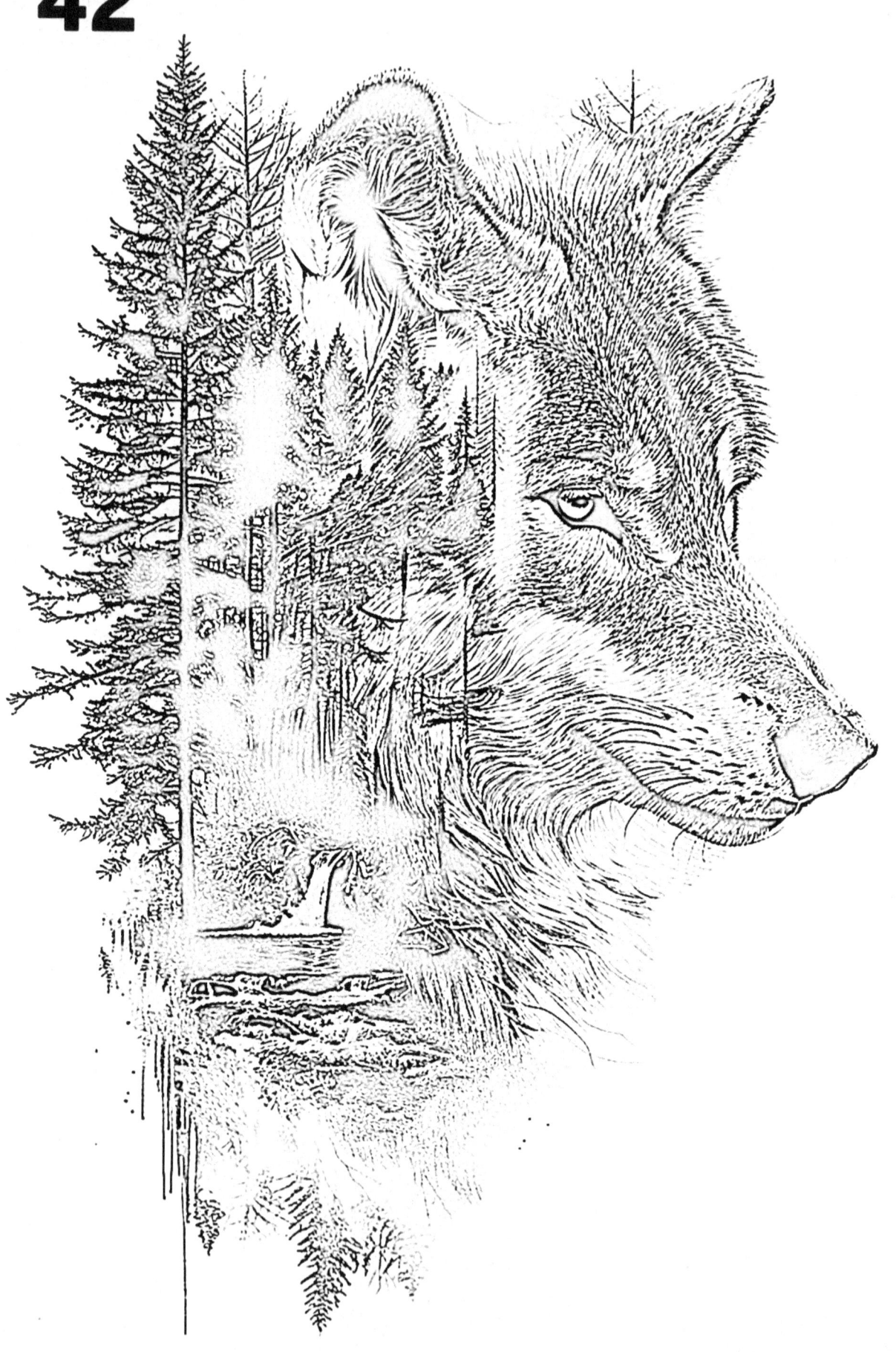

42

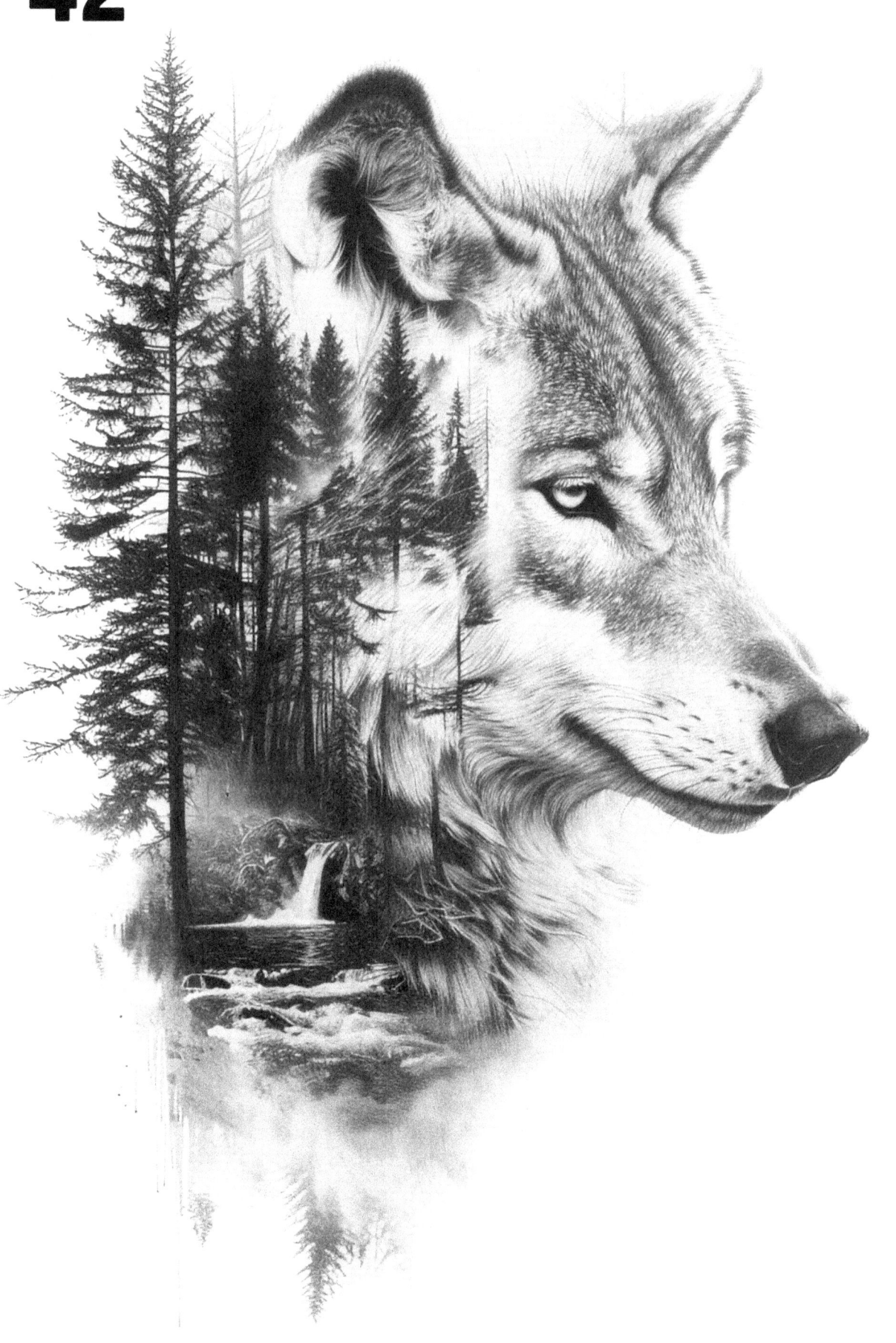

43

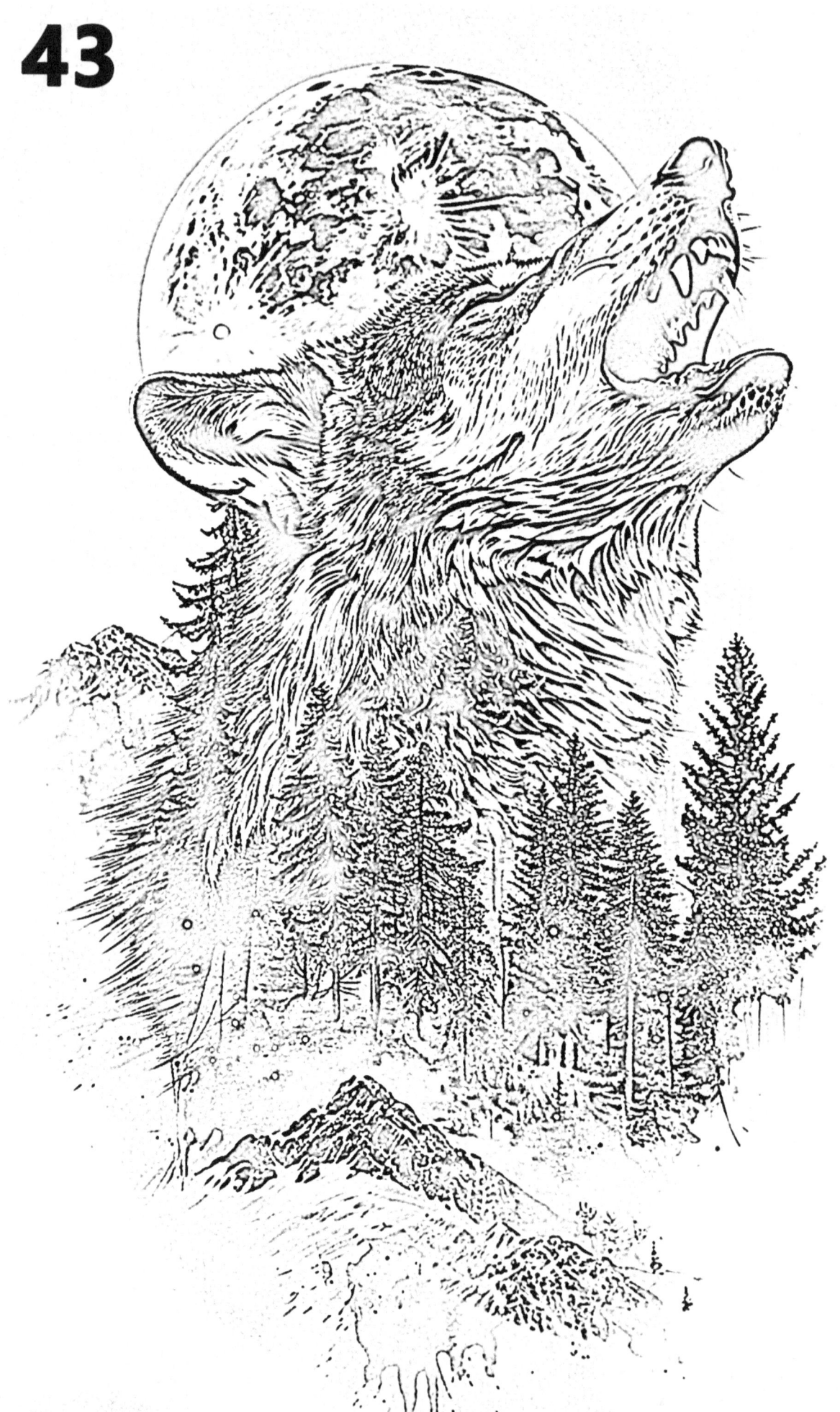

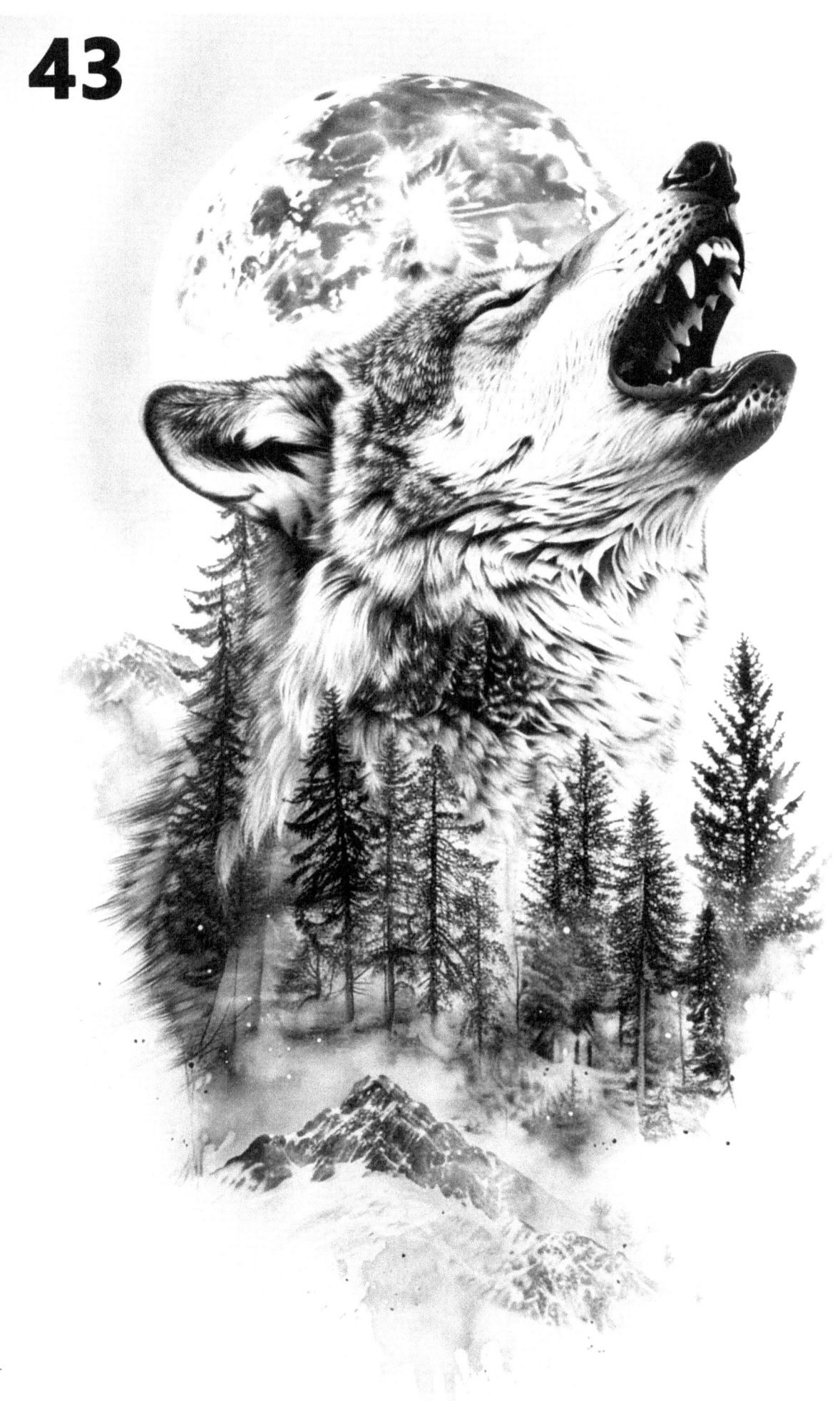

44

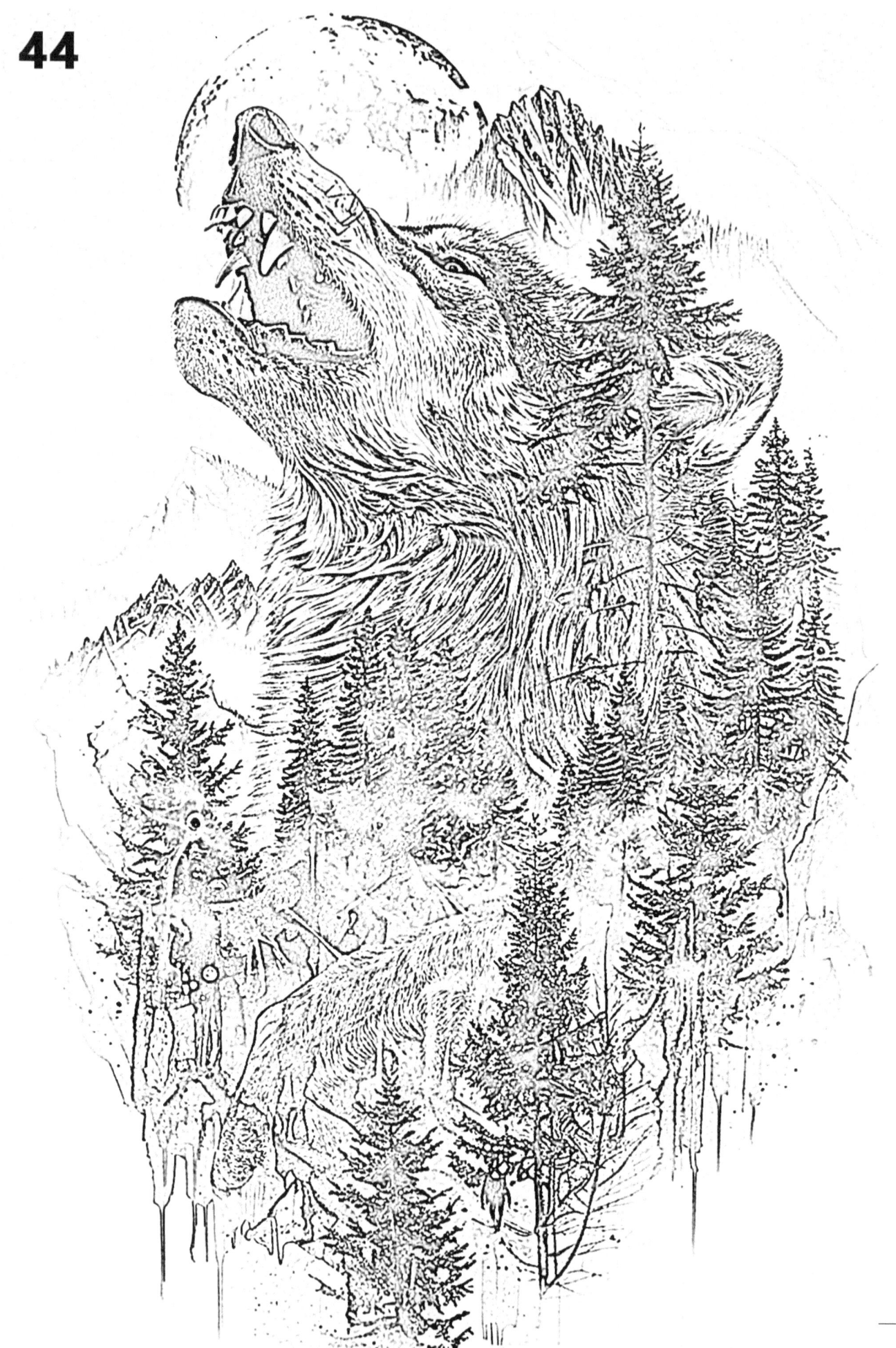

44

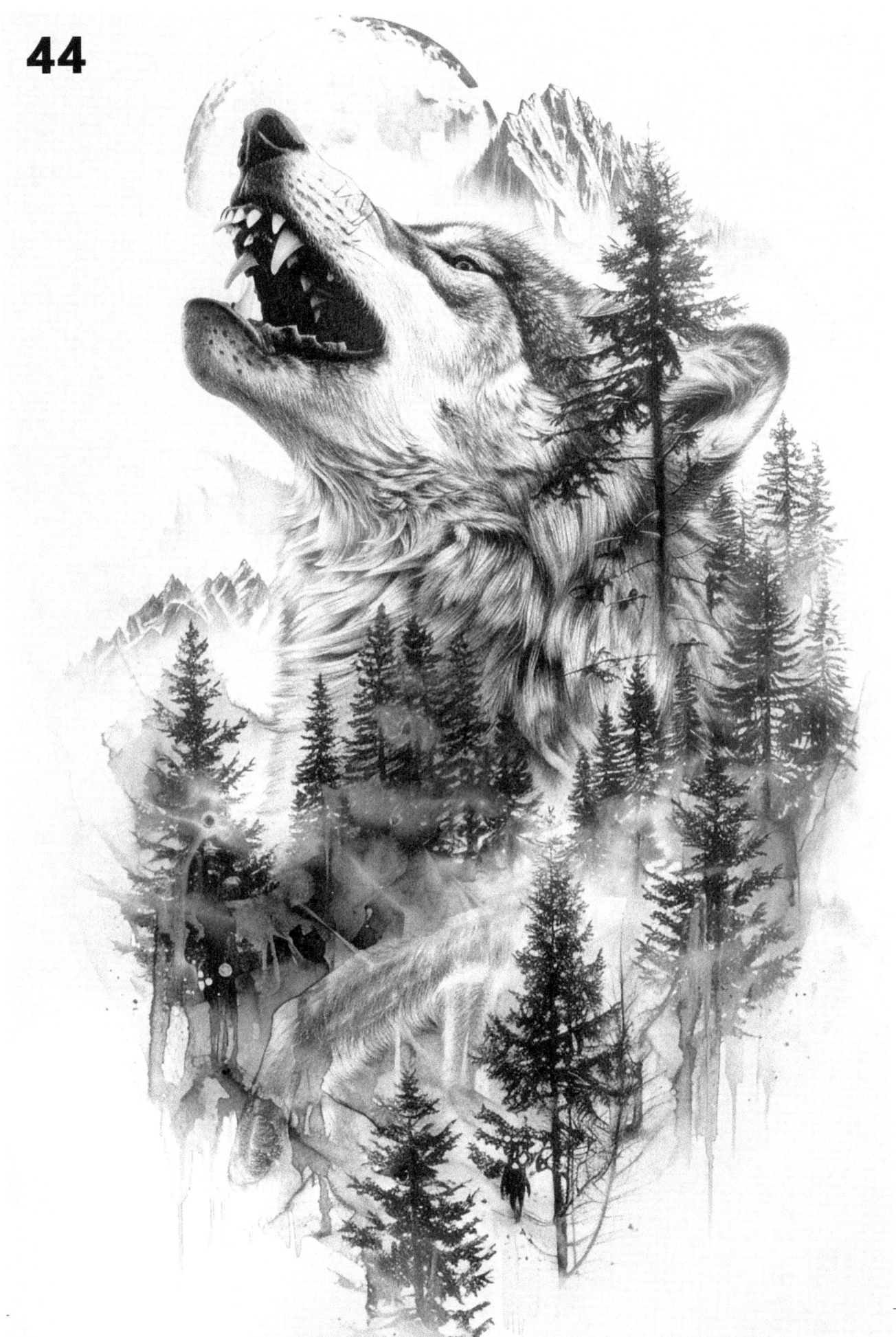

45

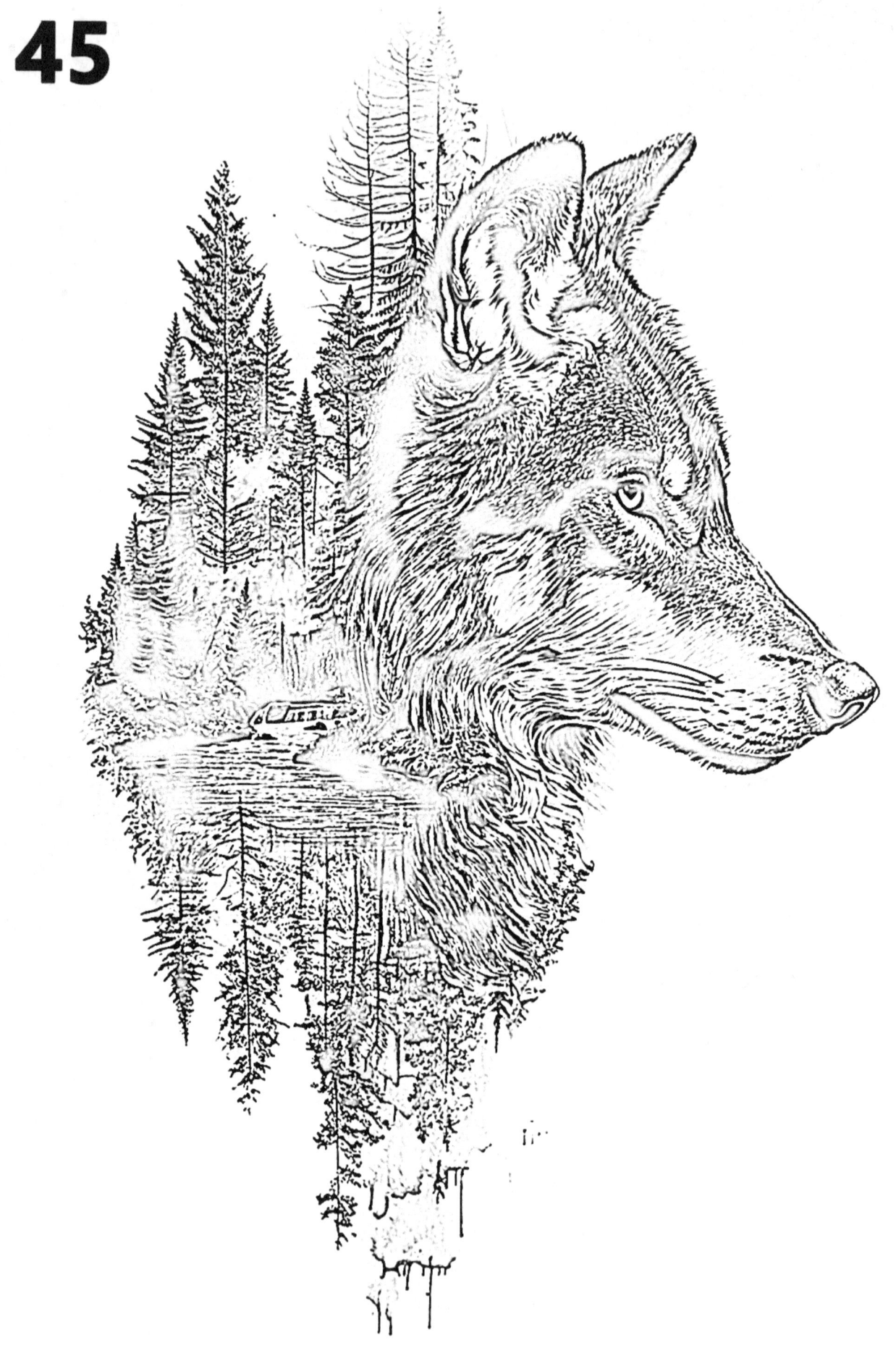

45

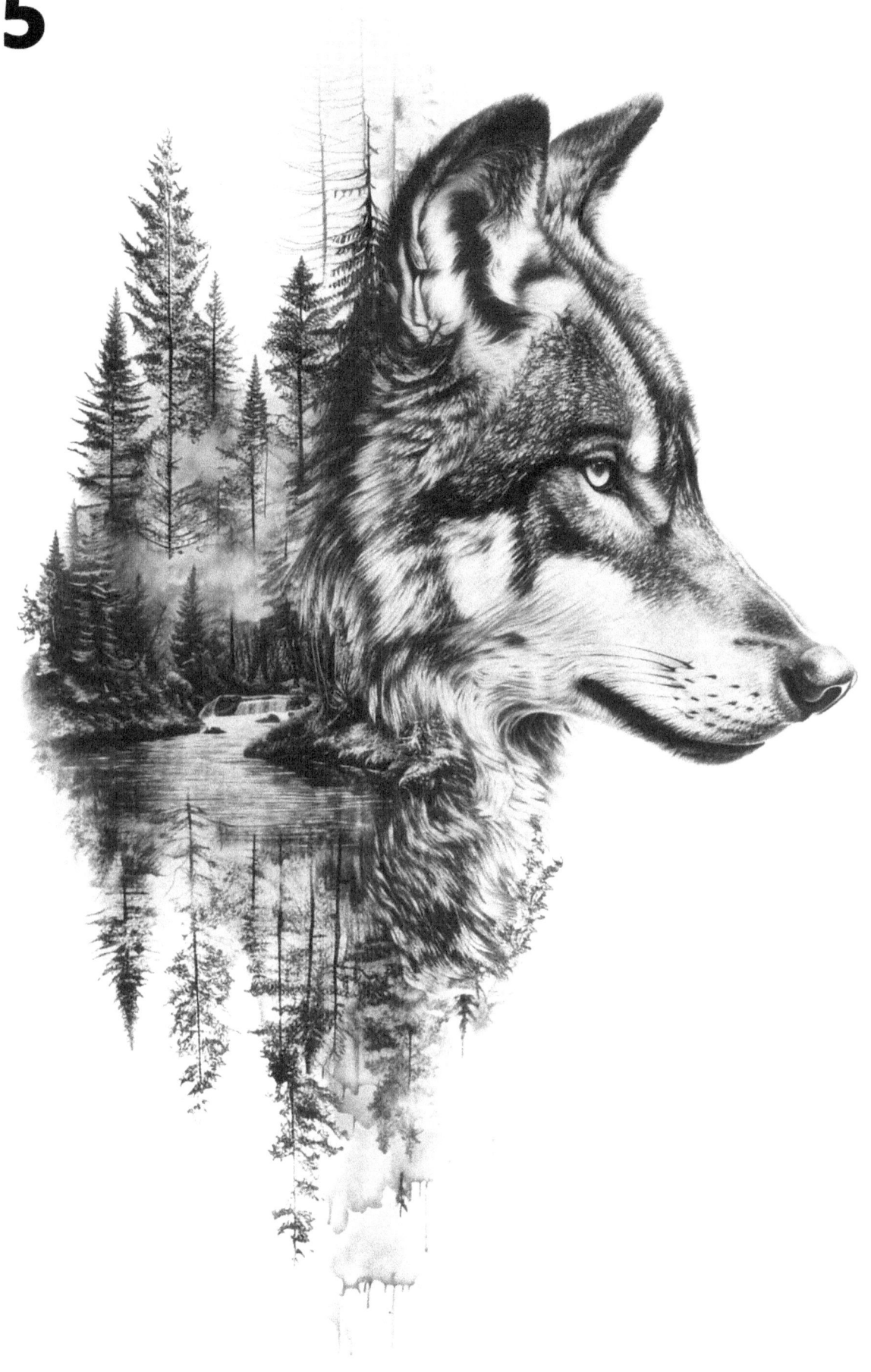

46

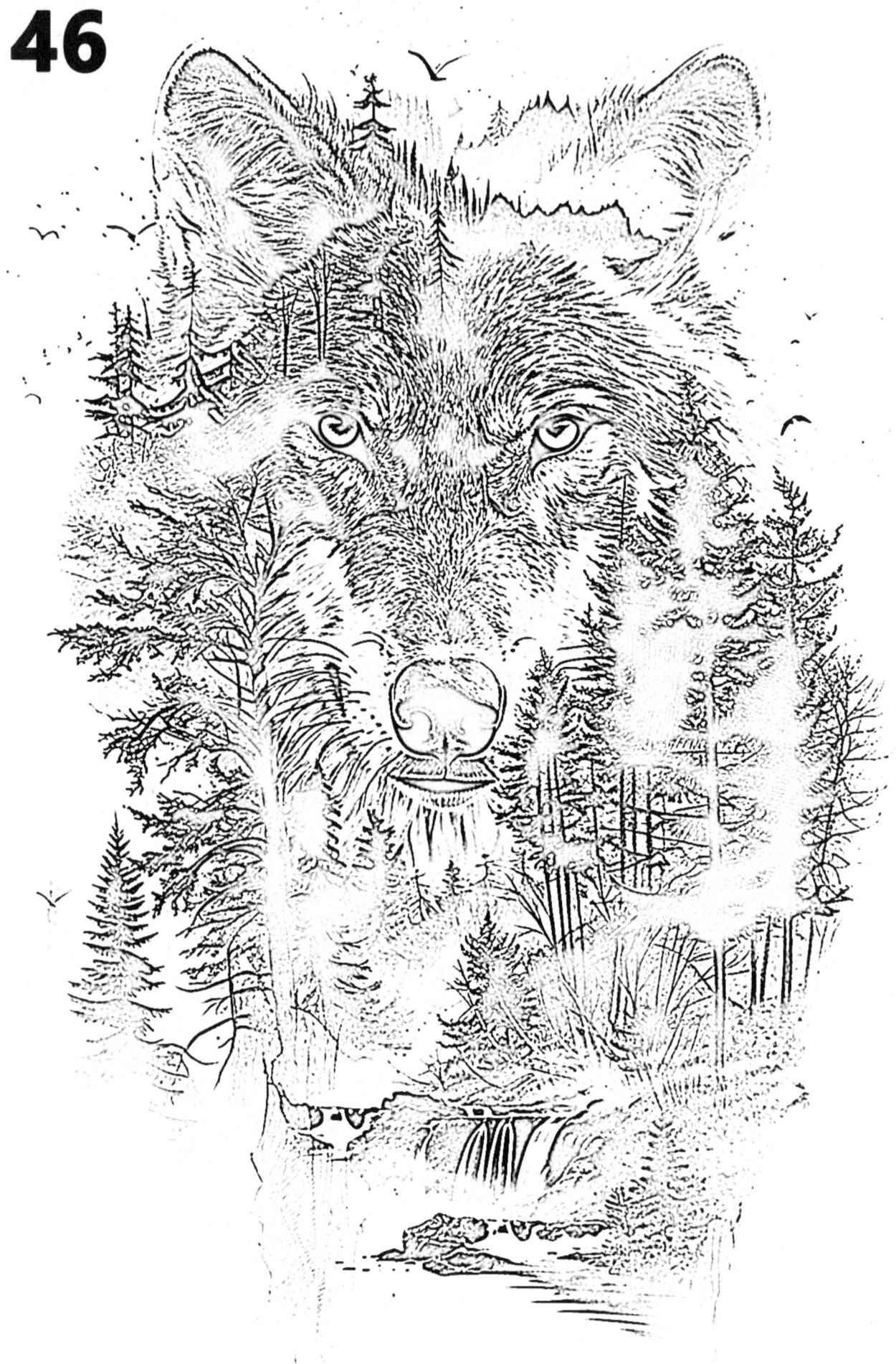

46

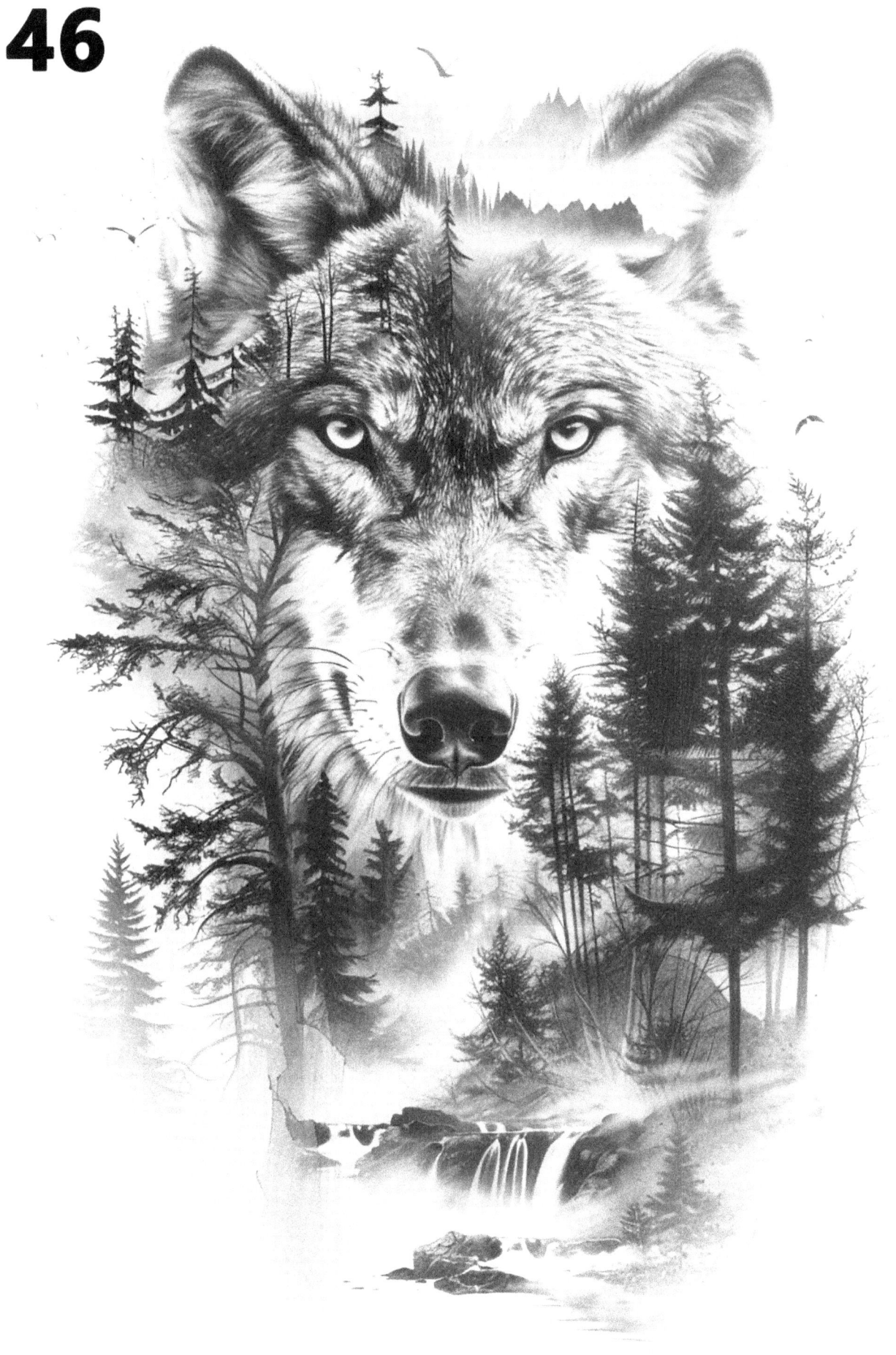

47

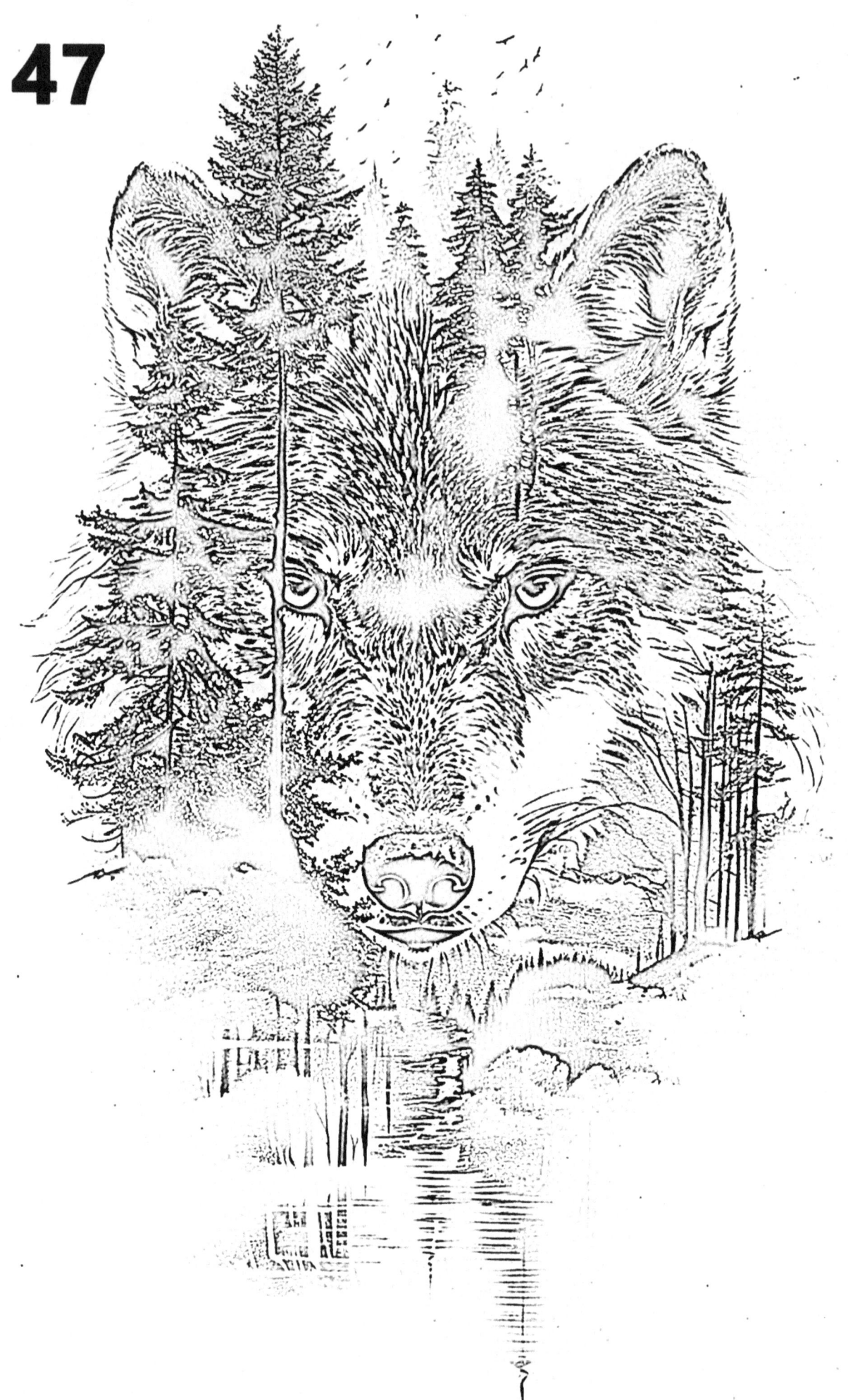

47

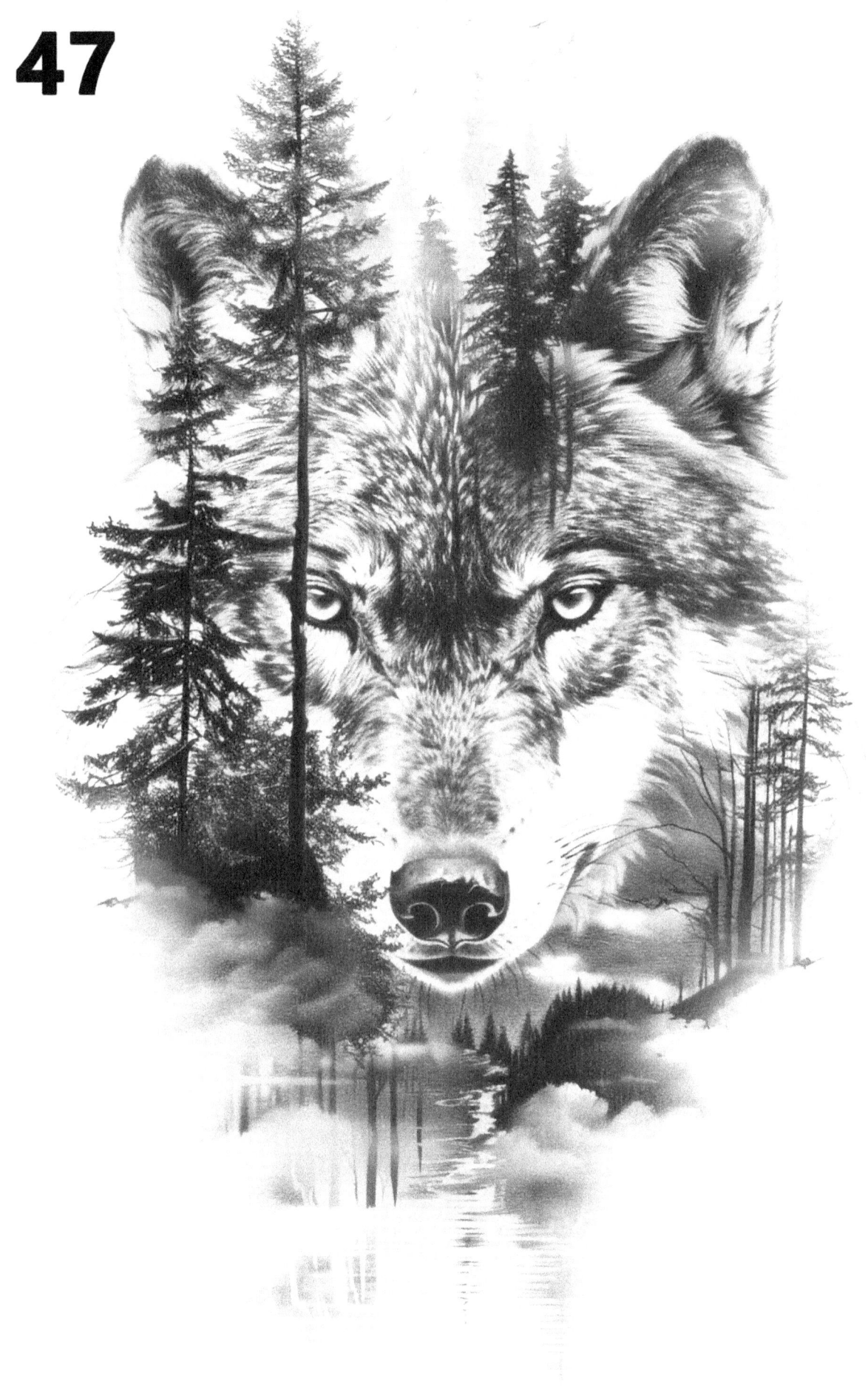

48

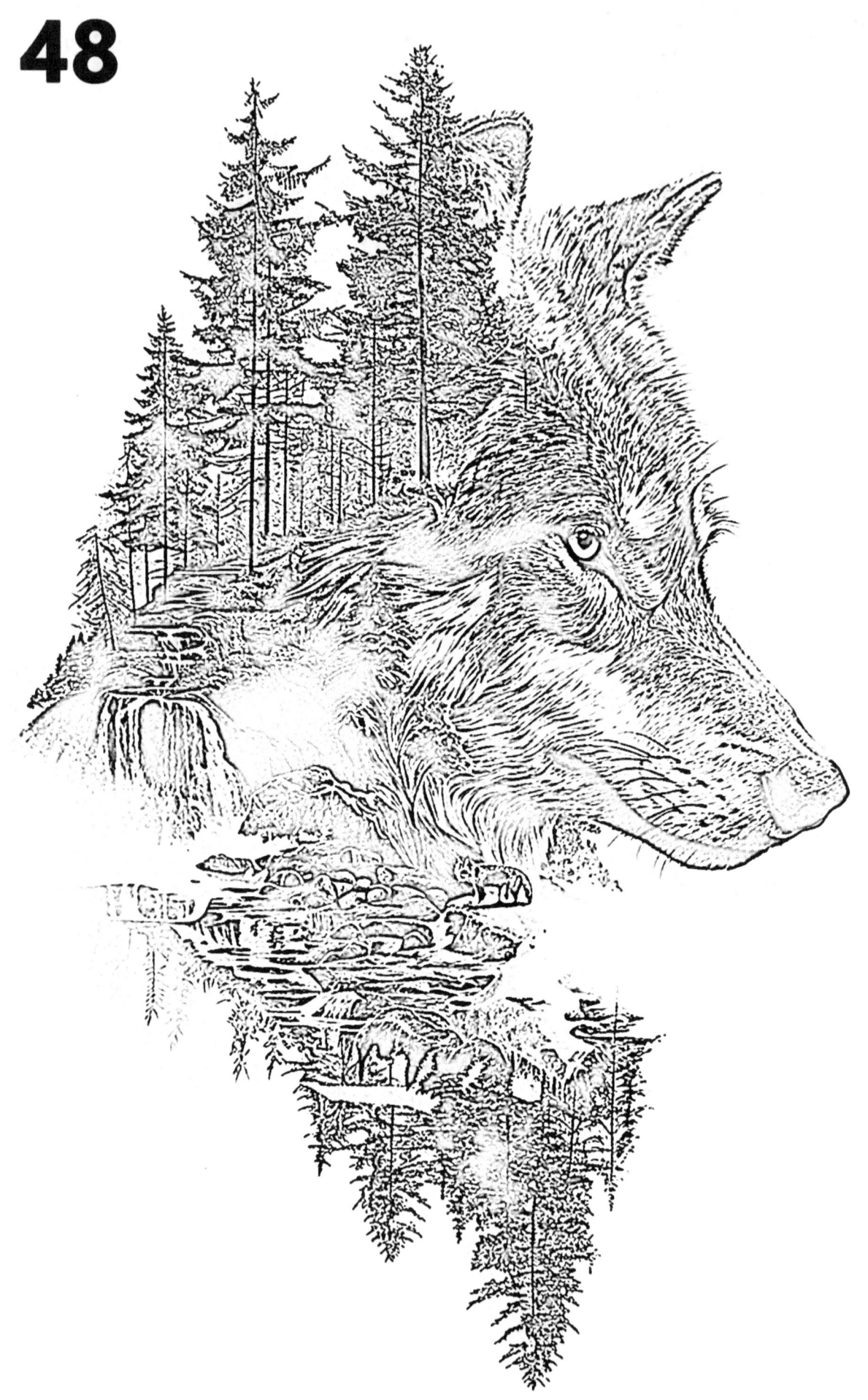

48

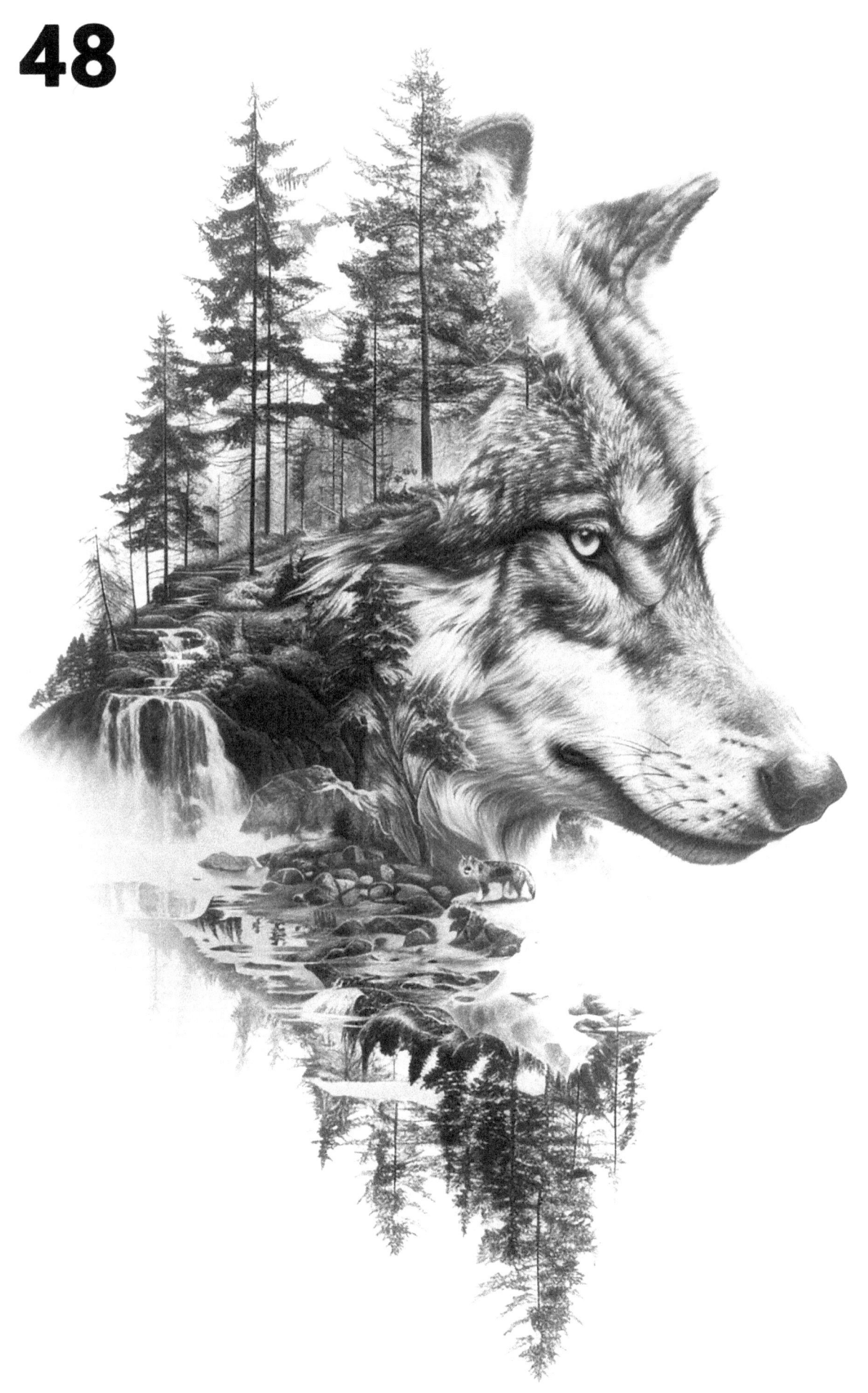

49

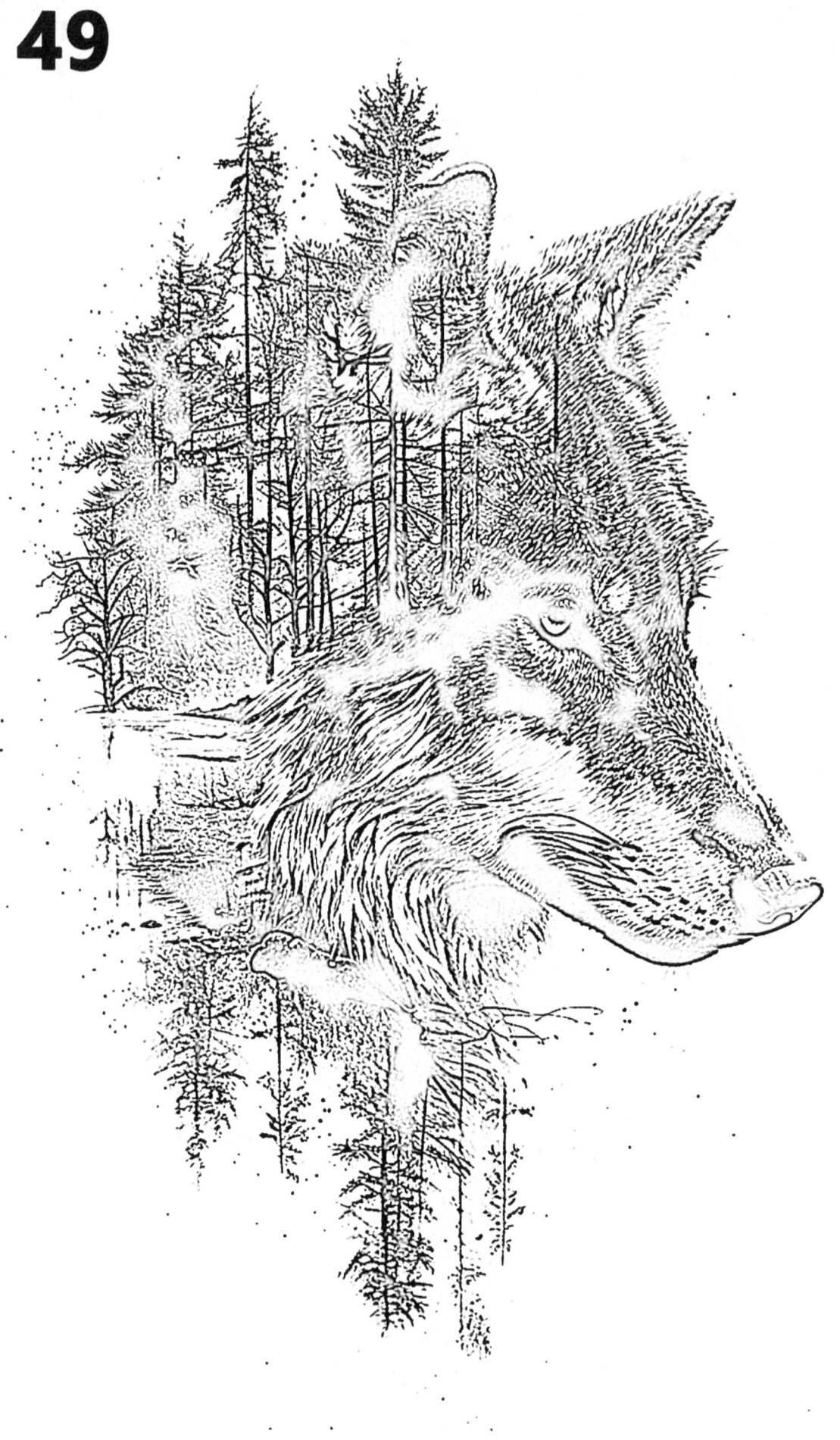

49

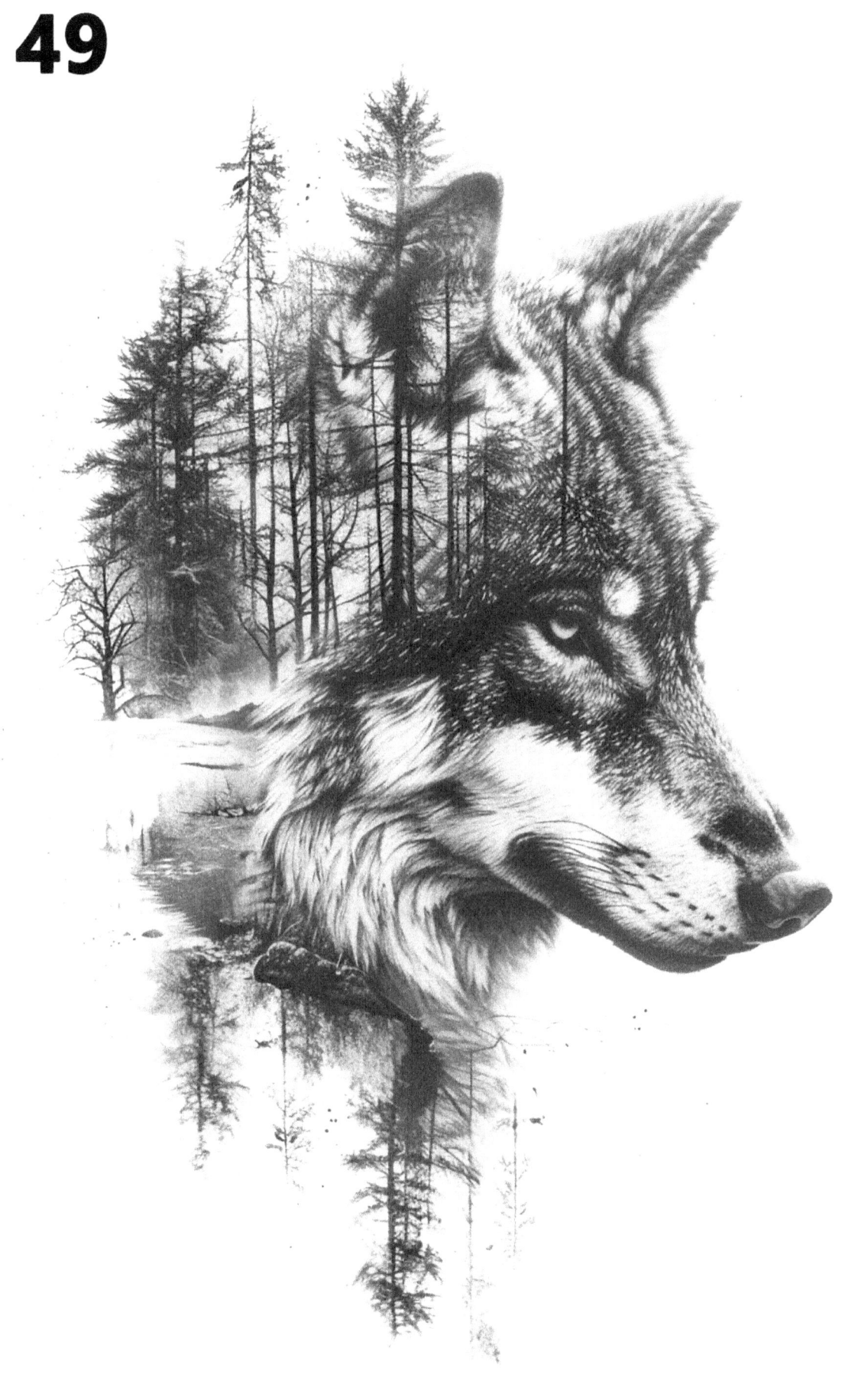

50

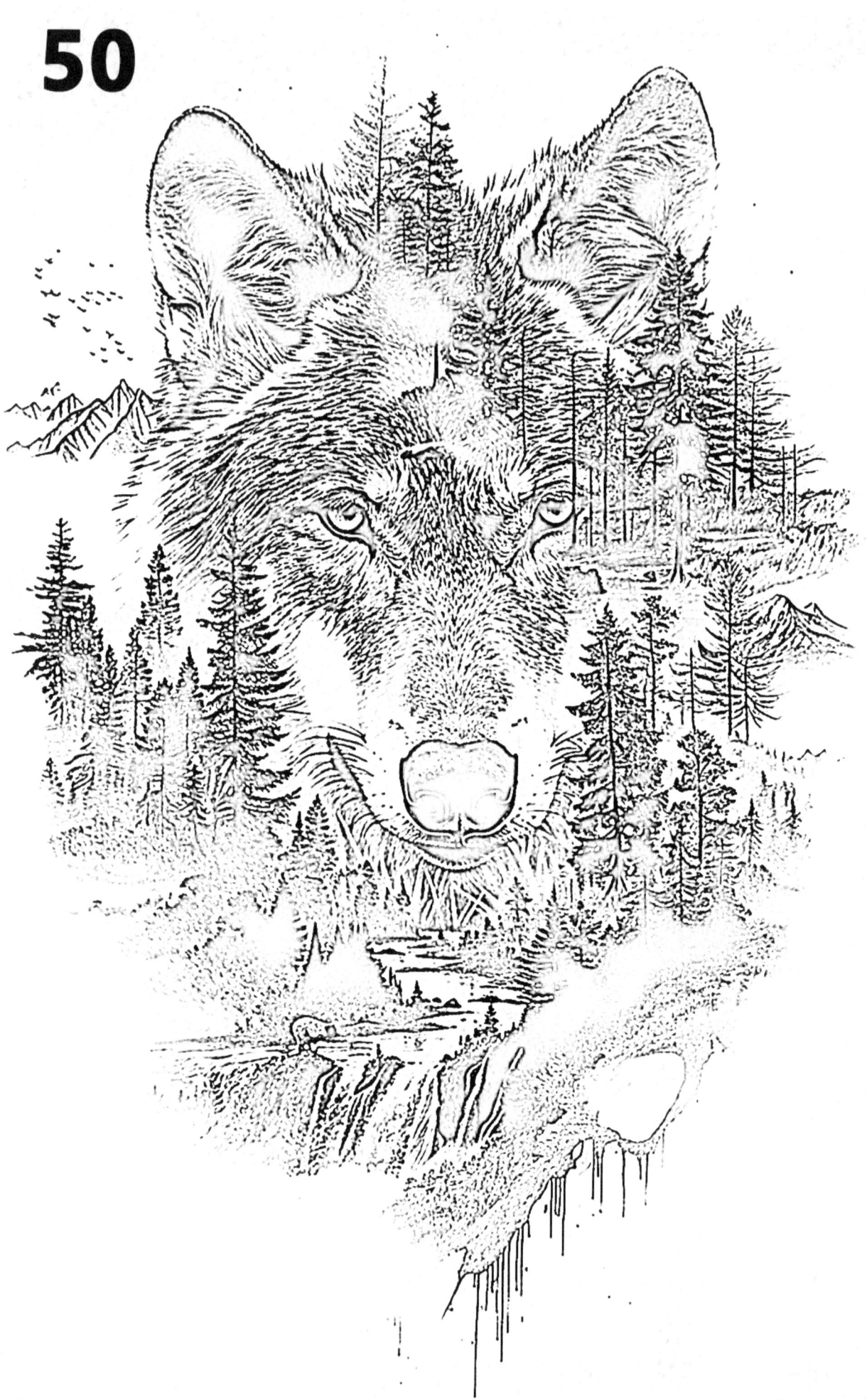

50

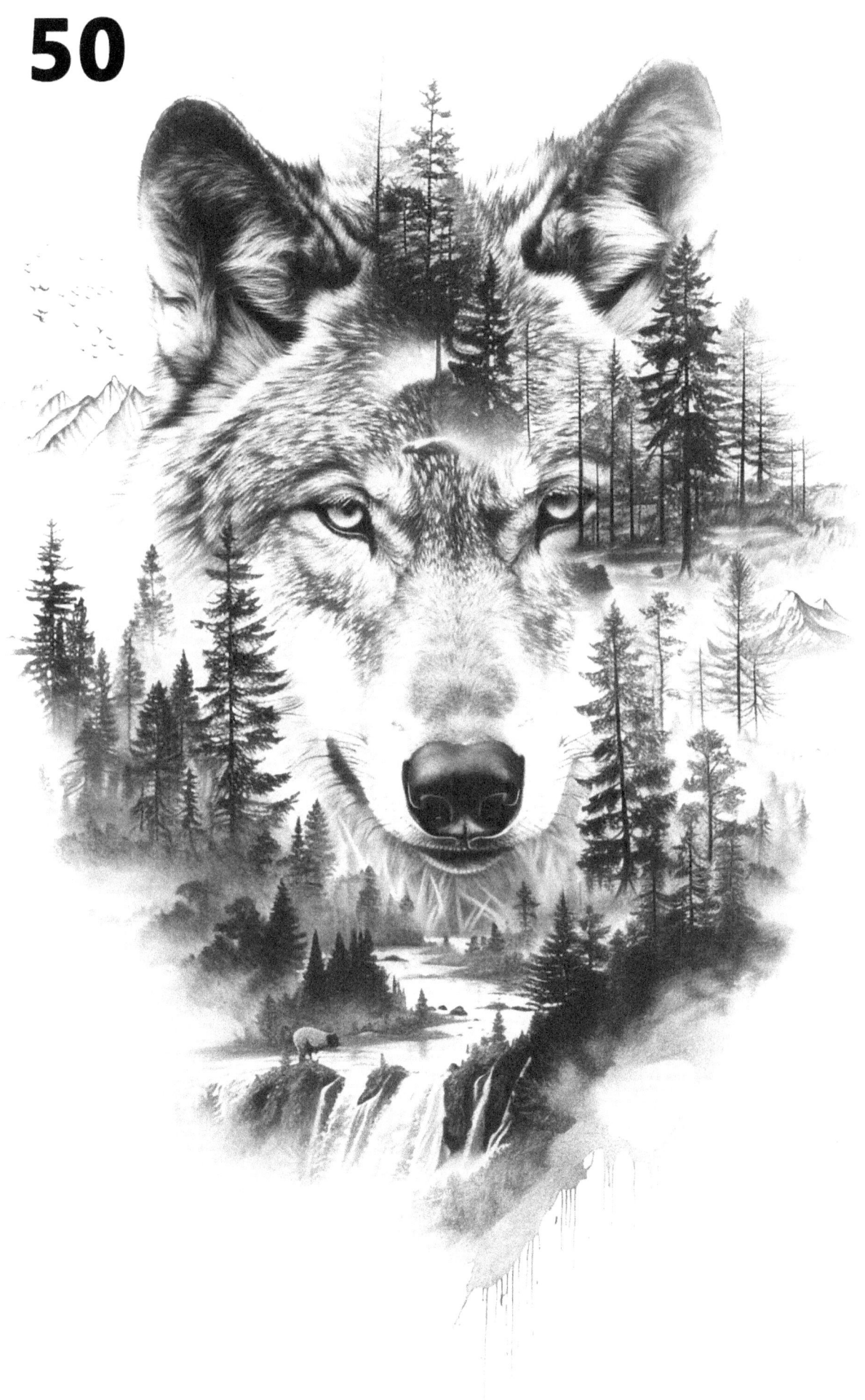

51

51

52

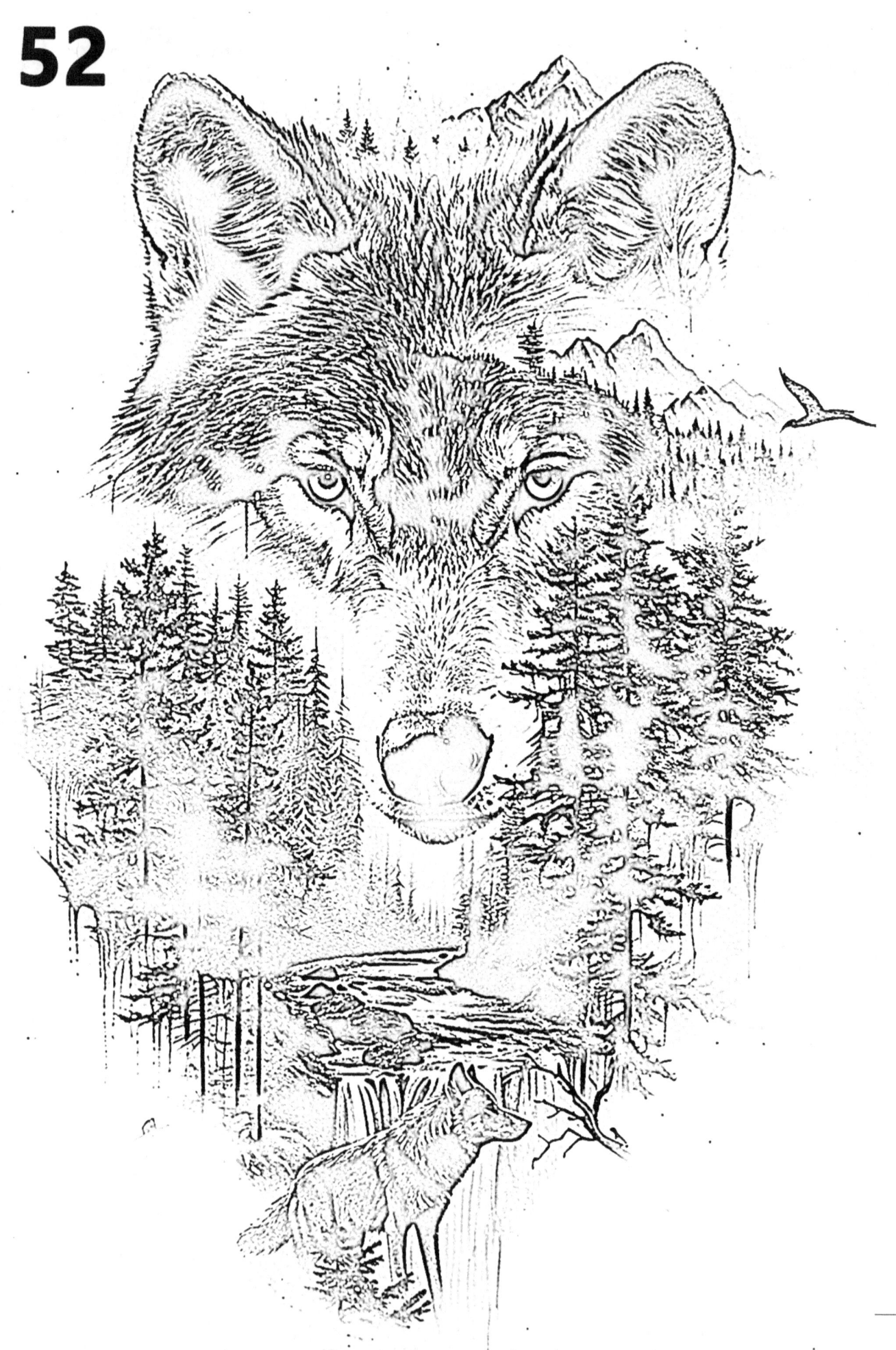

52

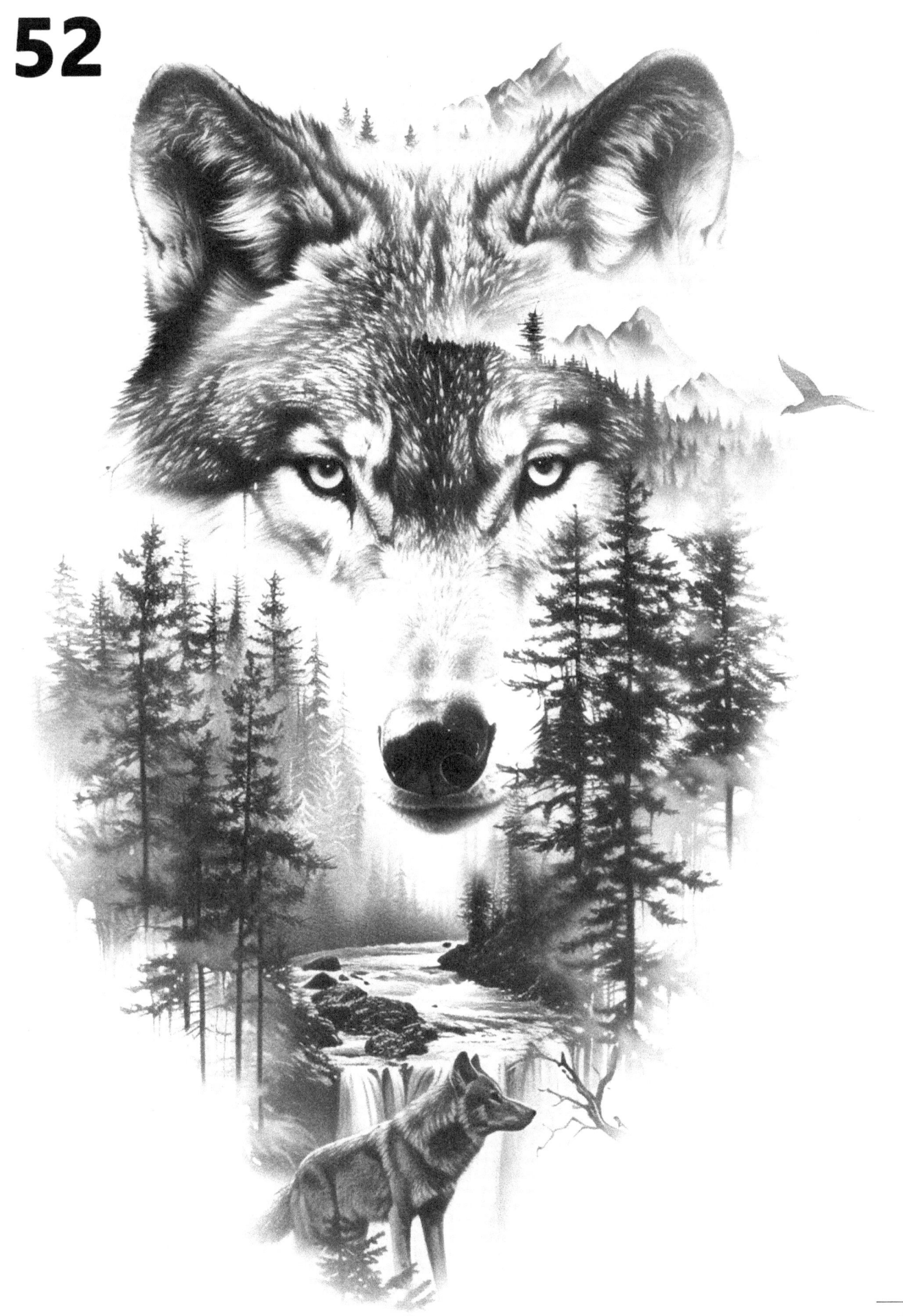

53

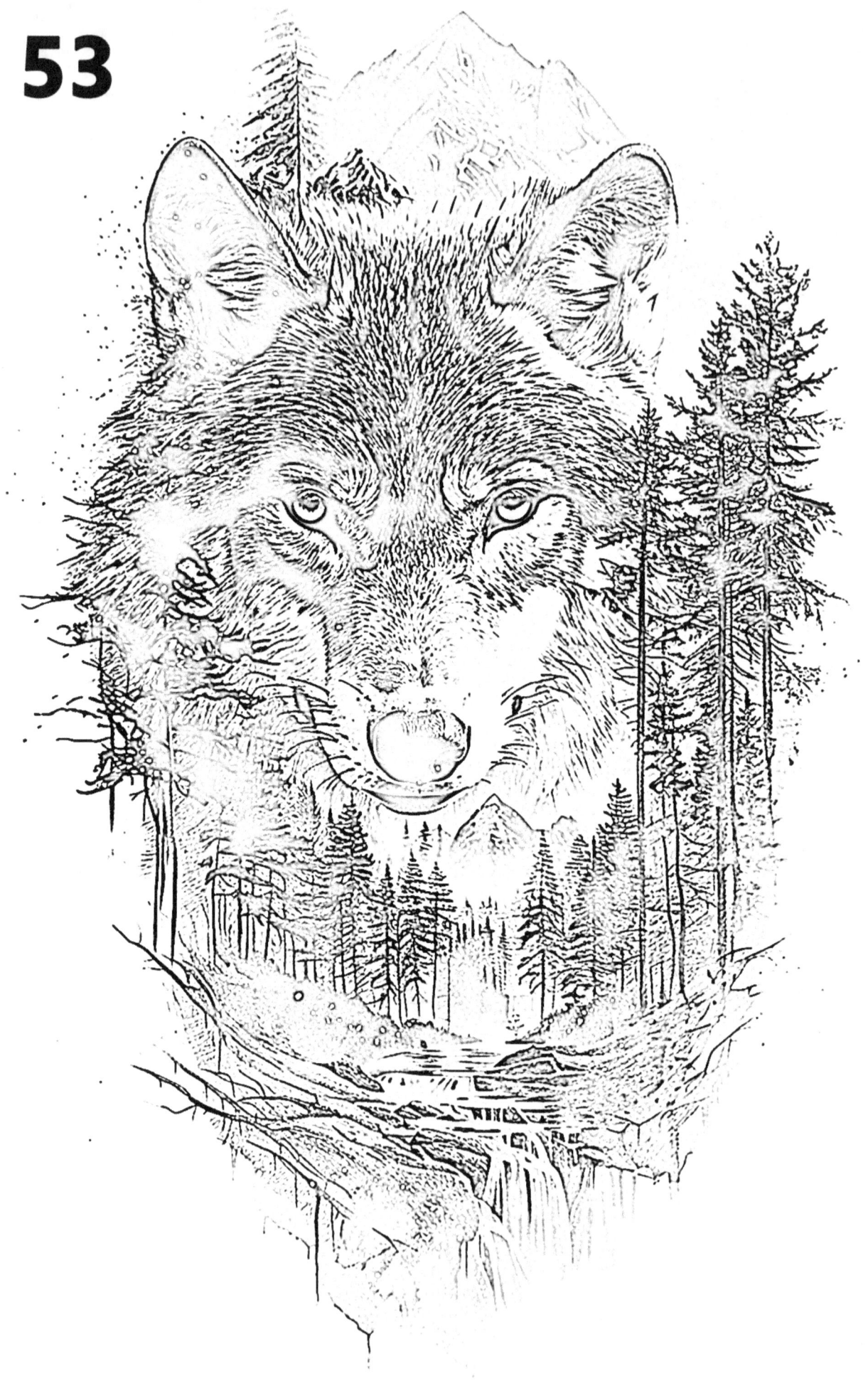

53

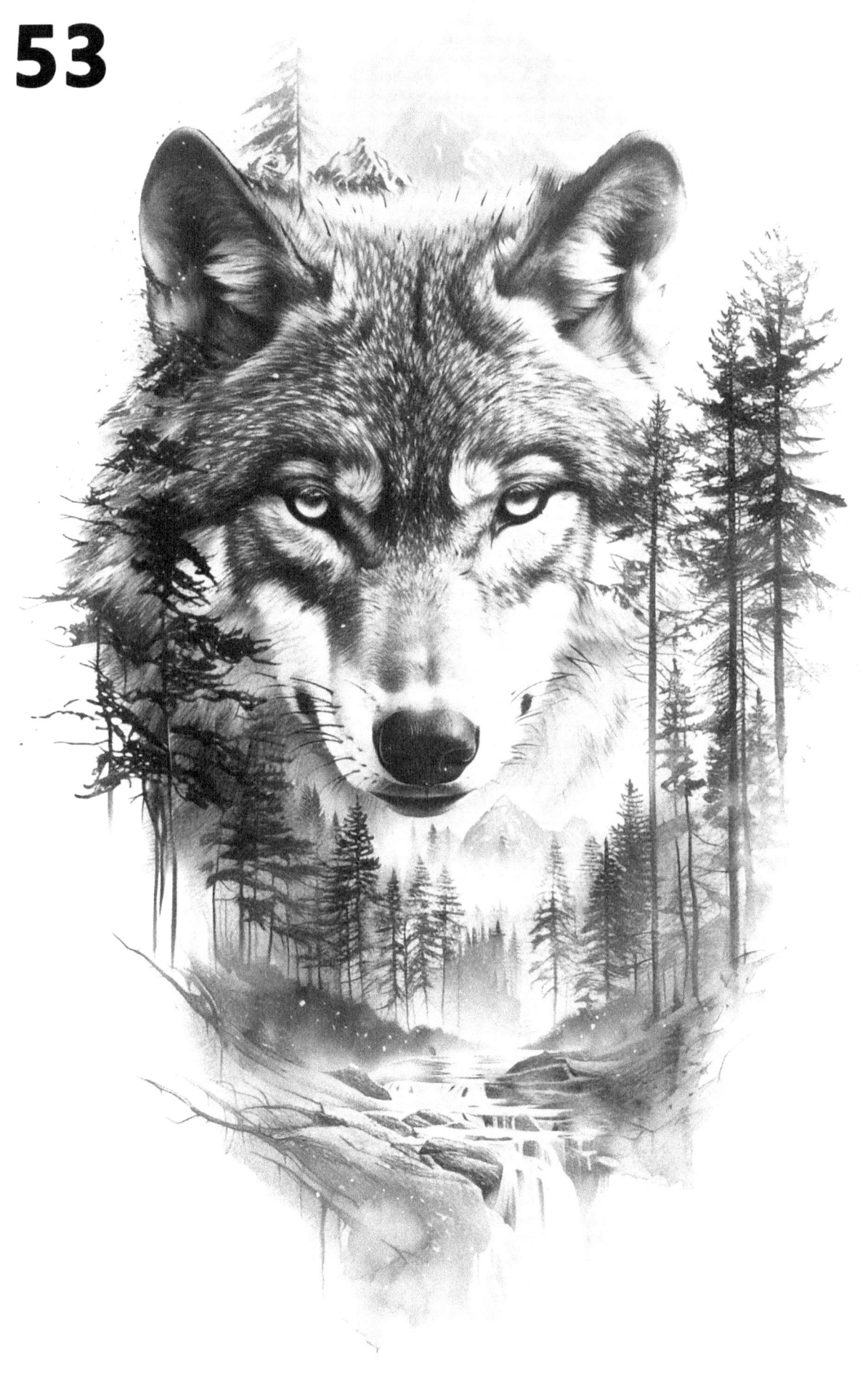

54

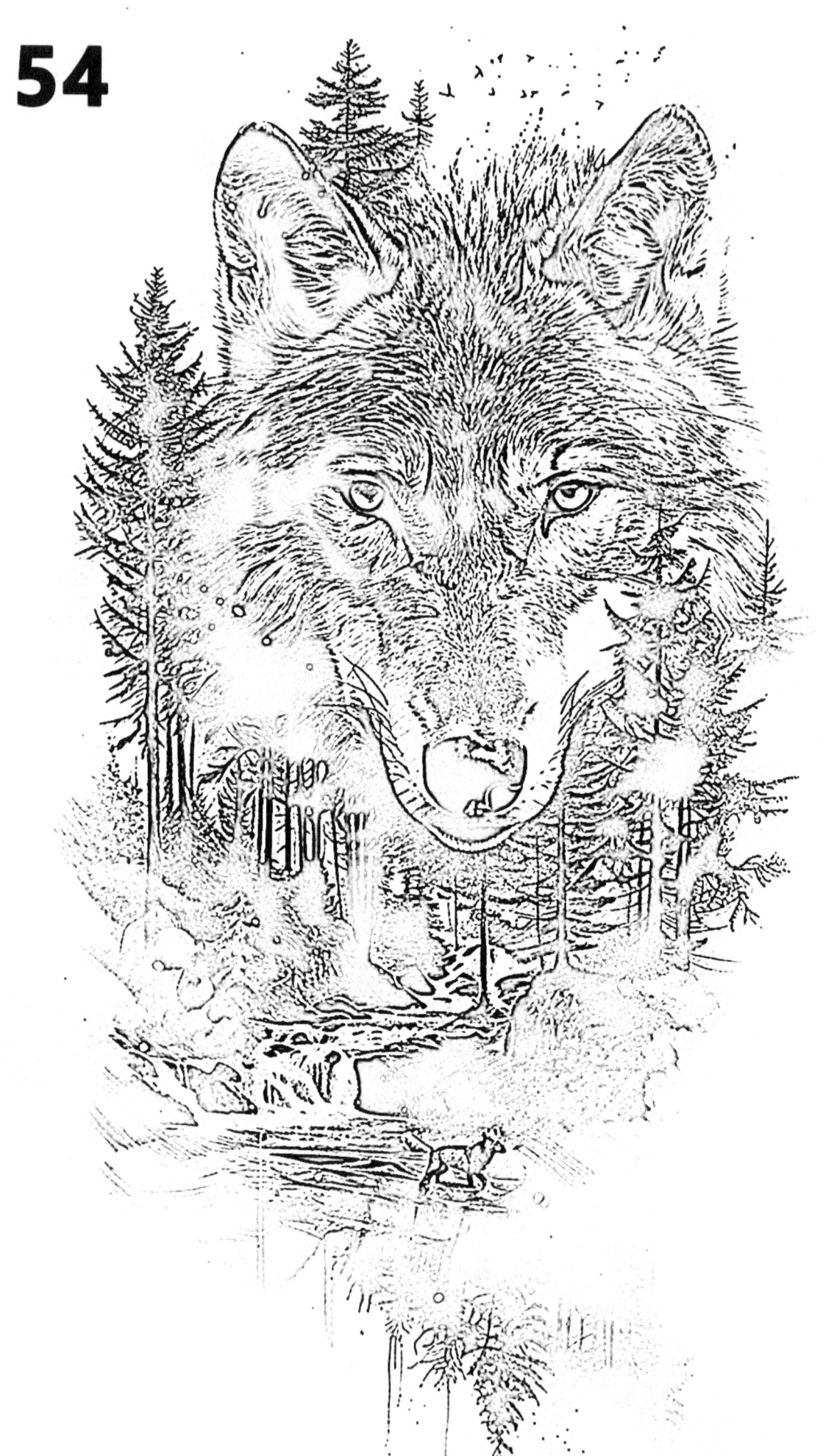

54

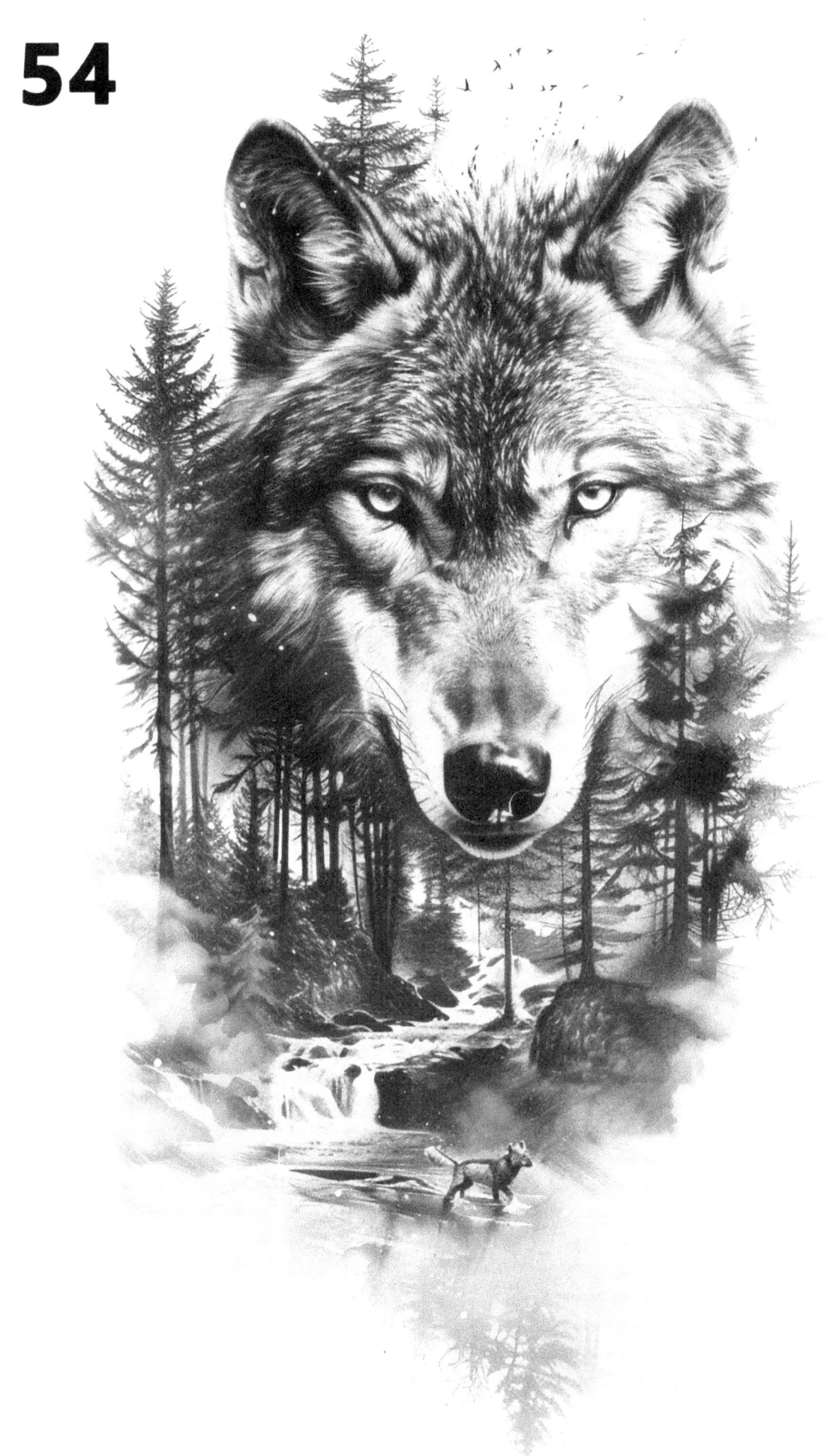

55

55

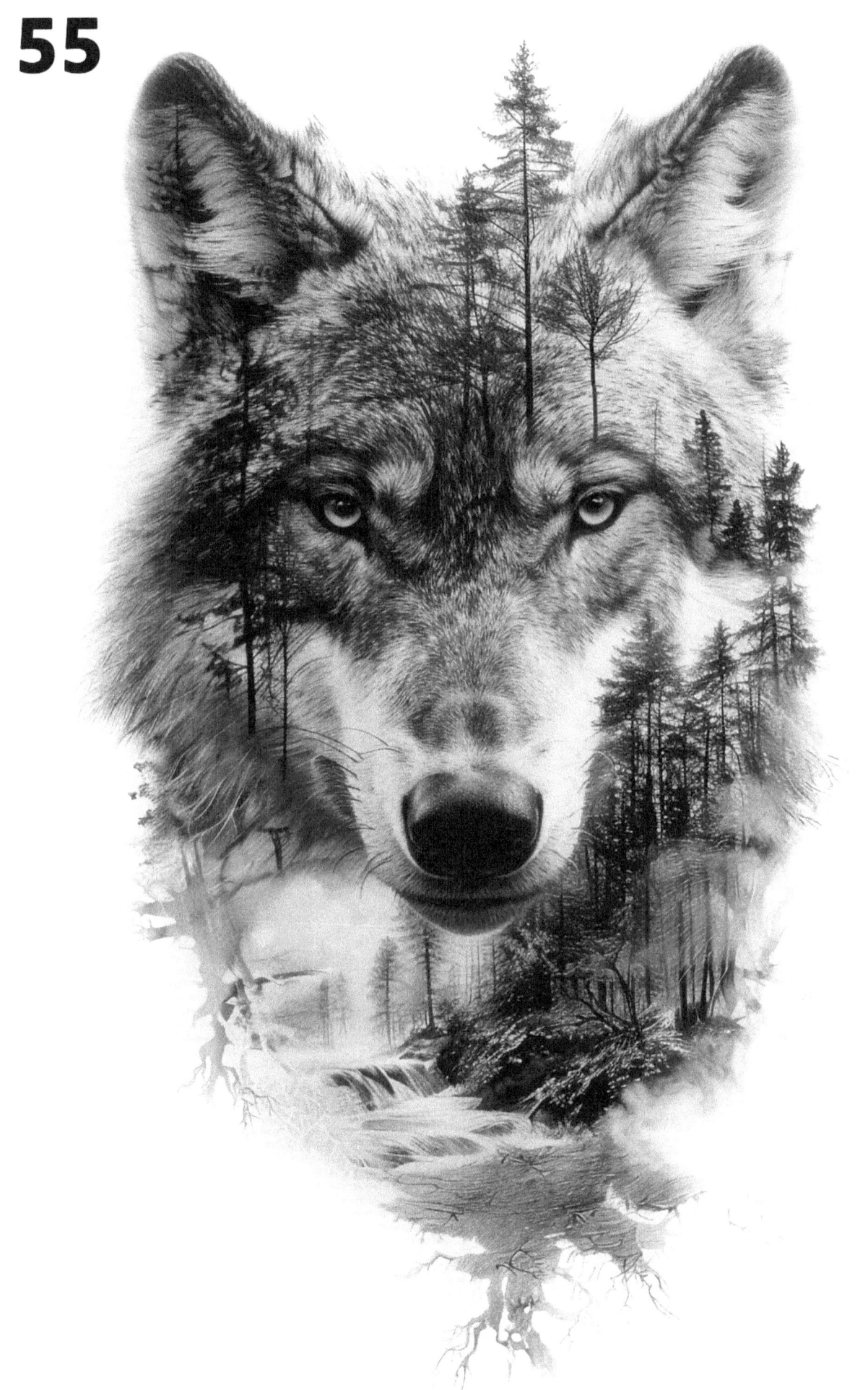

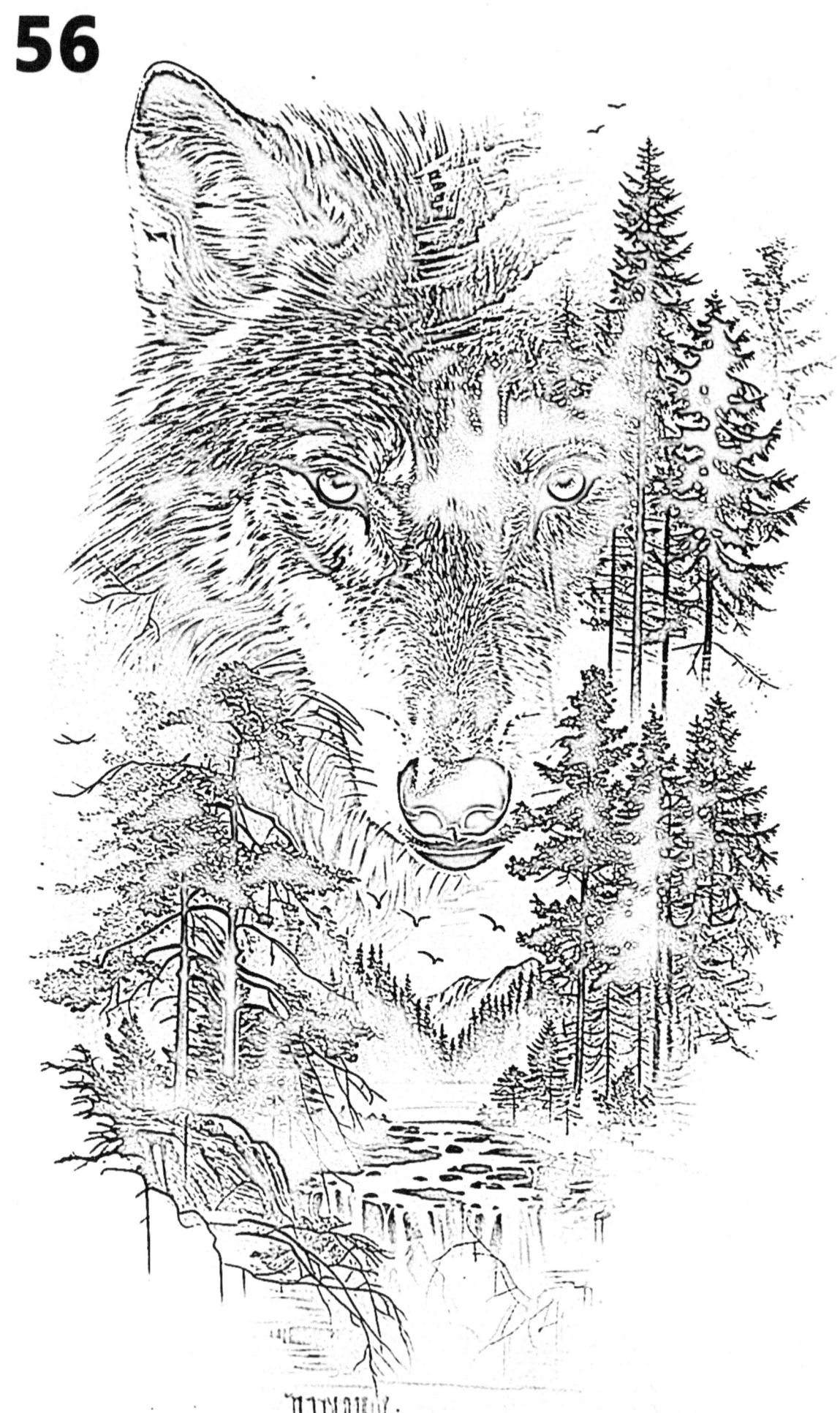

56

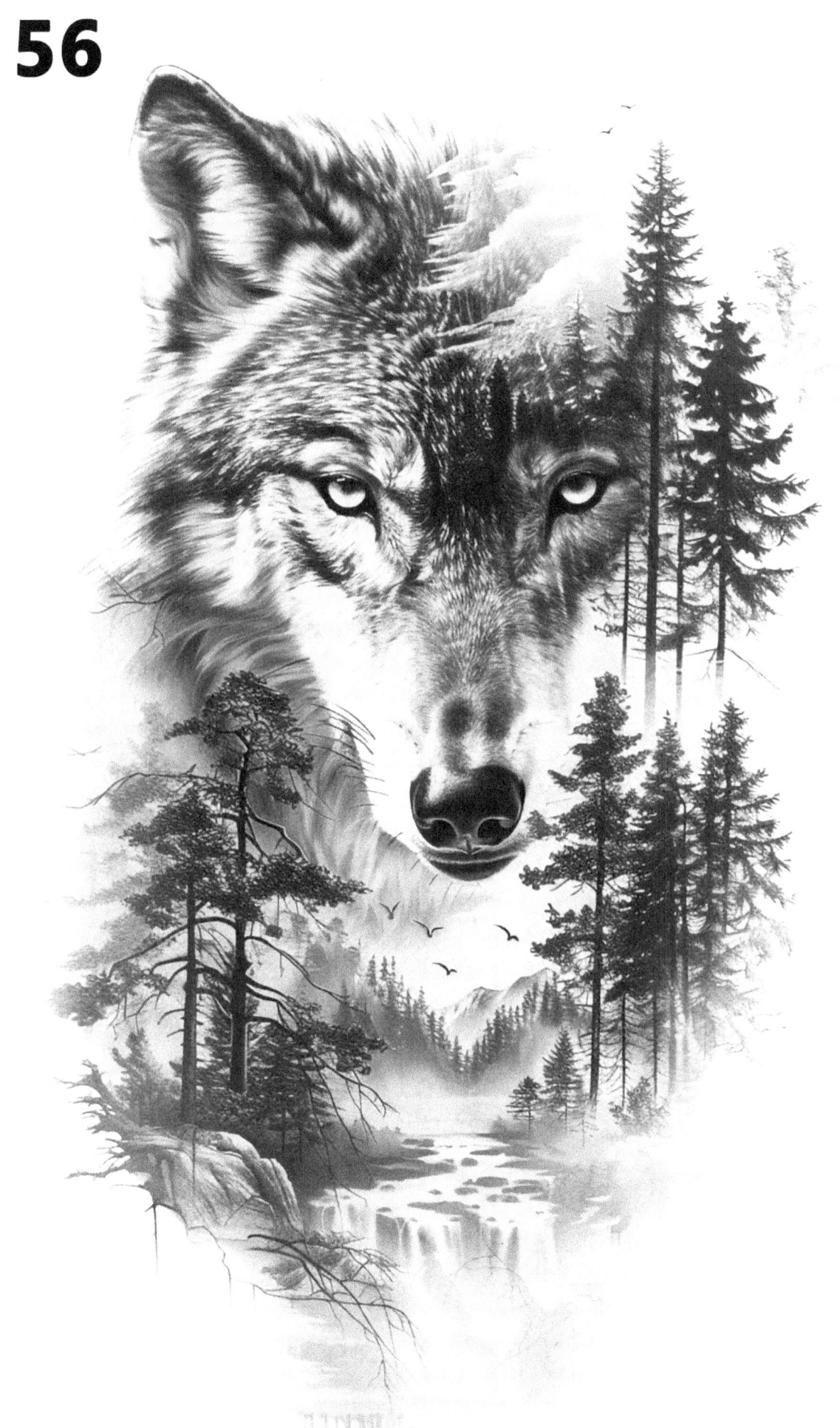

57

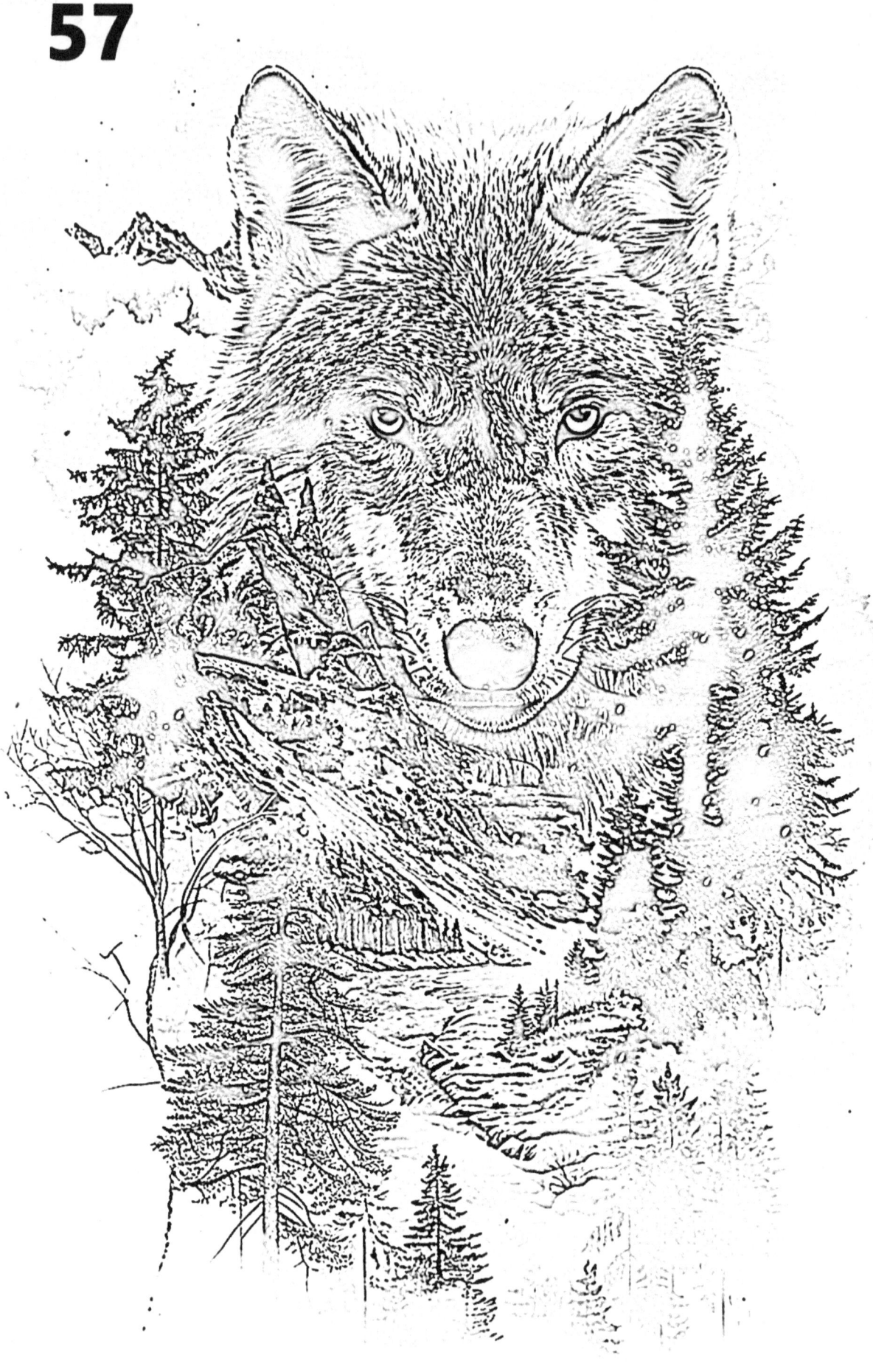

57

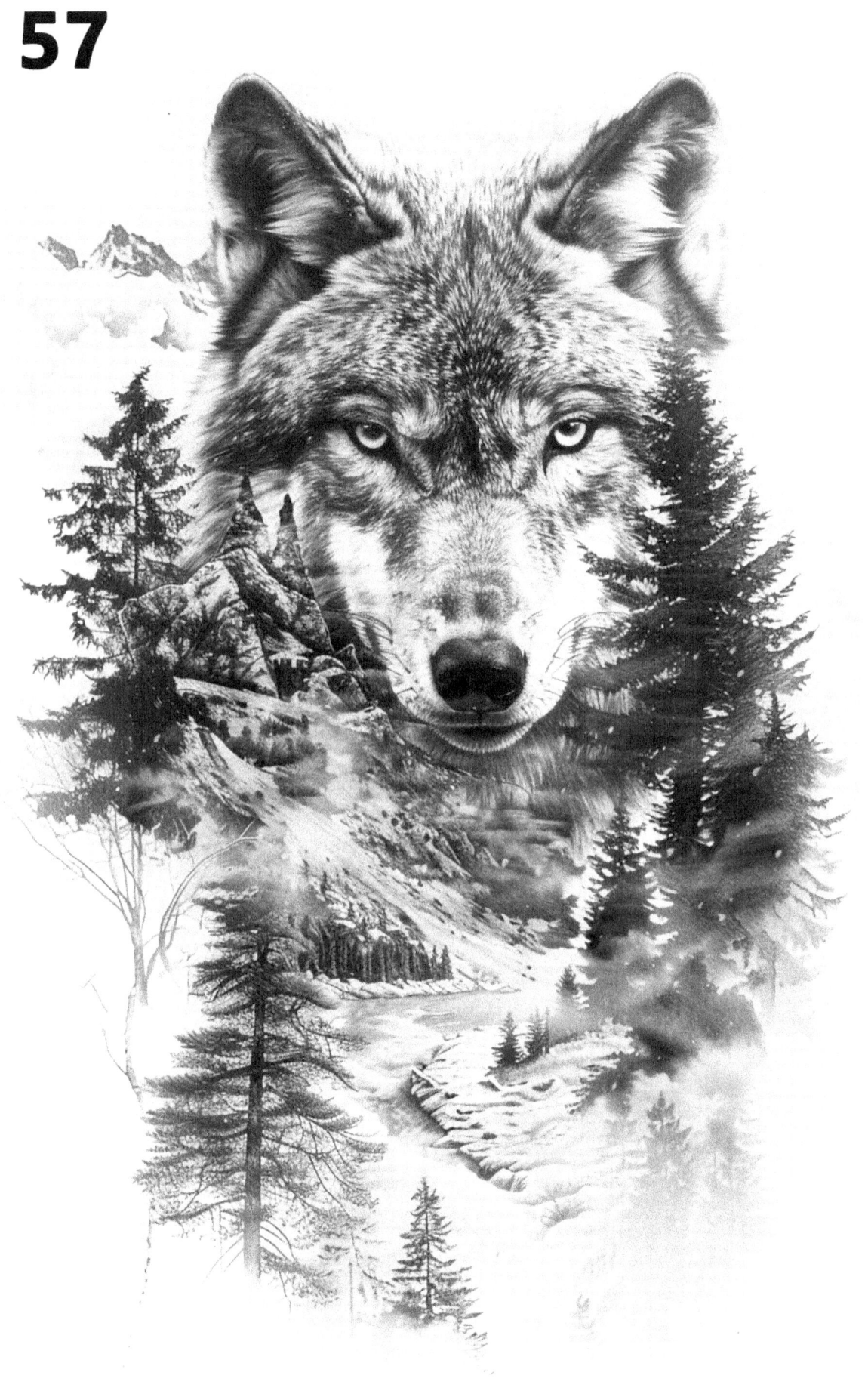

58

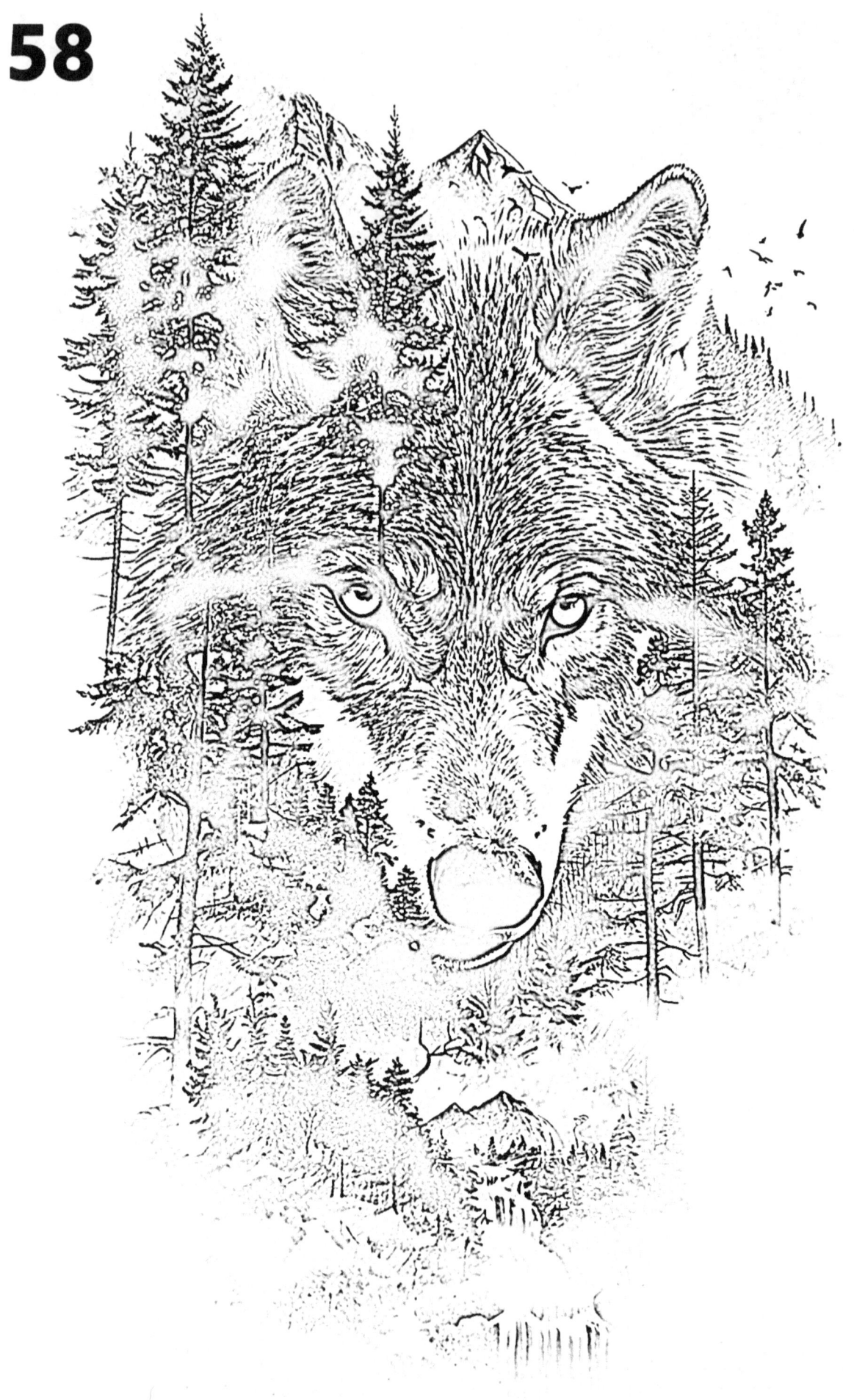

58

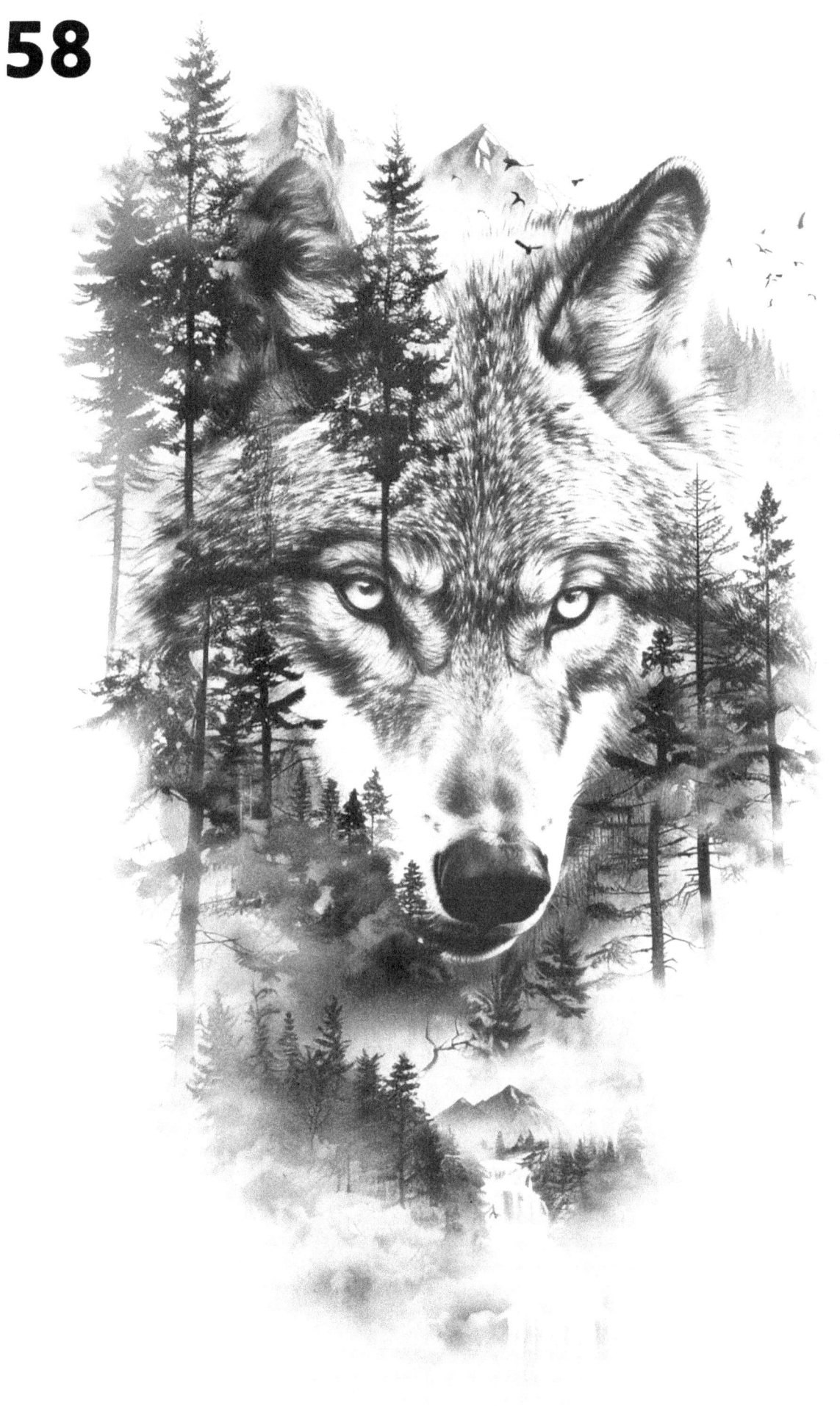

59

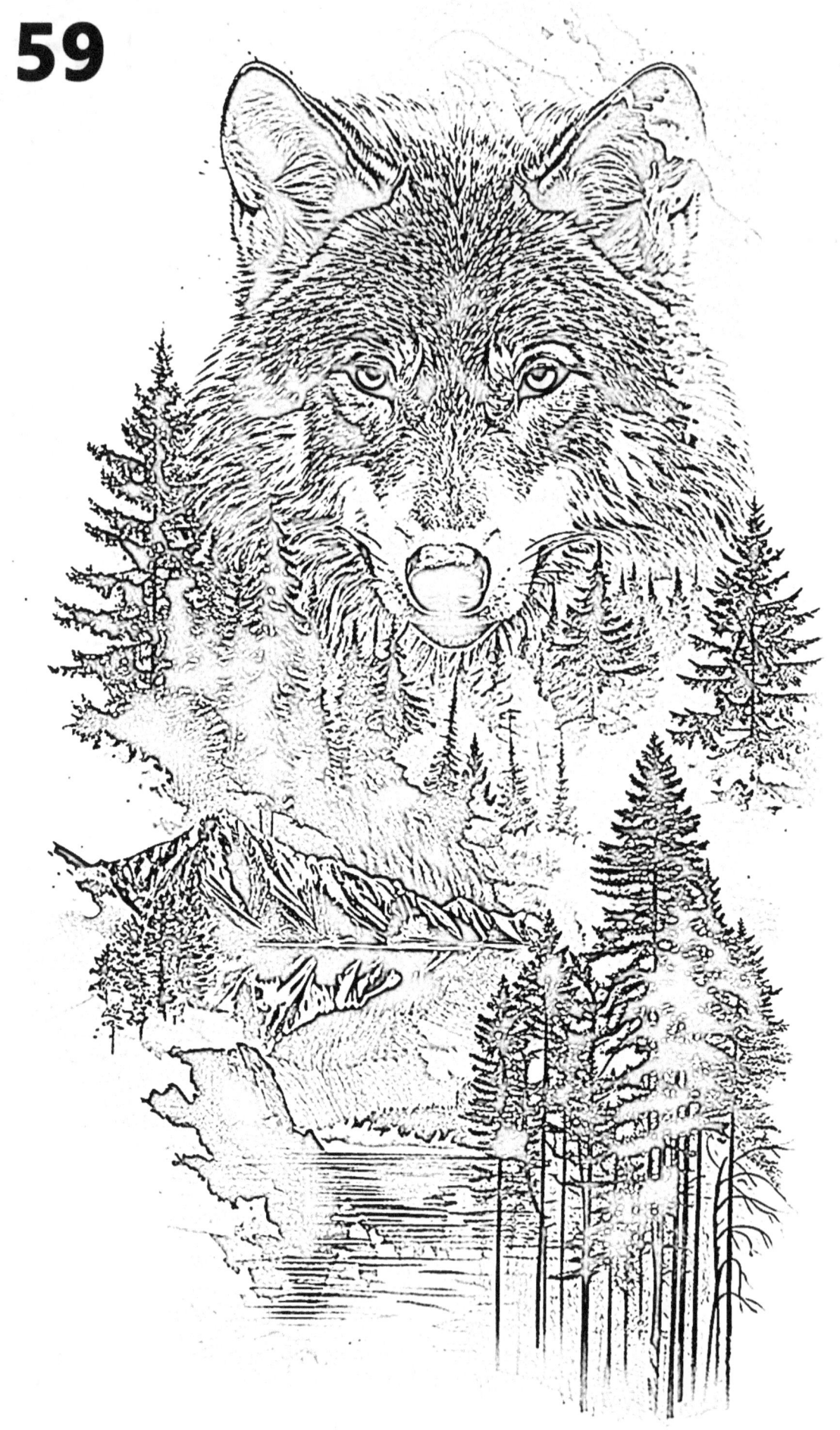

59

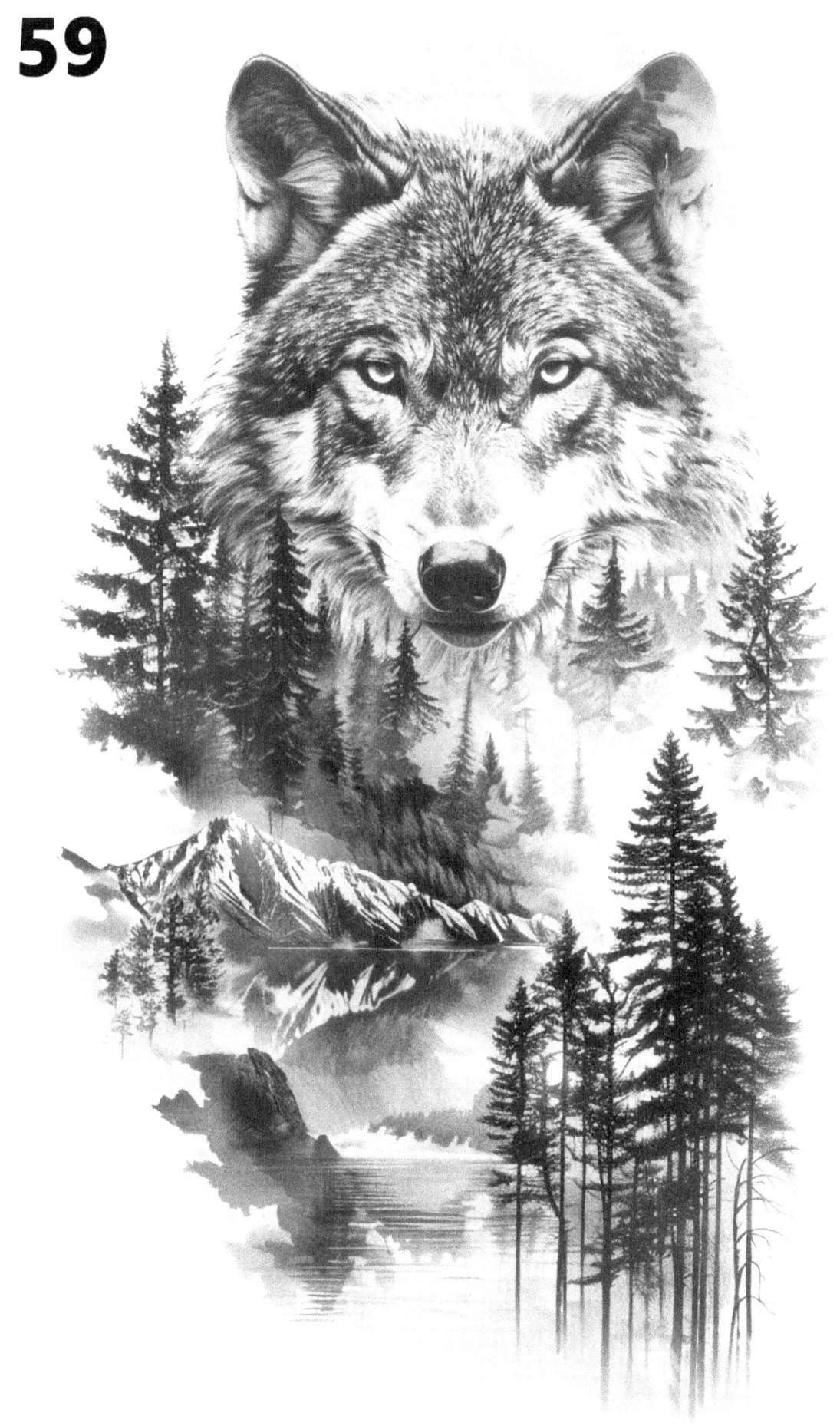

60

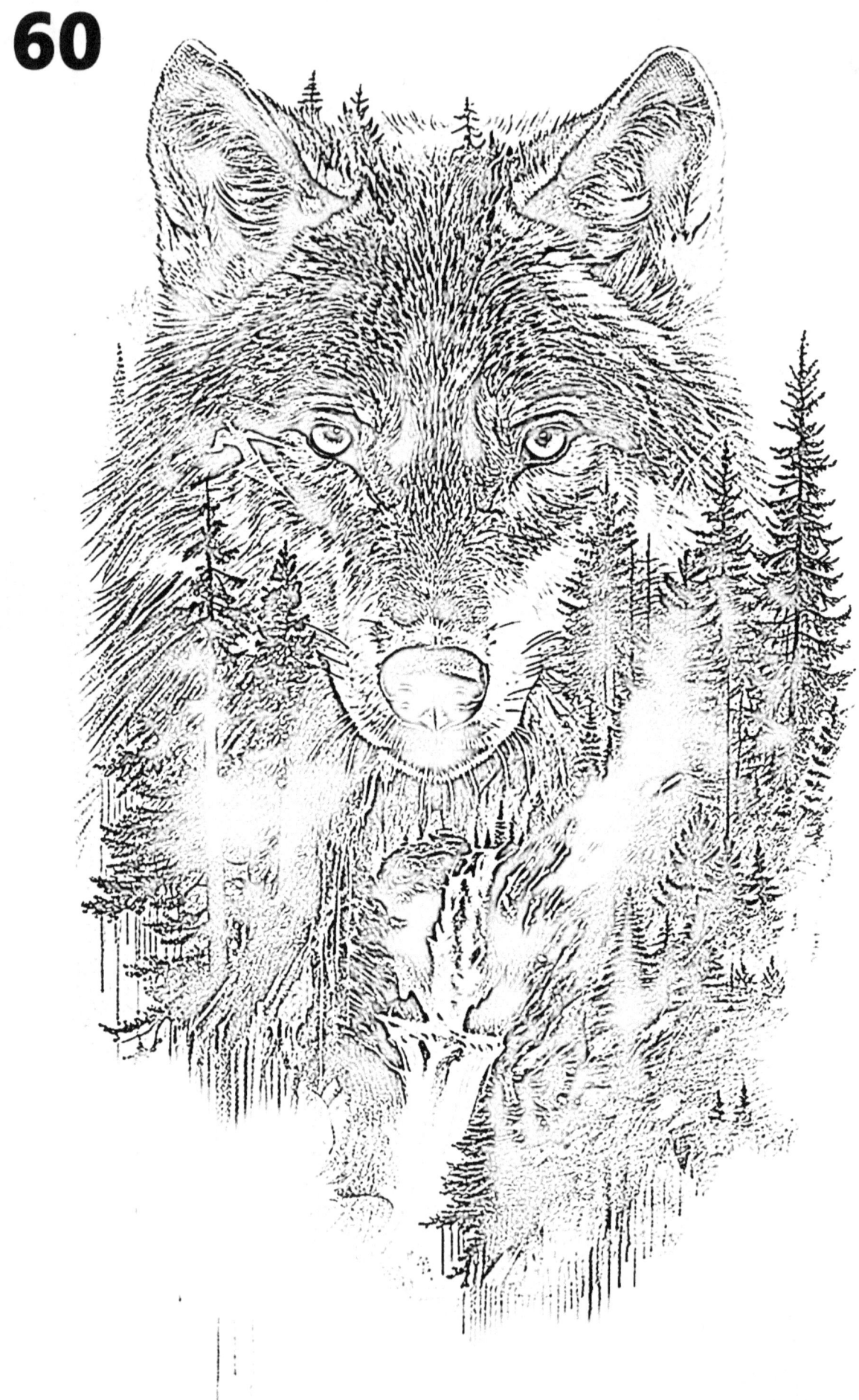

60

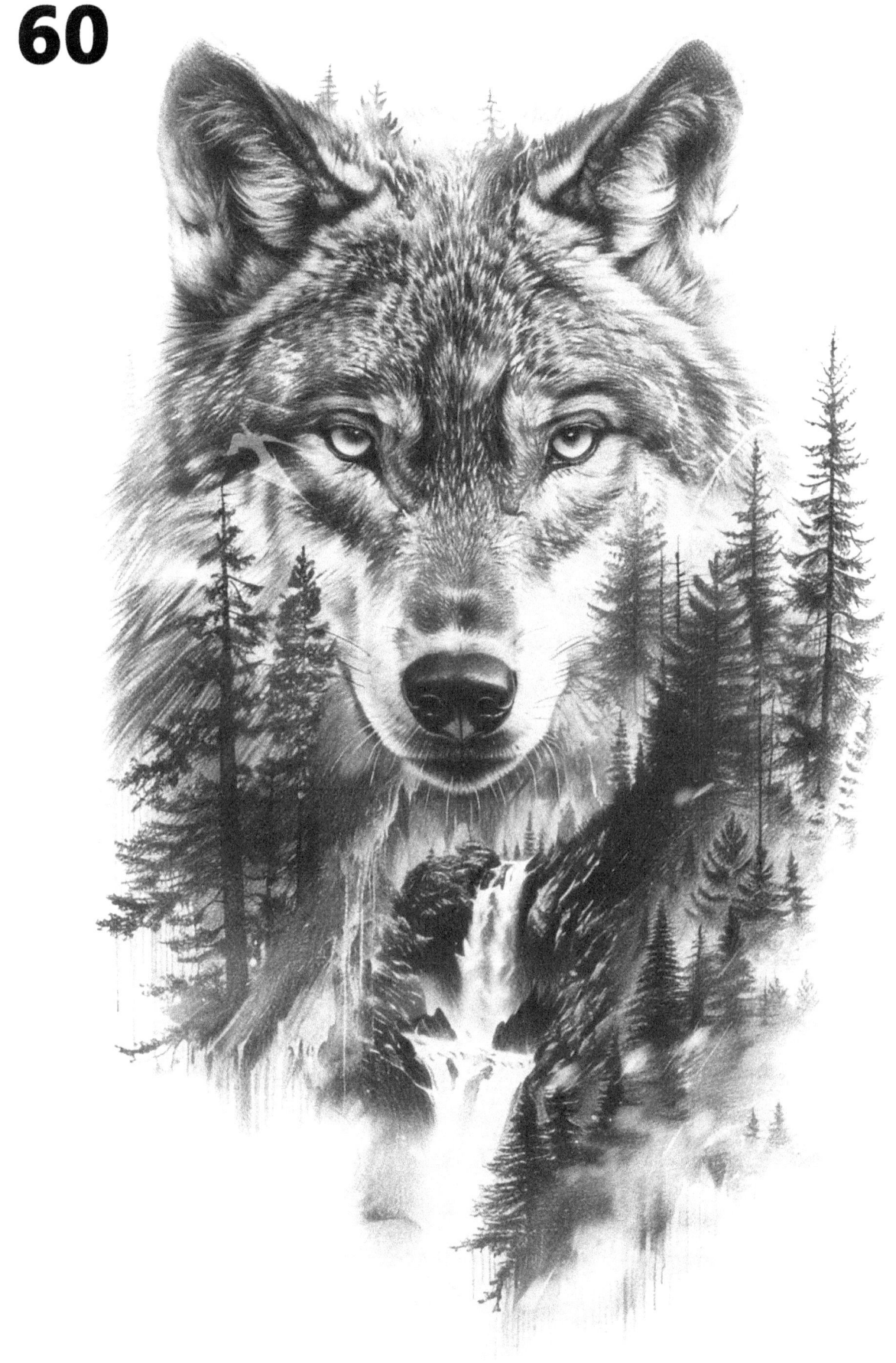

61

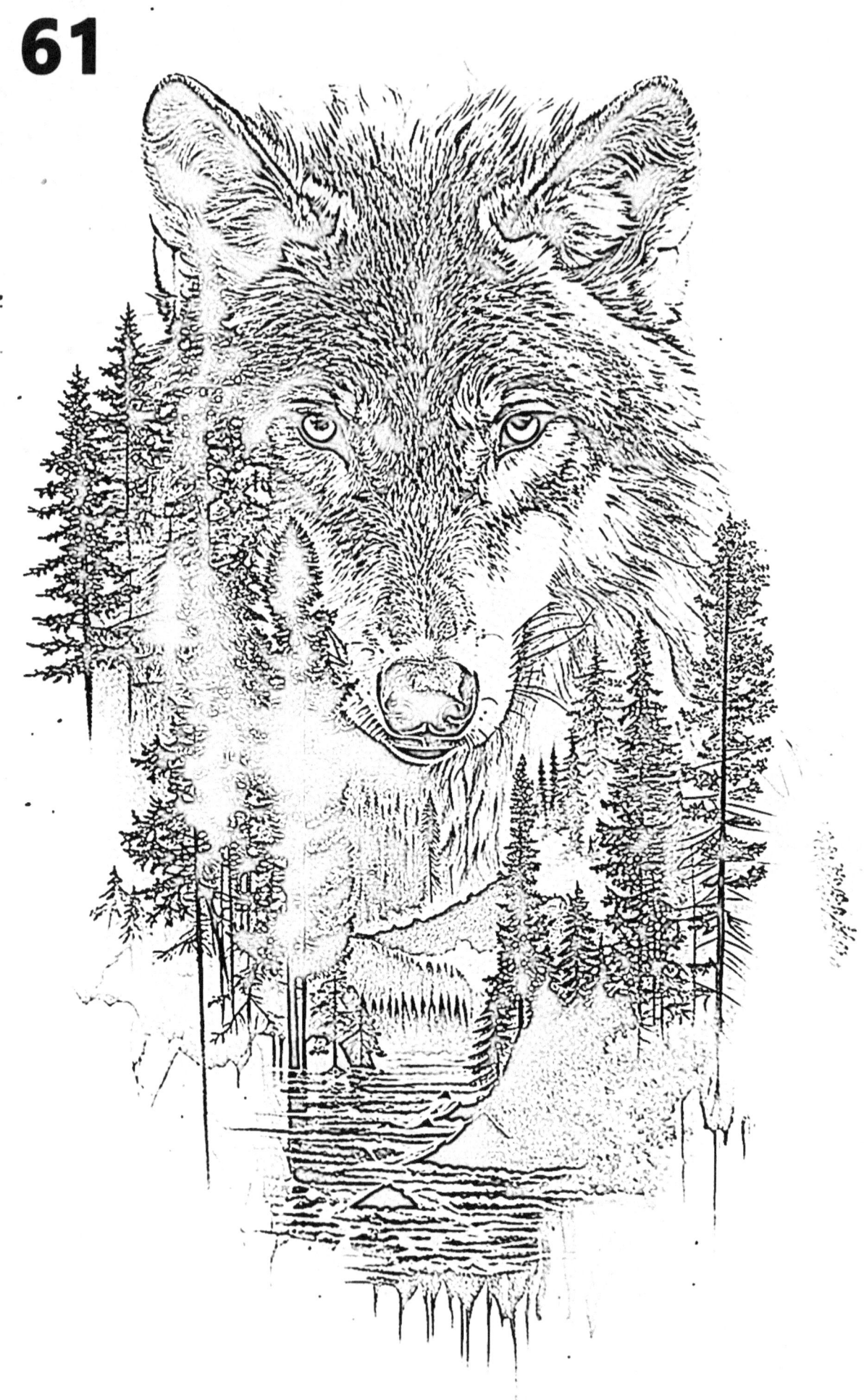

61

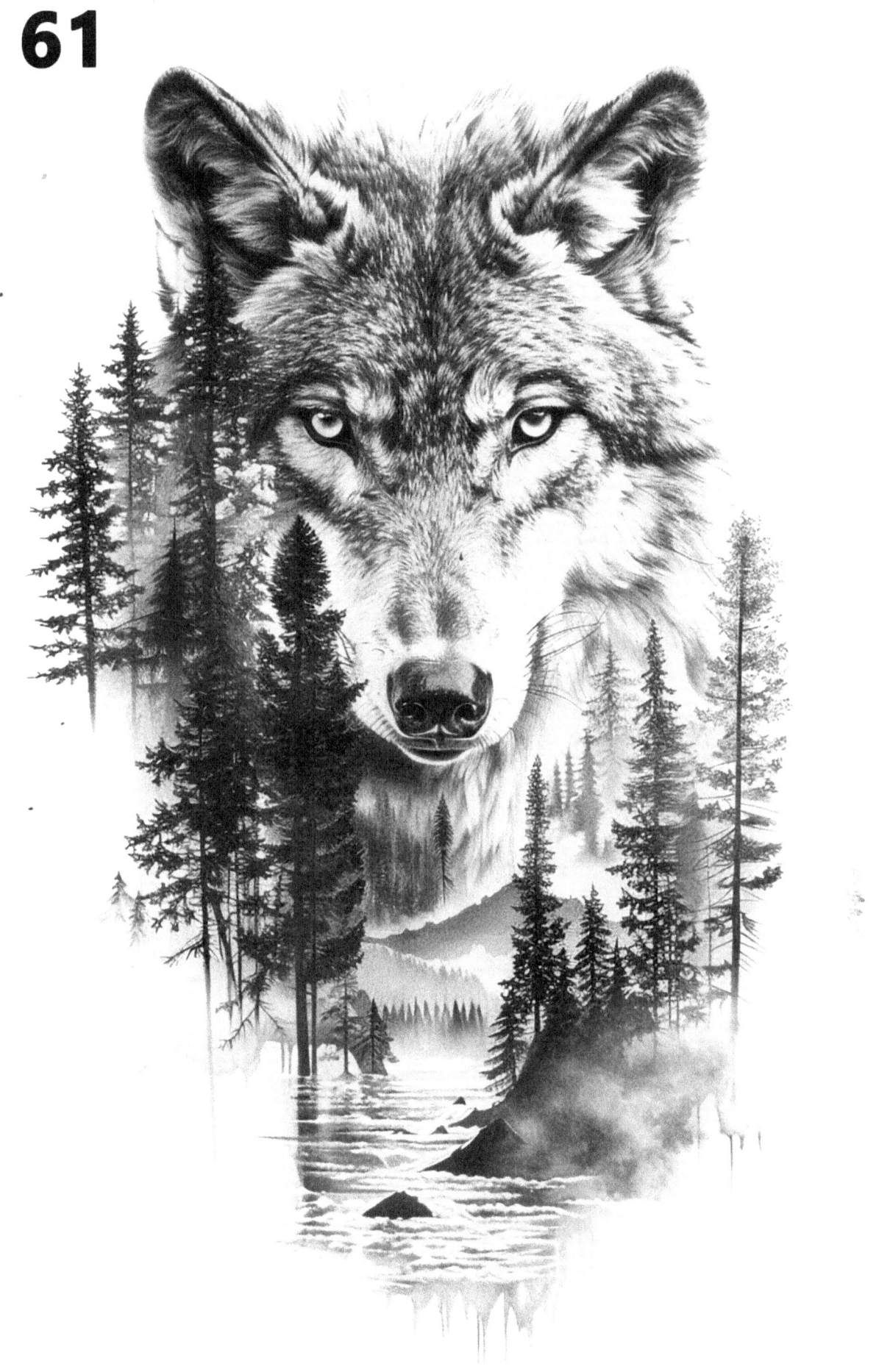

62

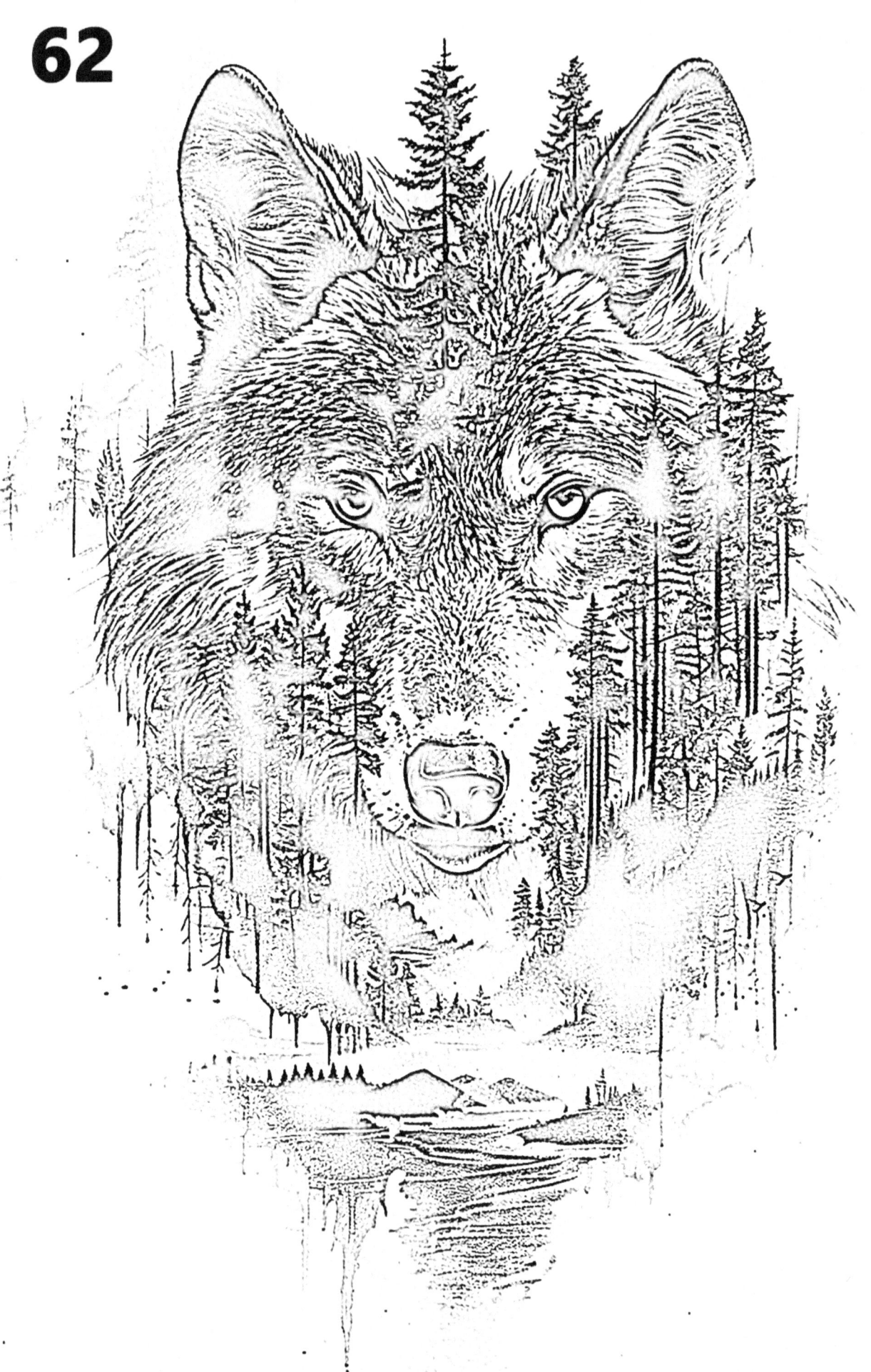

62

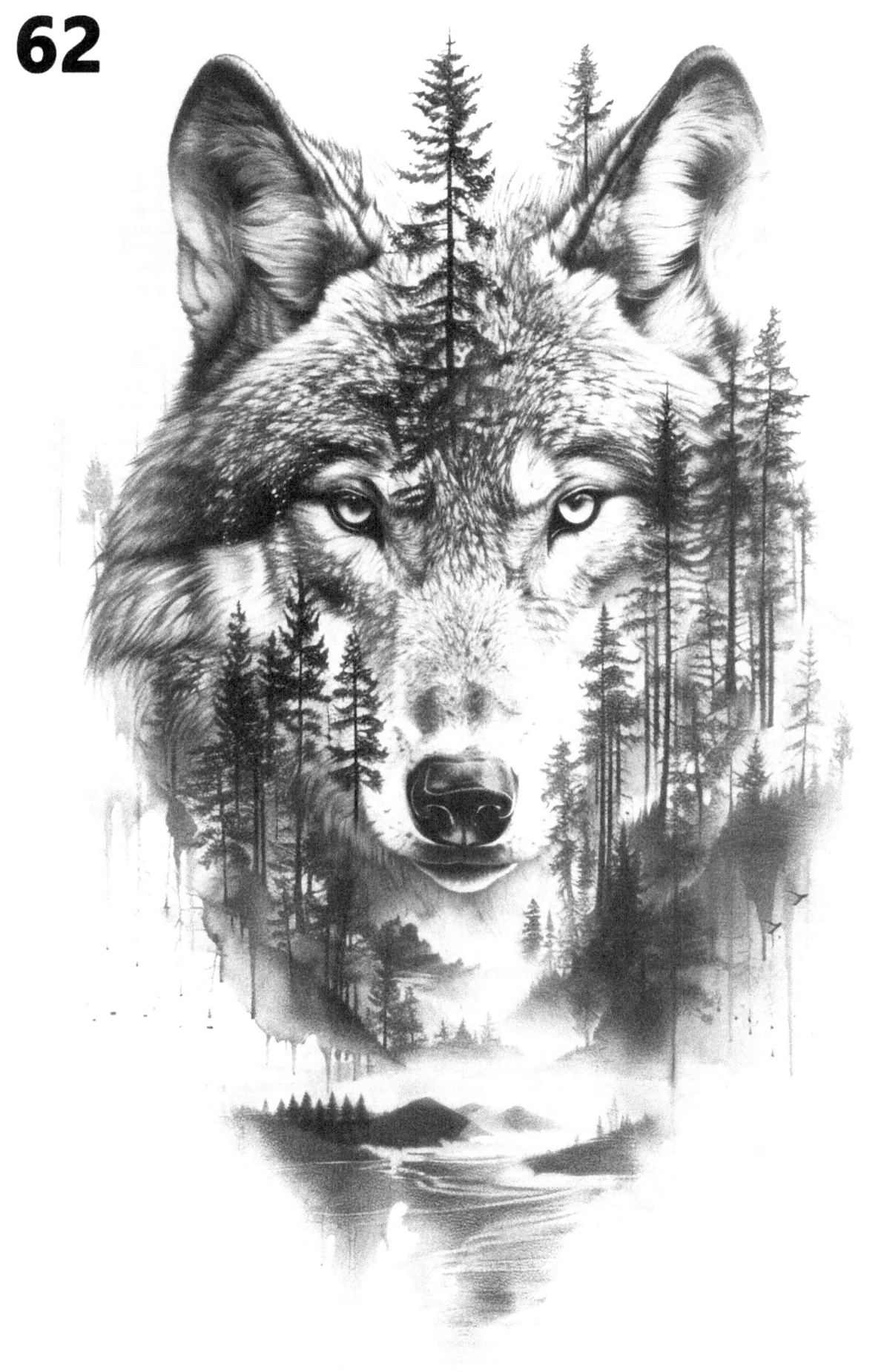

63

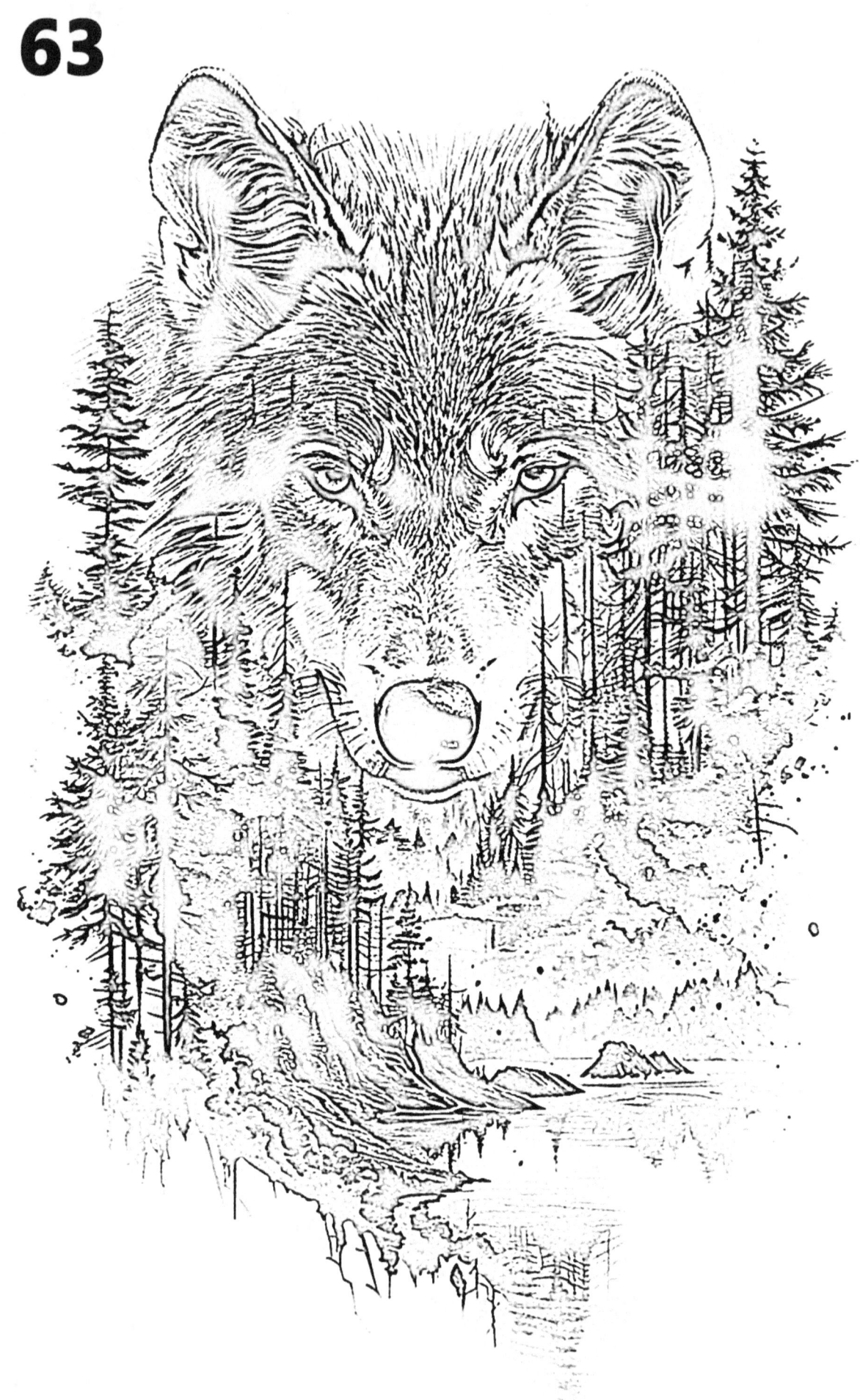

63

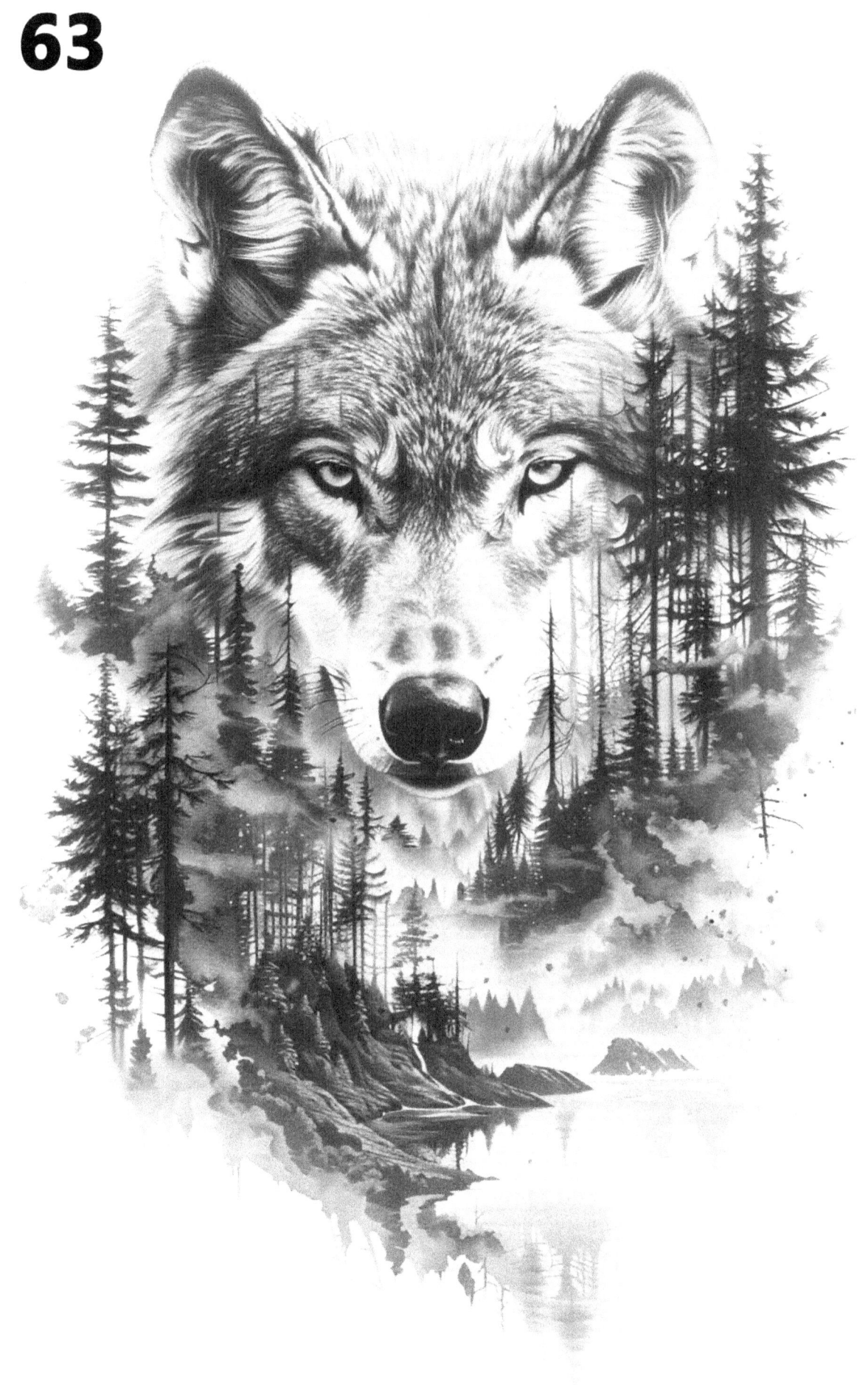

64

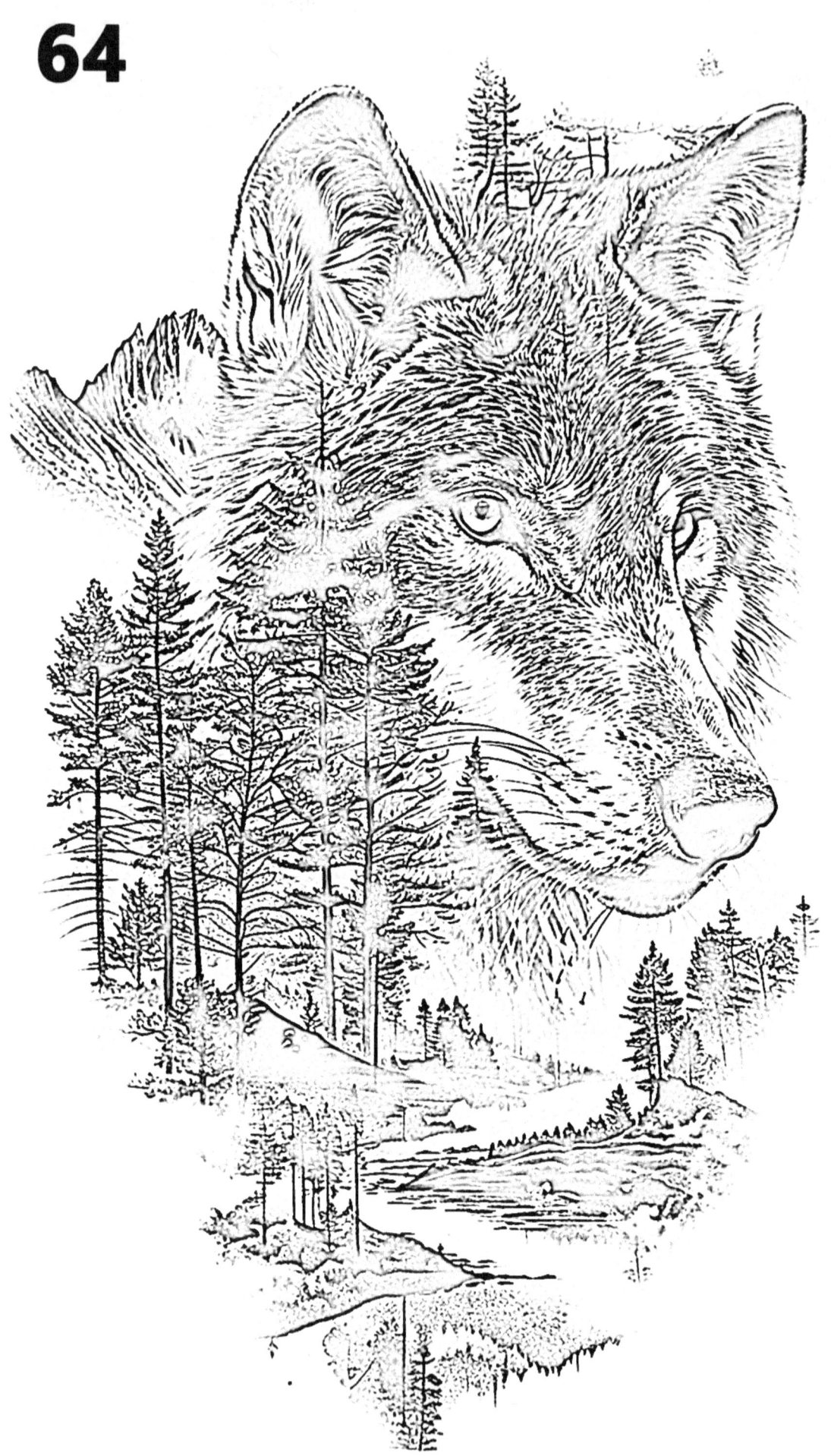

64

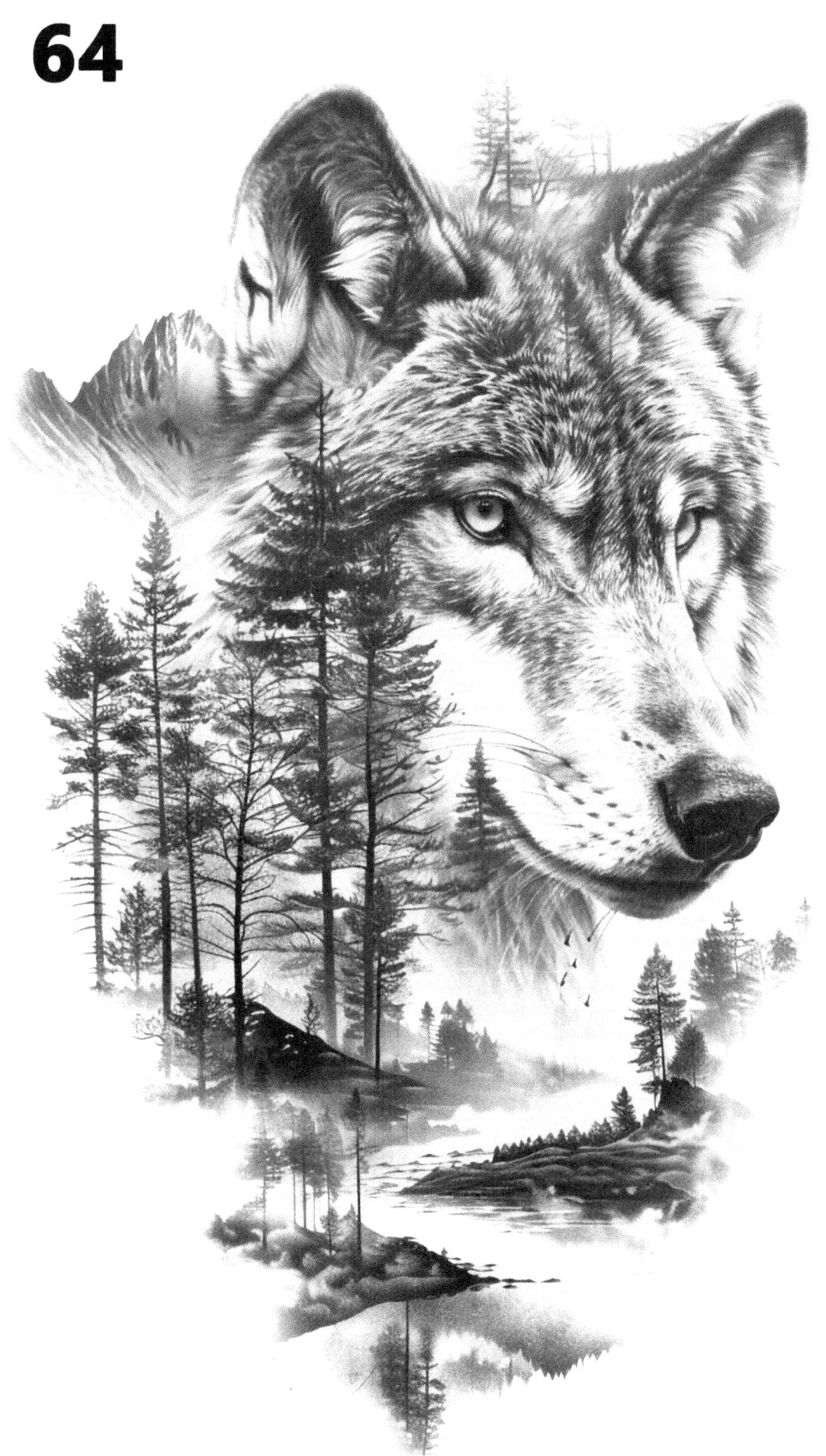

65

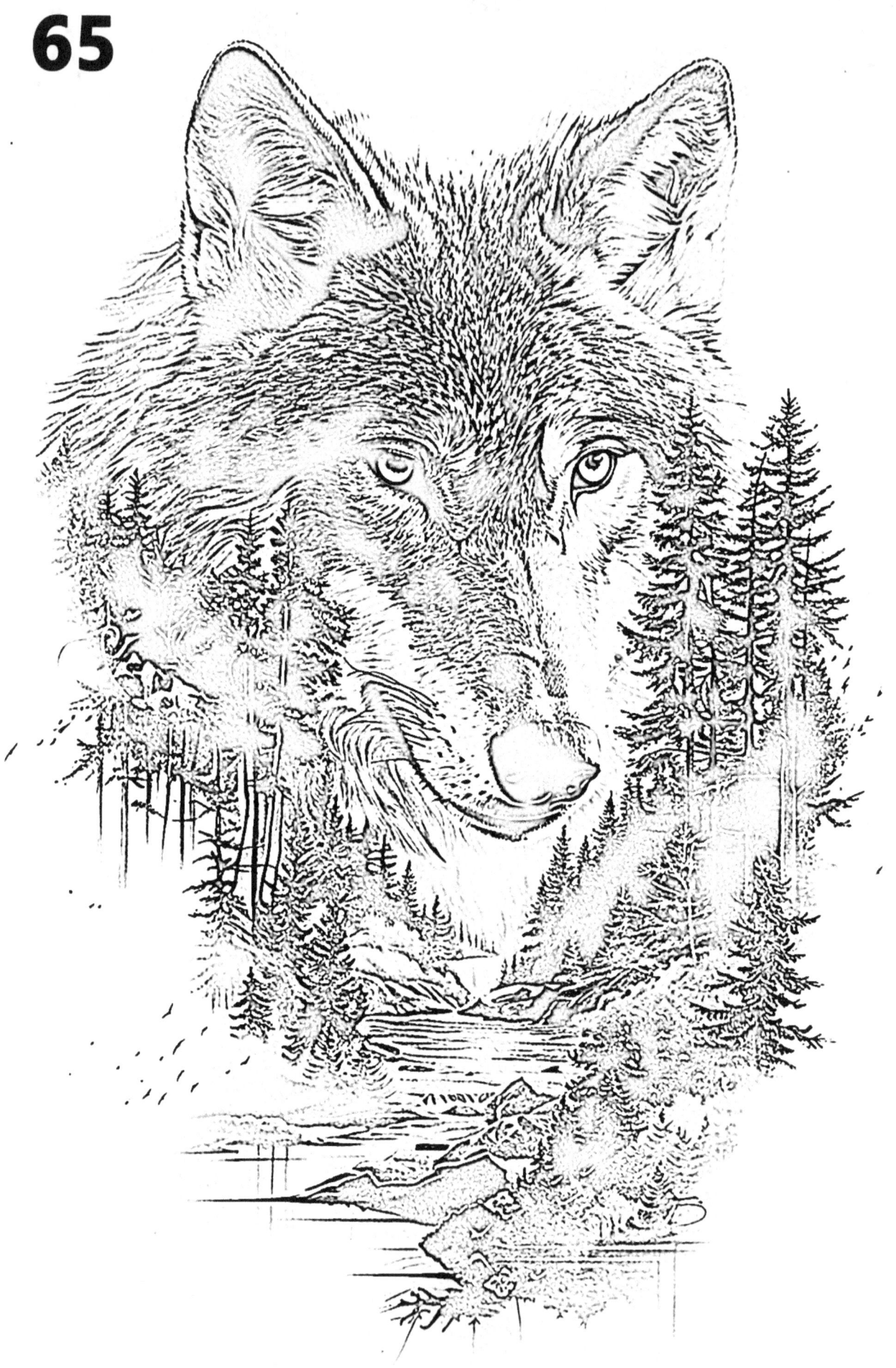

65

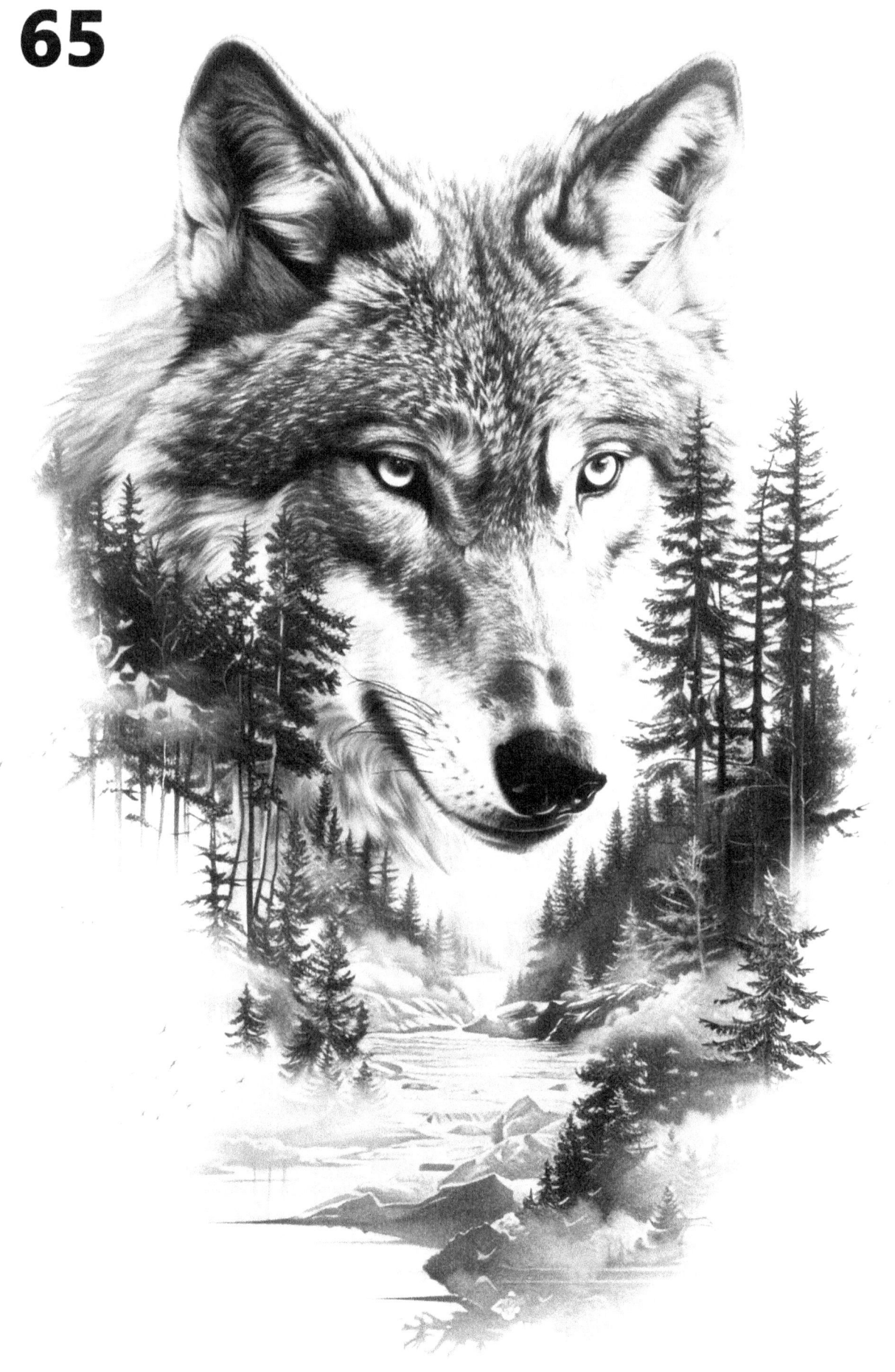

66

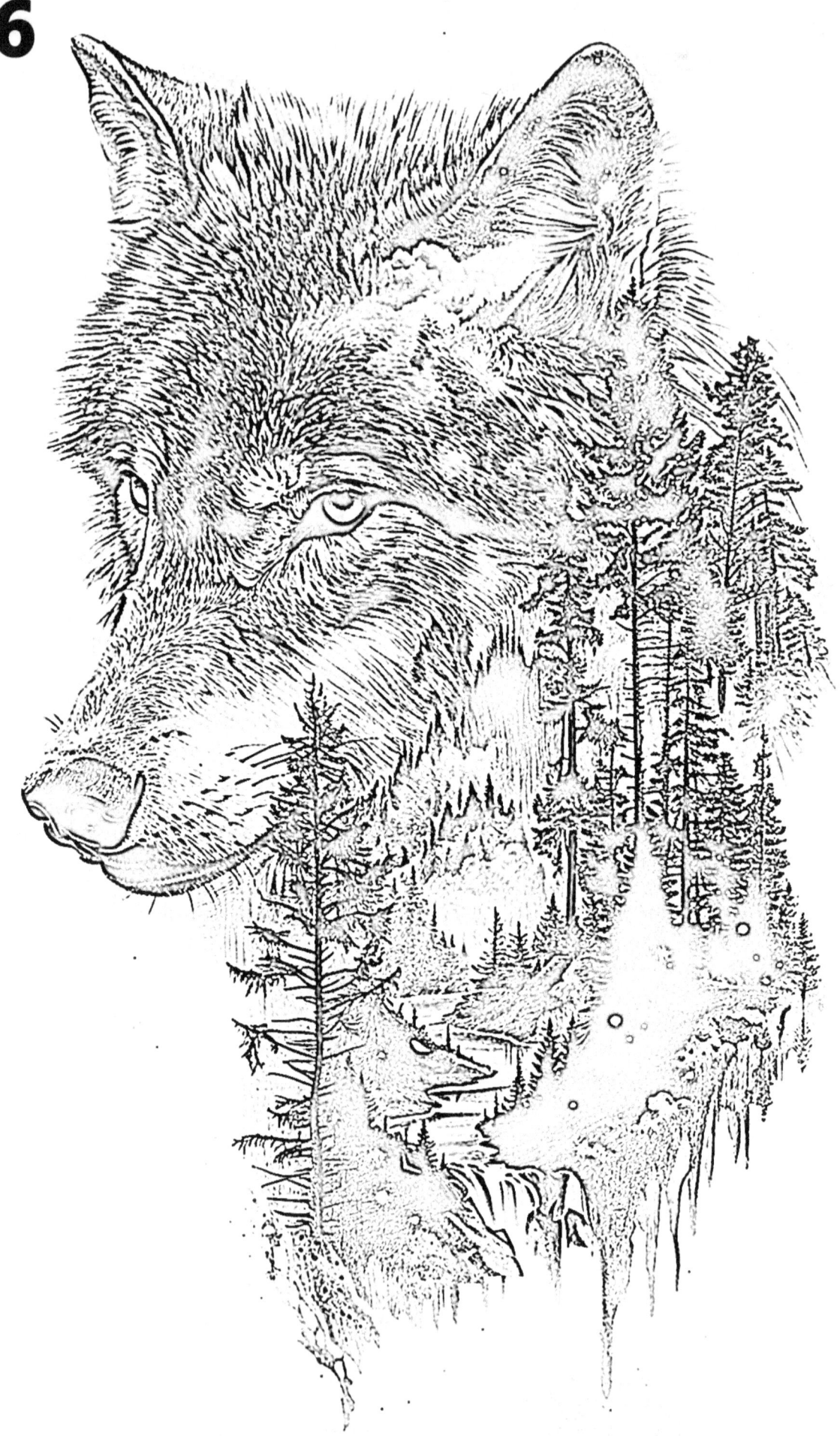

66

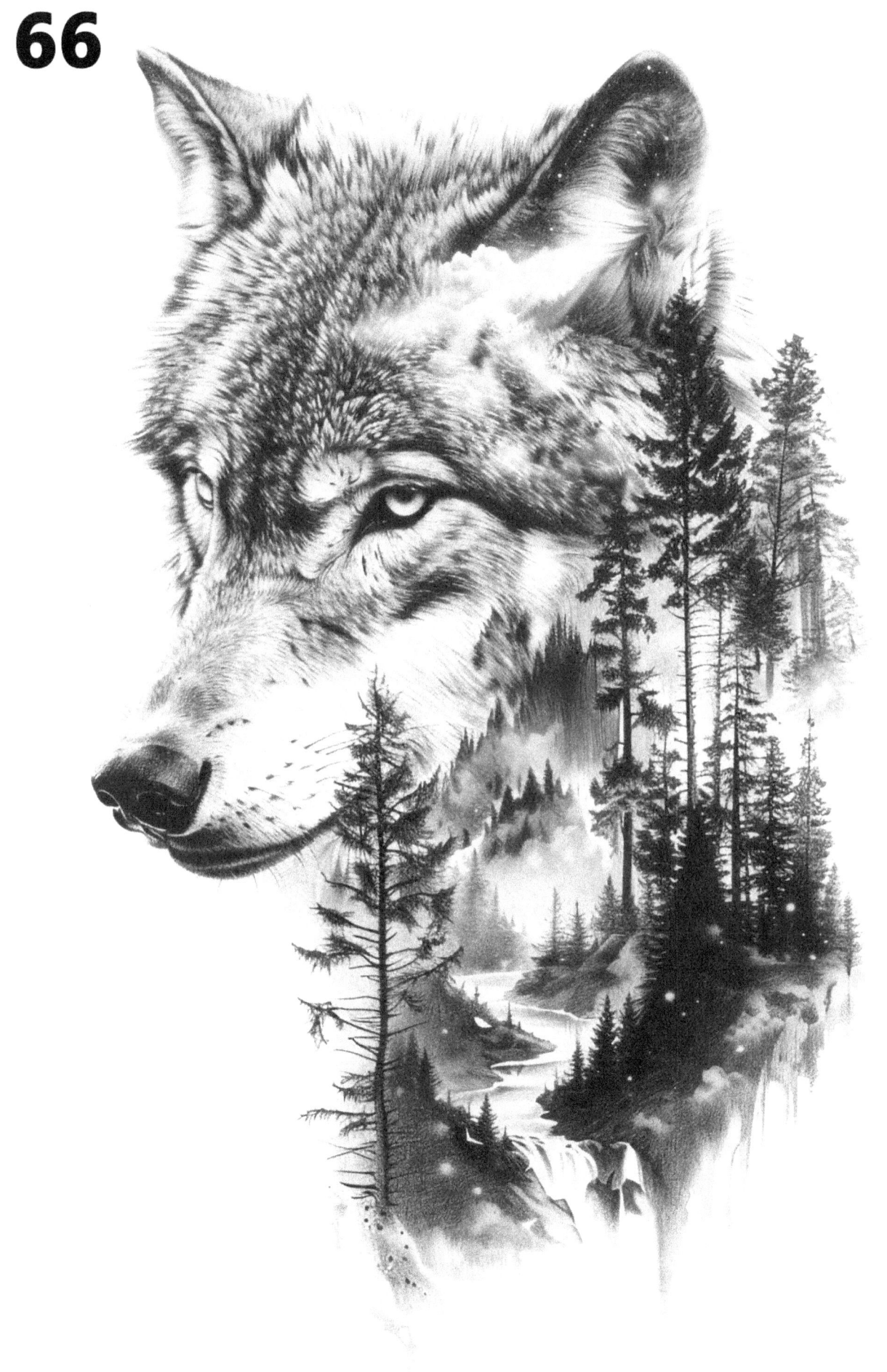

67

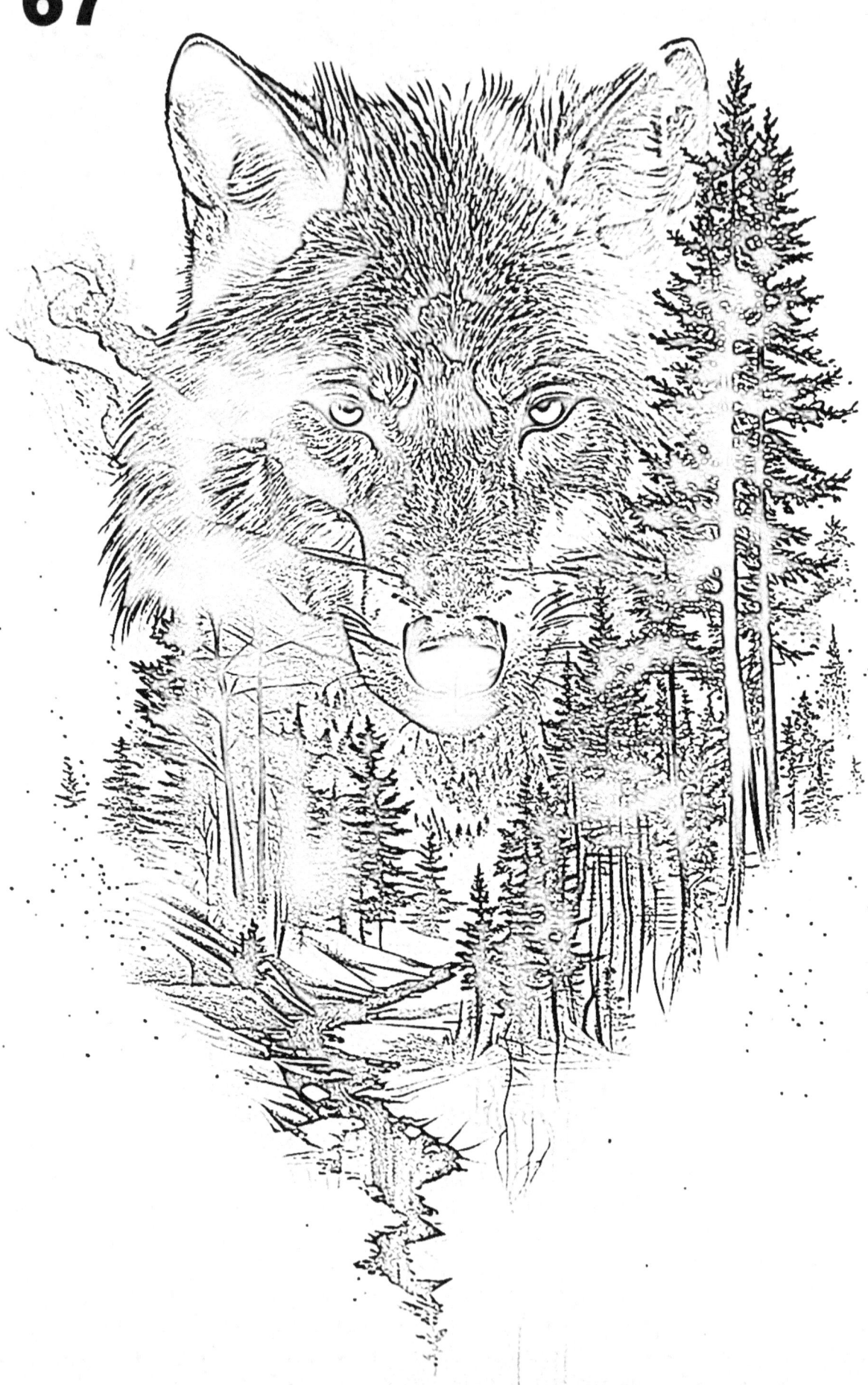

67

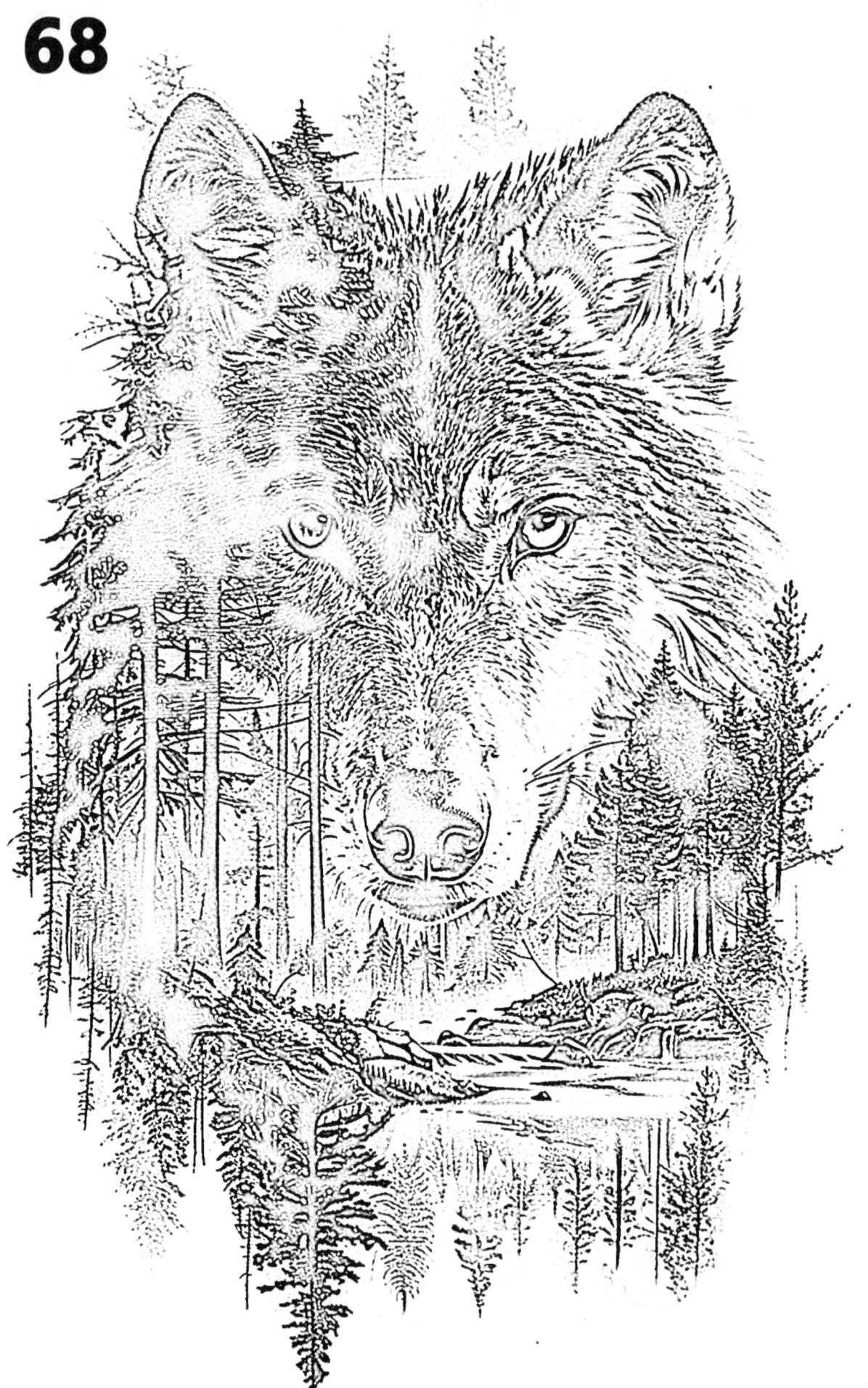

68

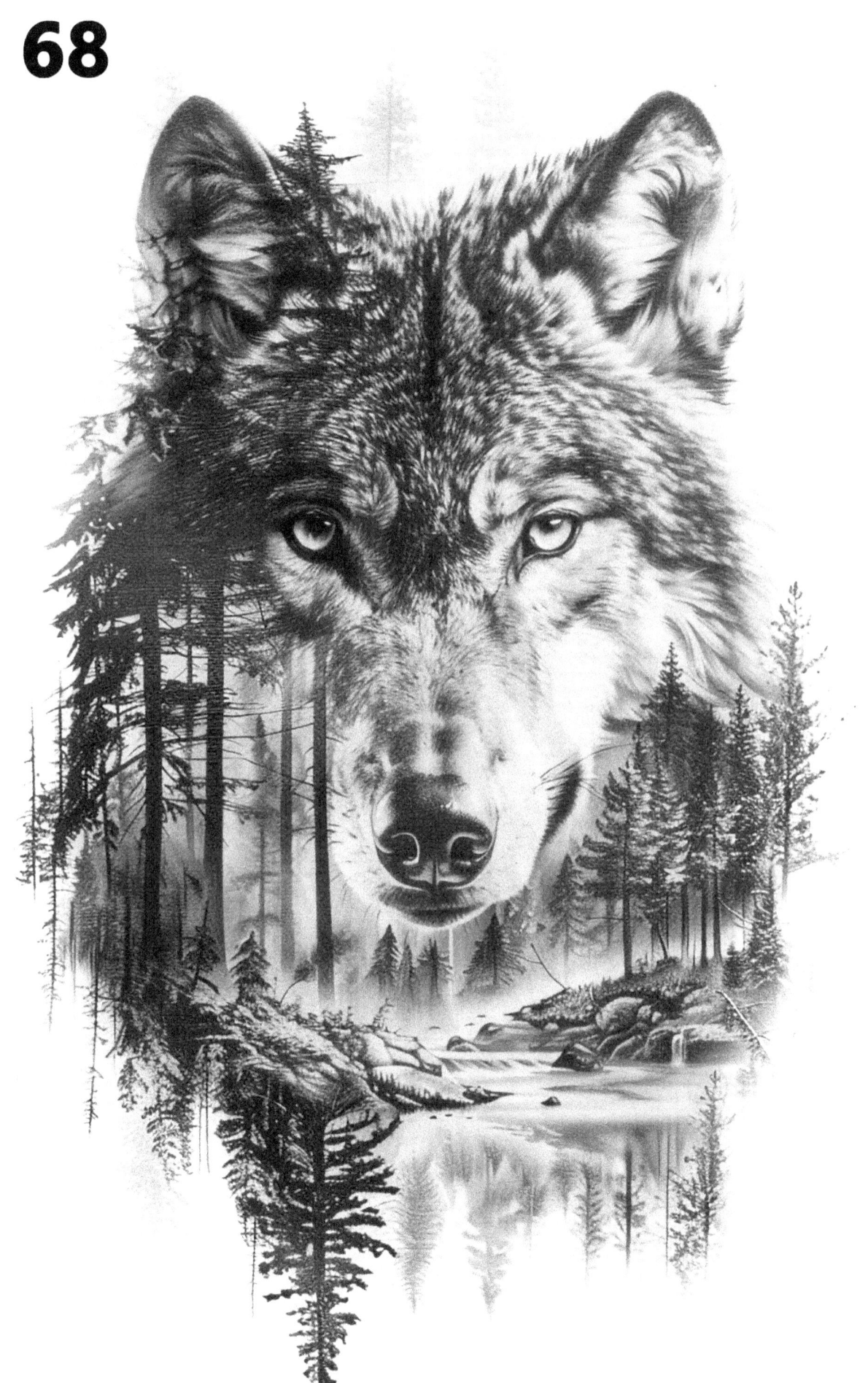

69

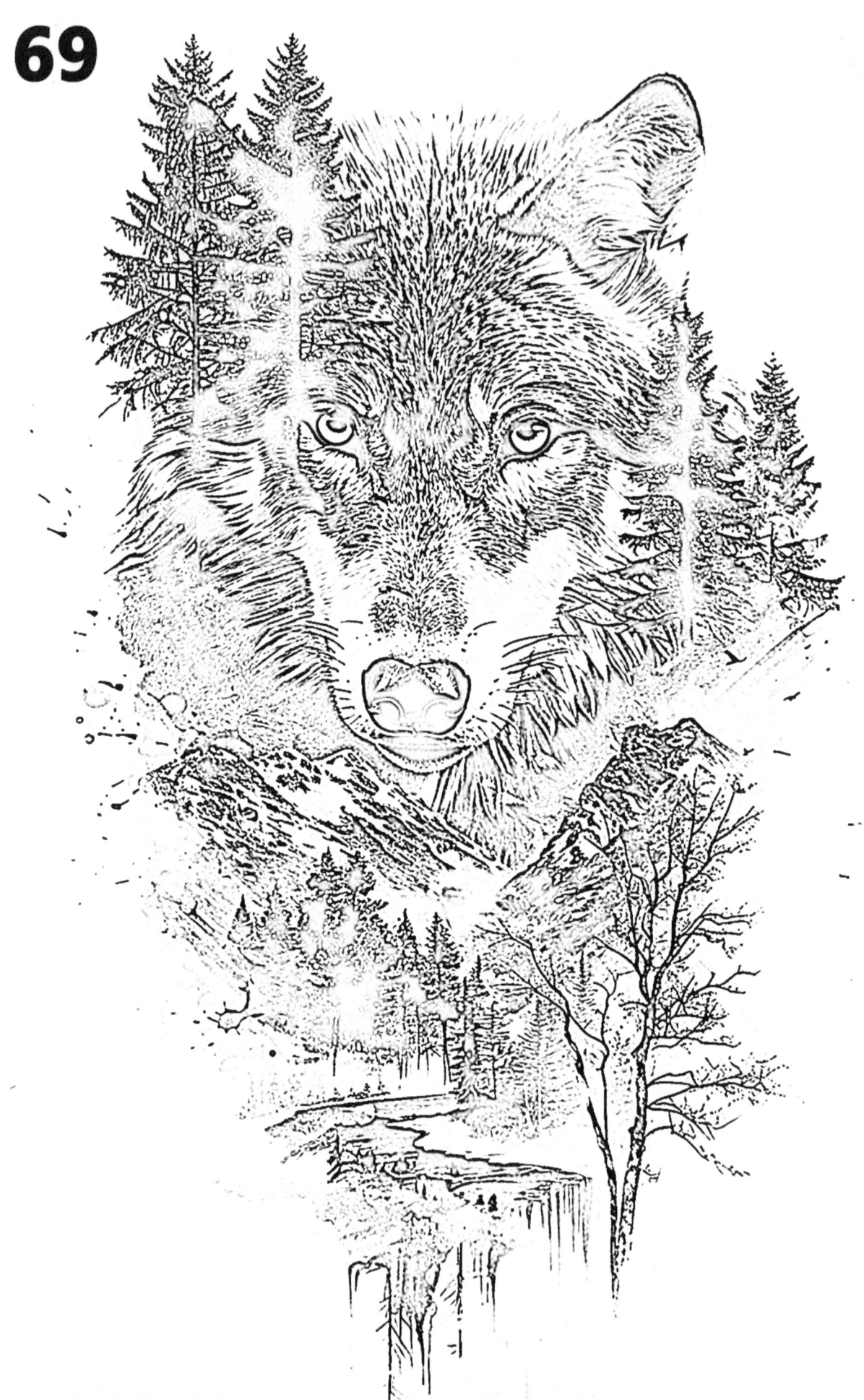

69

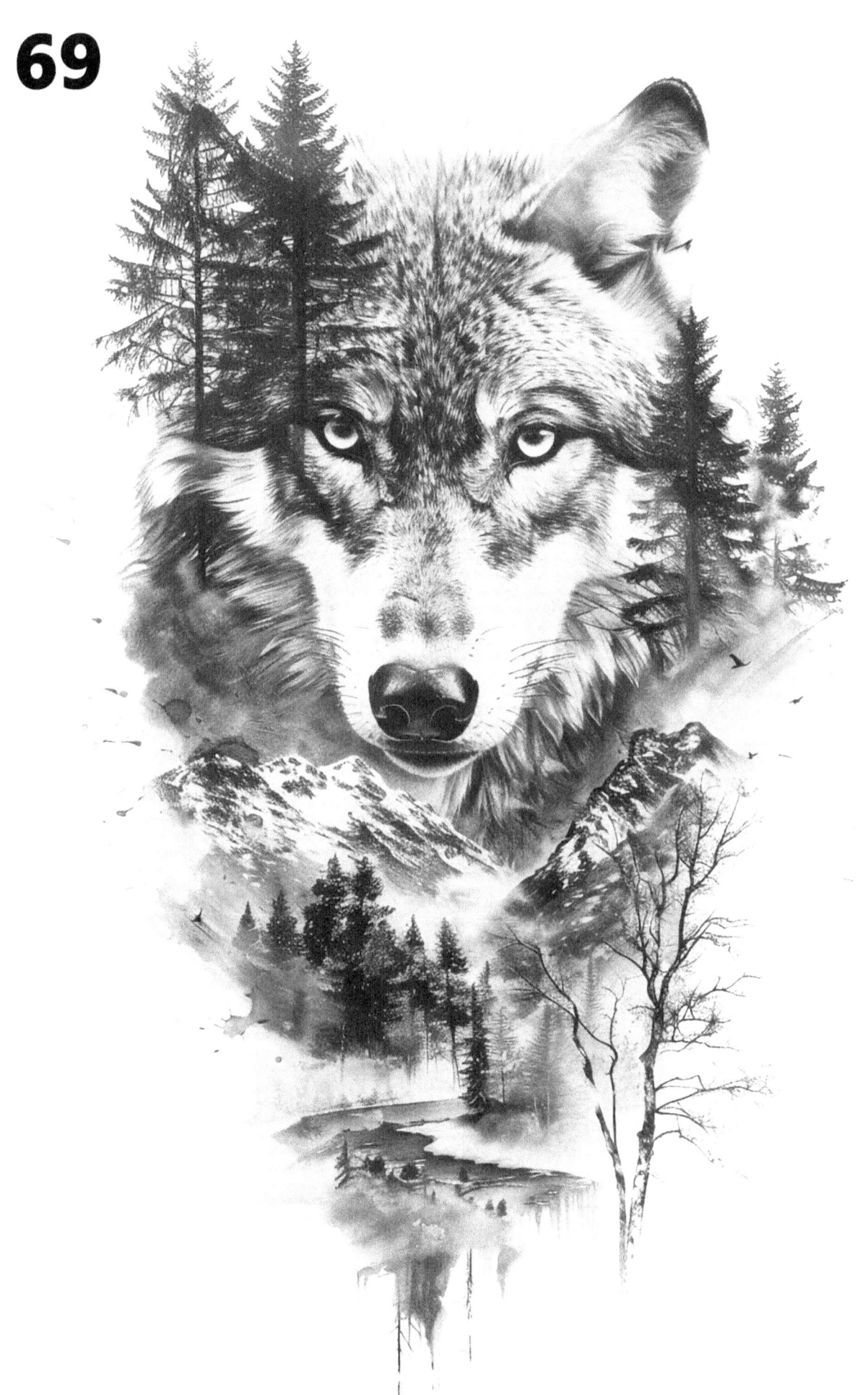

70

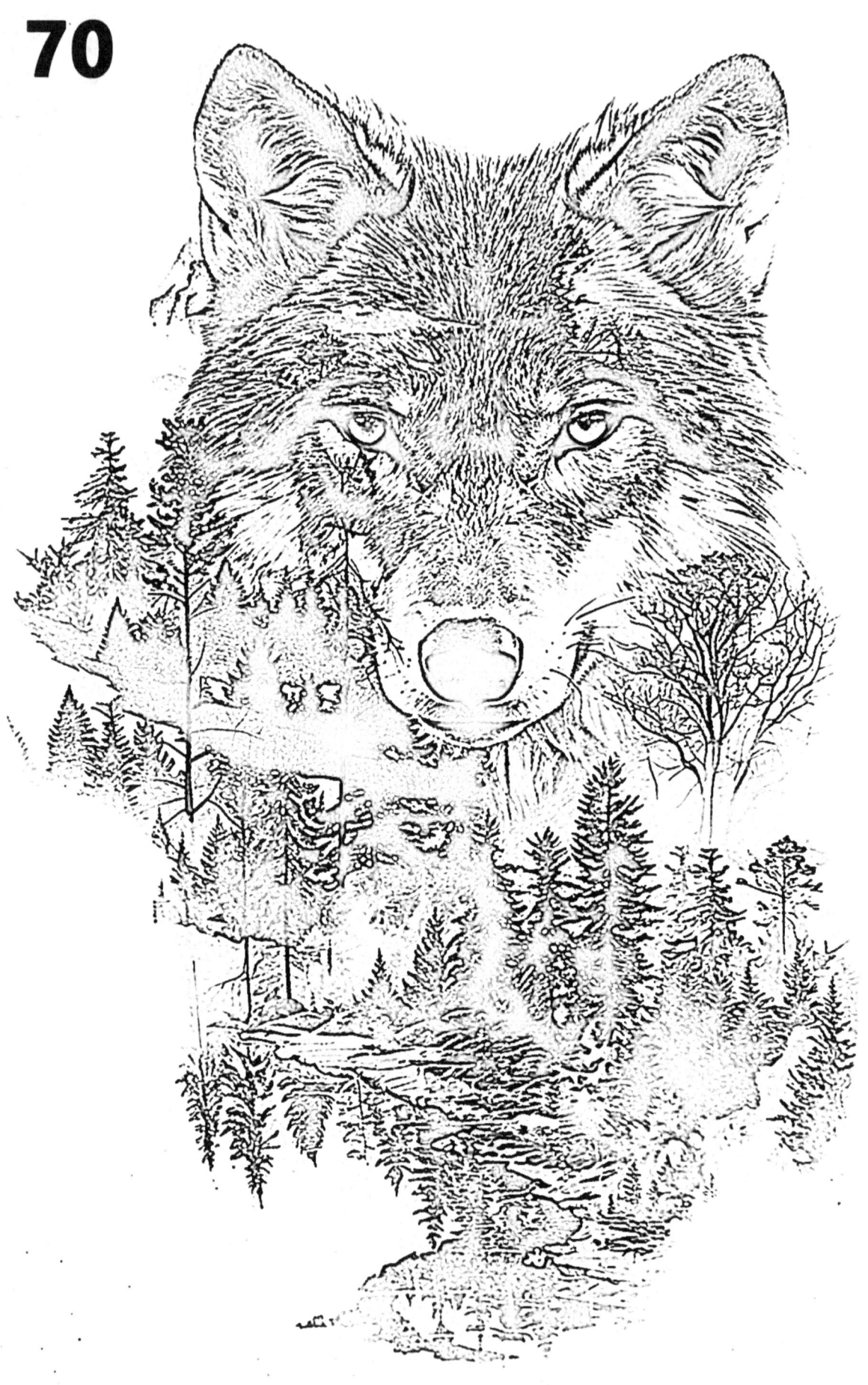

70

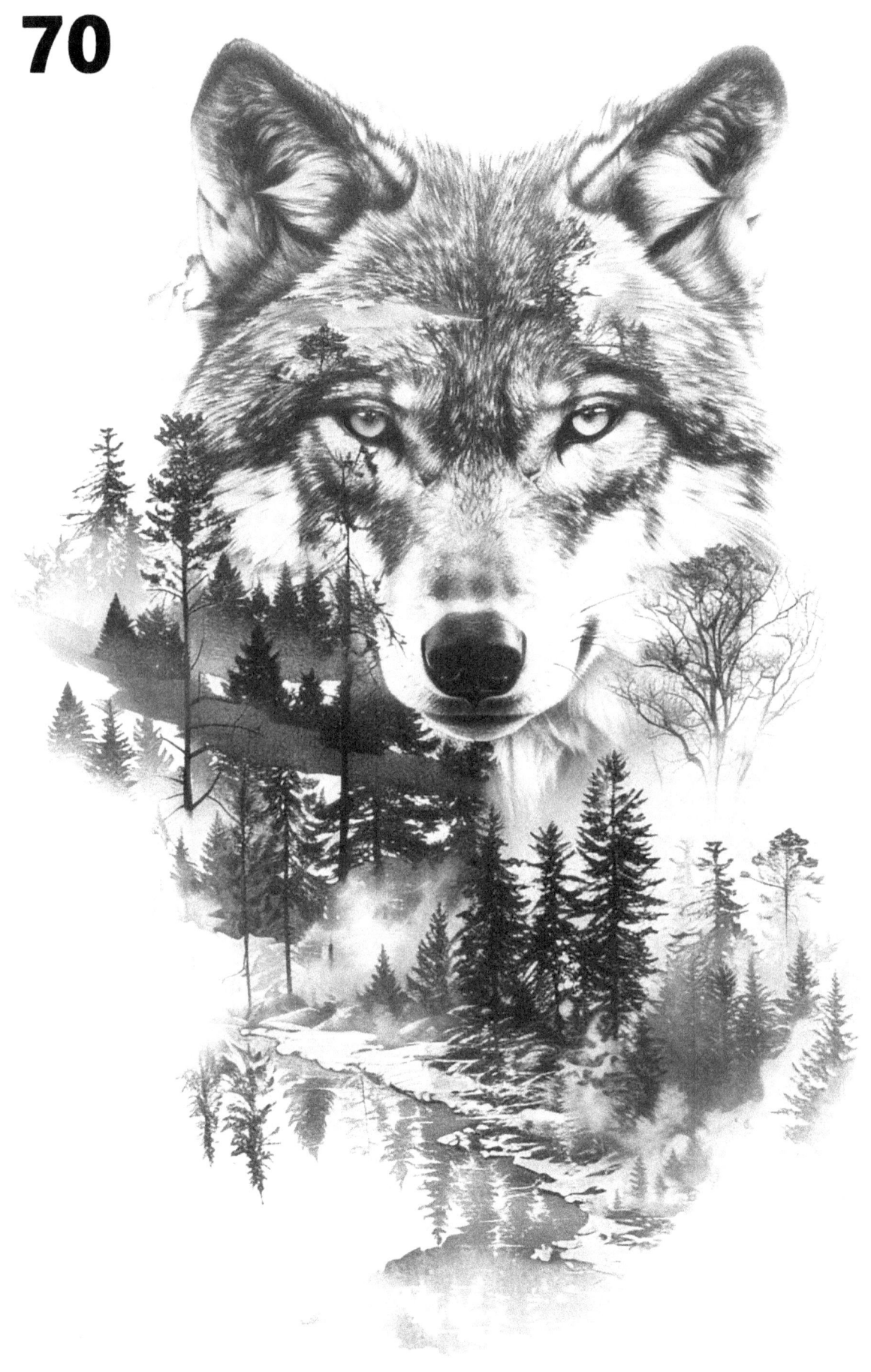

71

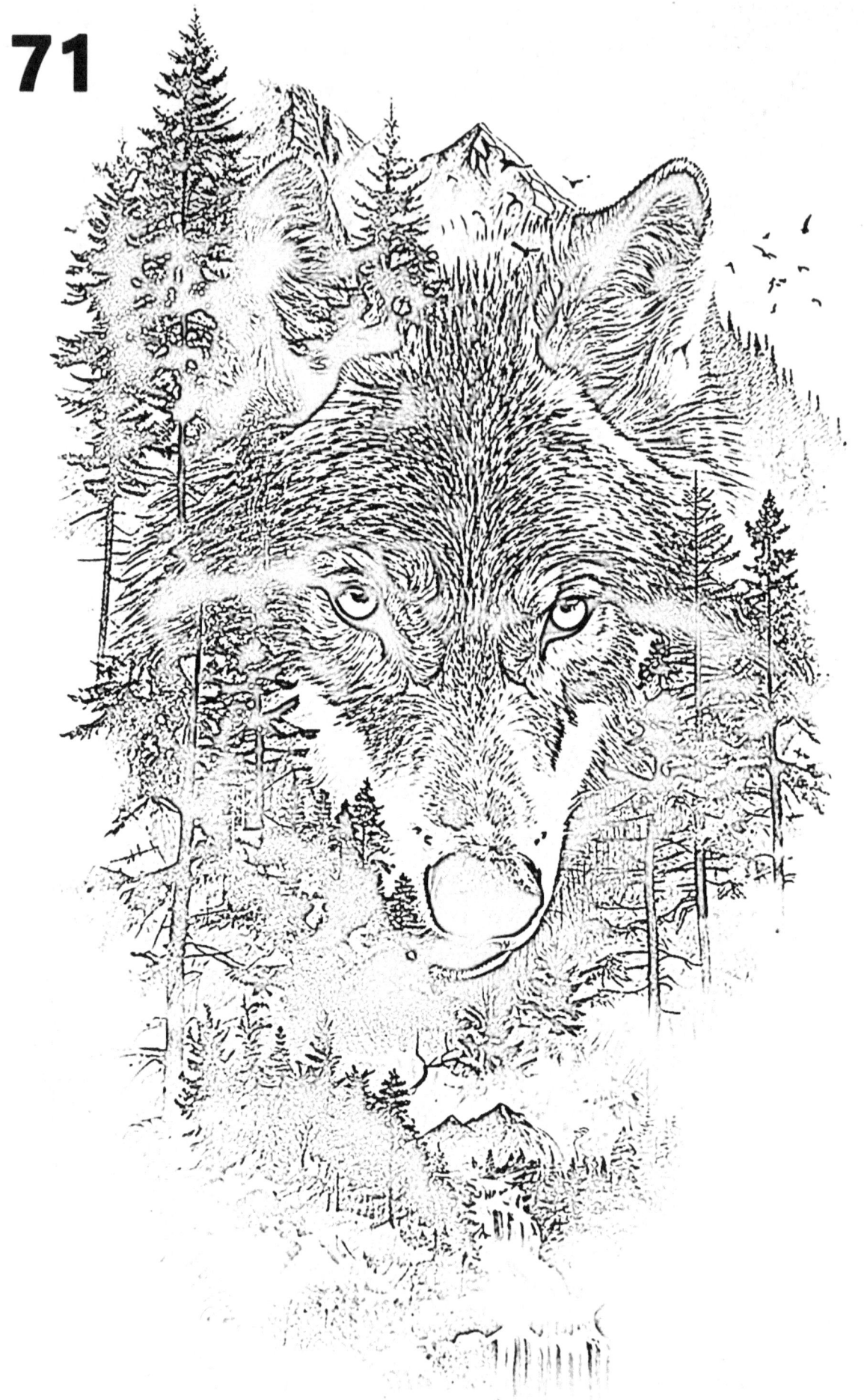

71

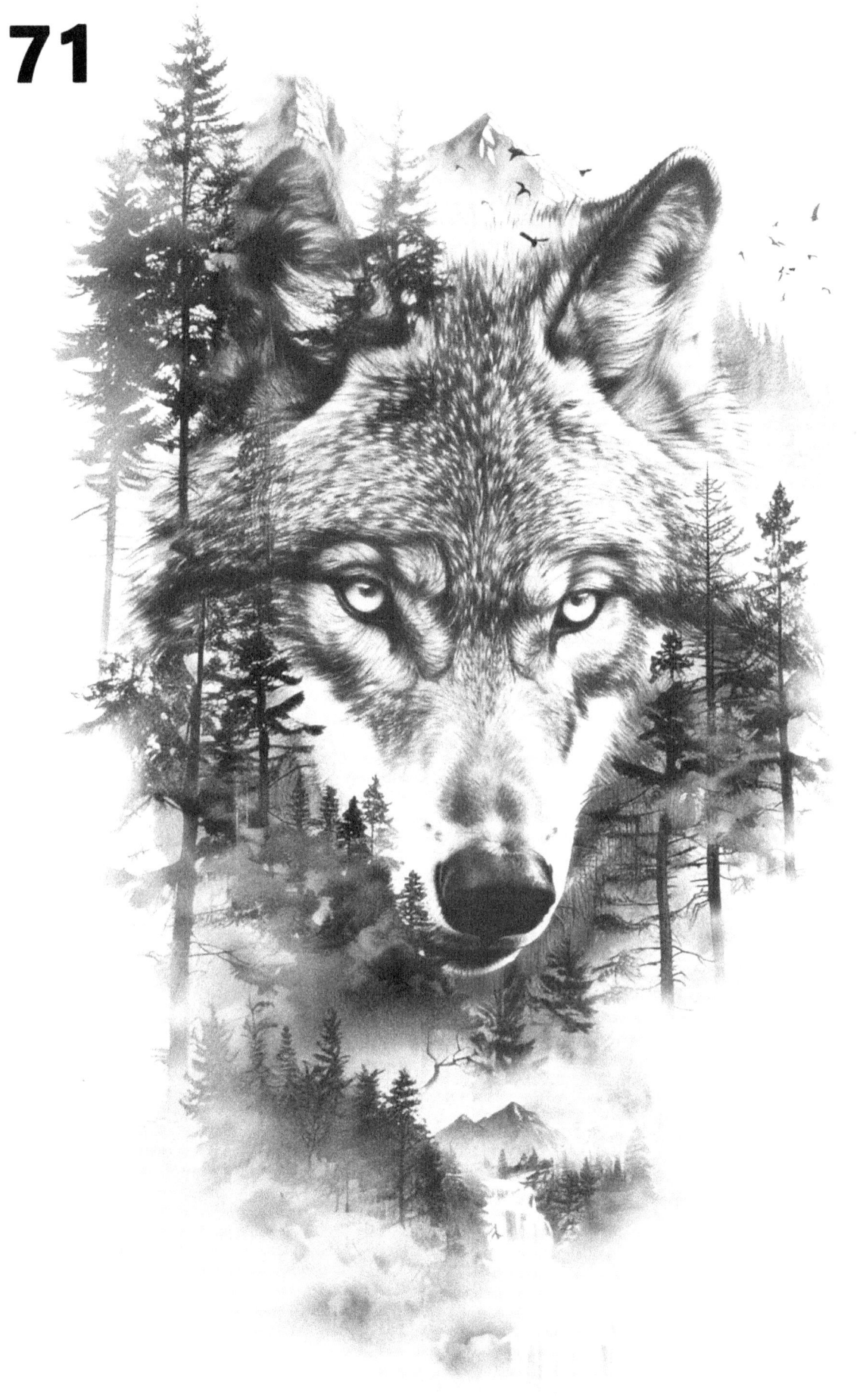

72

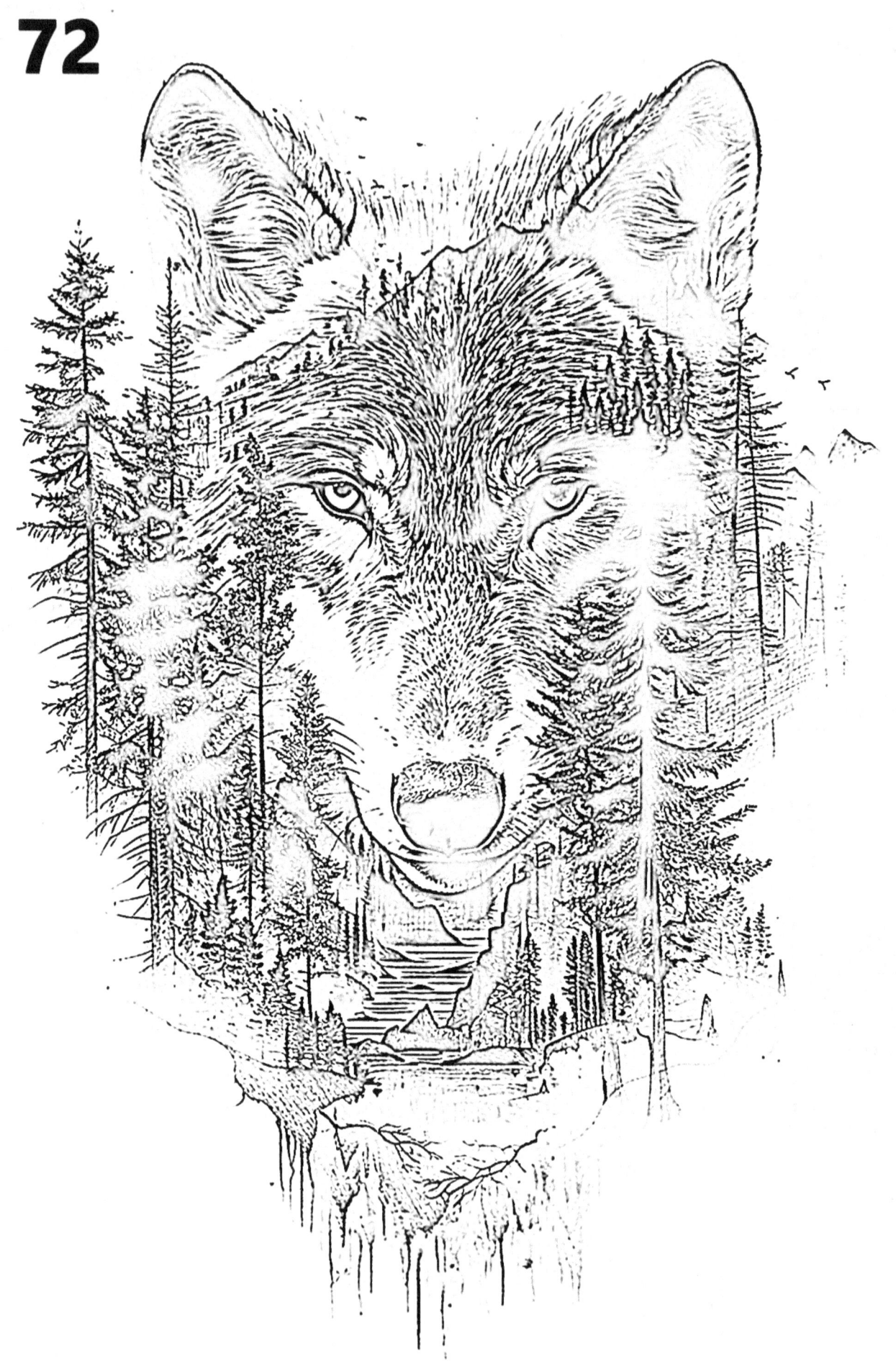

72

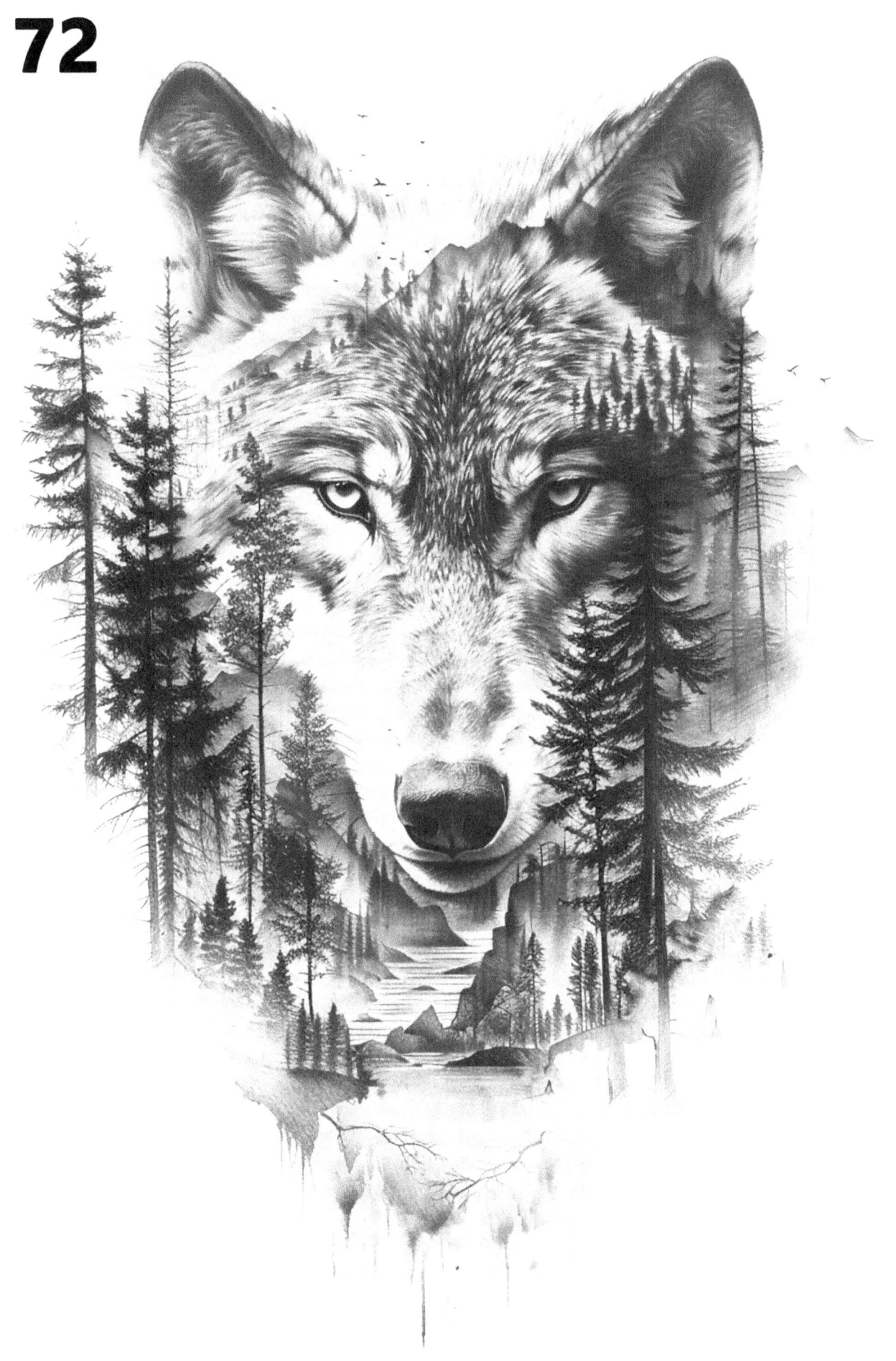

73

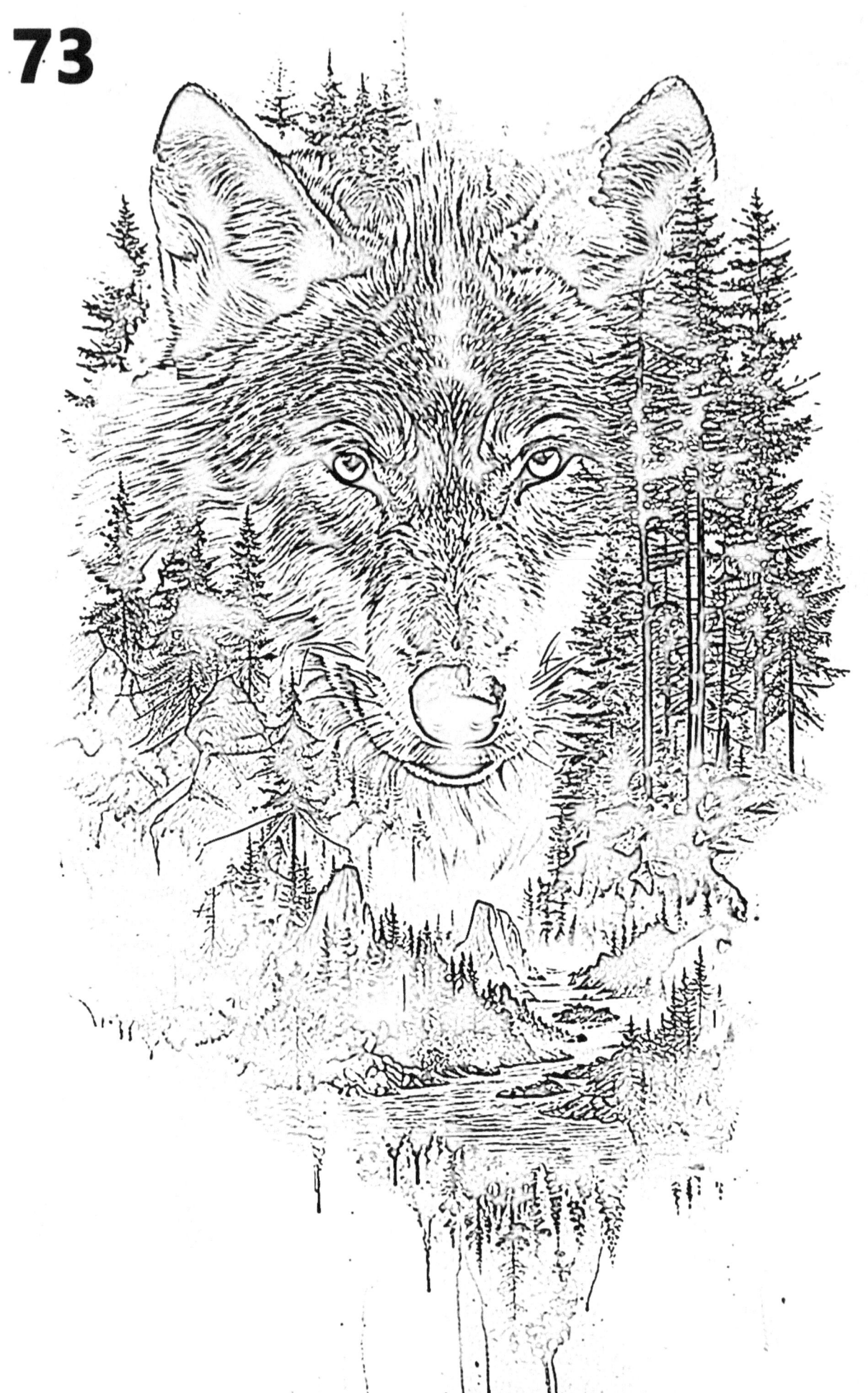

73

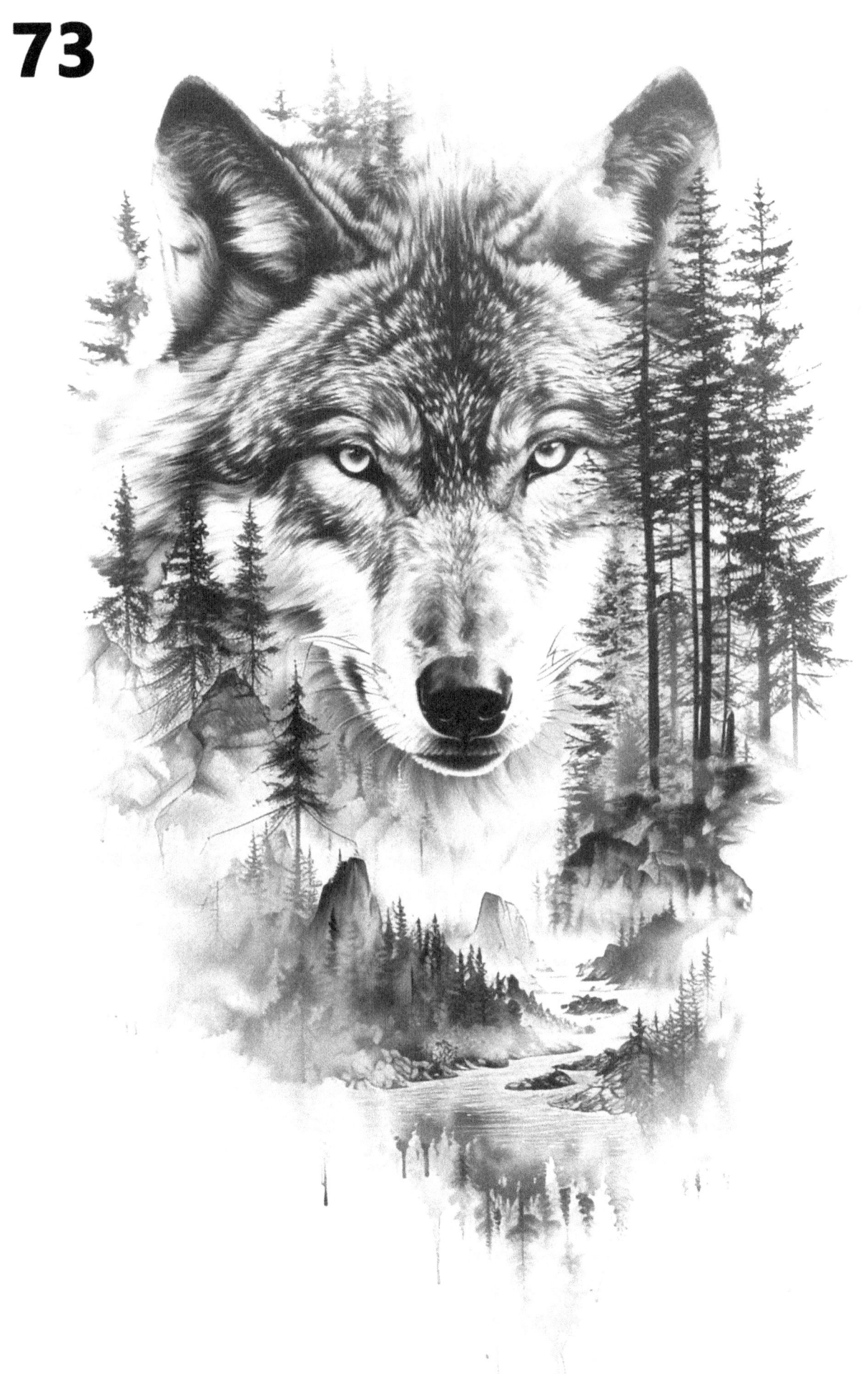

74

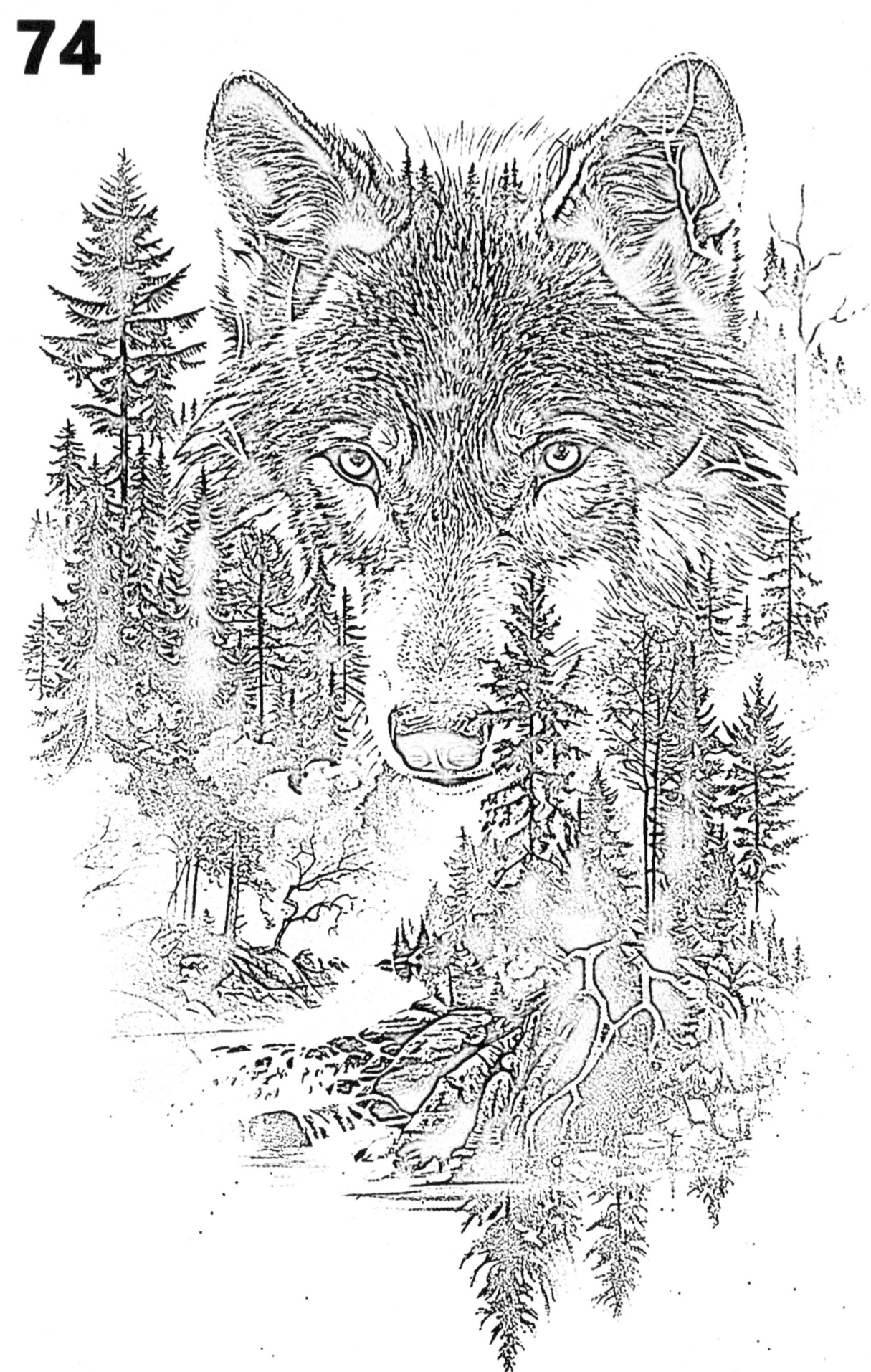

74

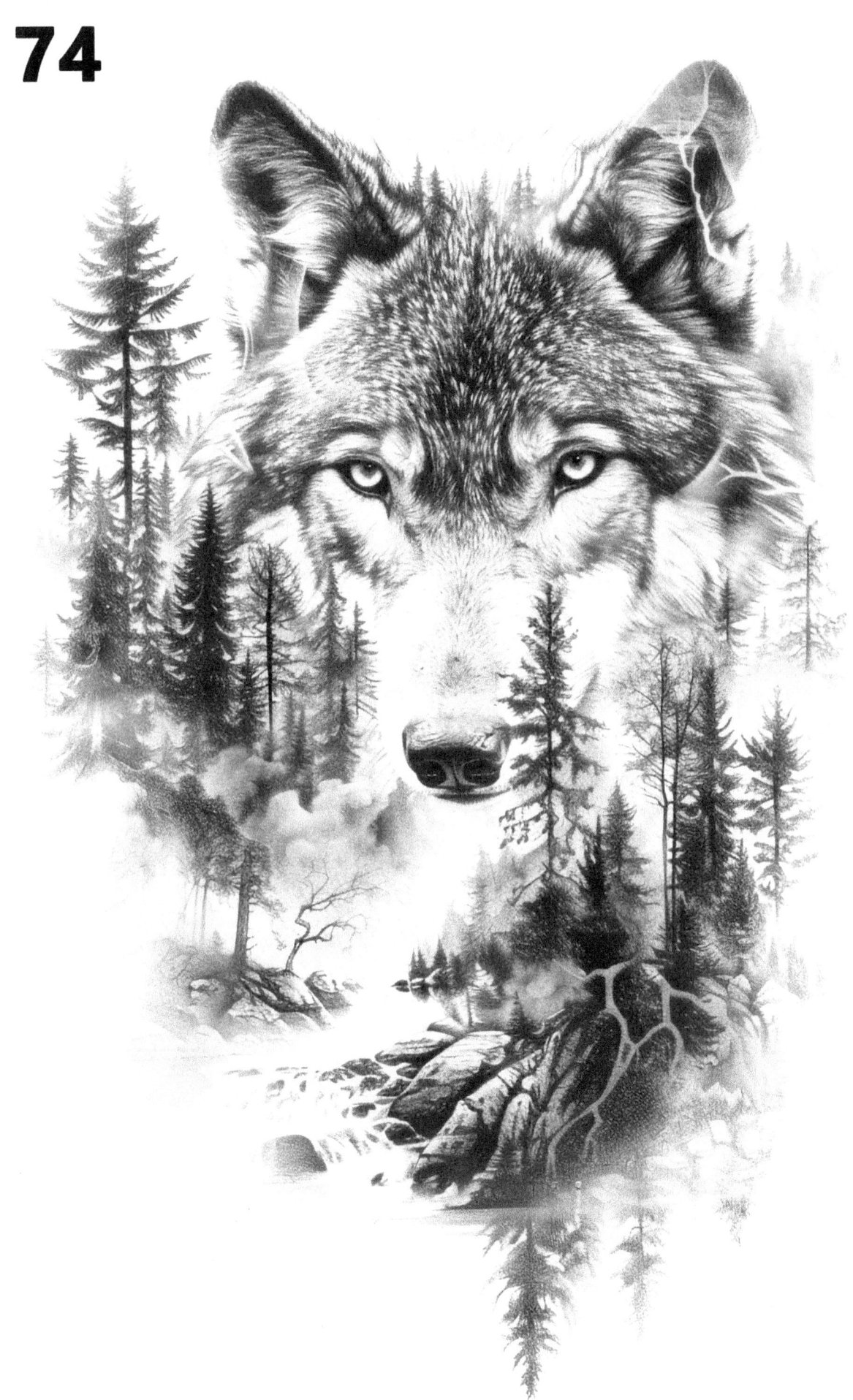

75

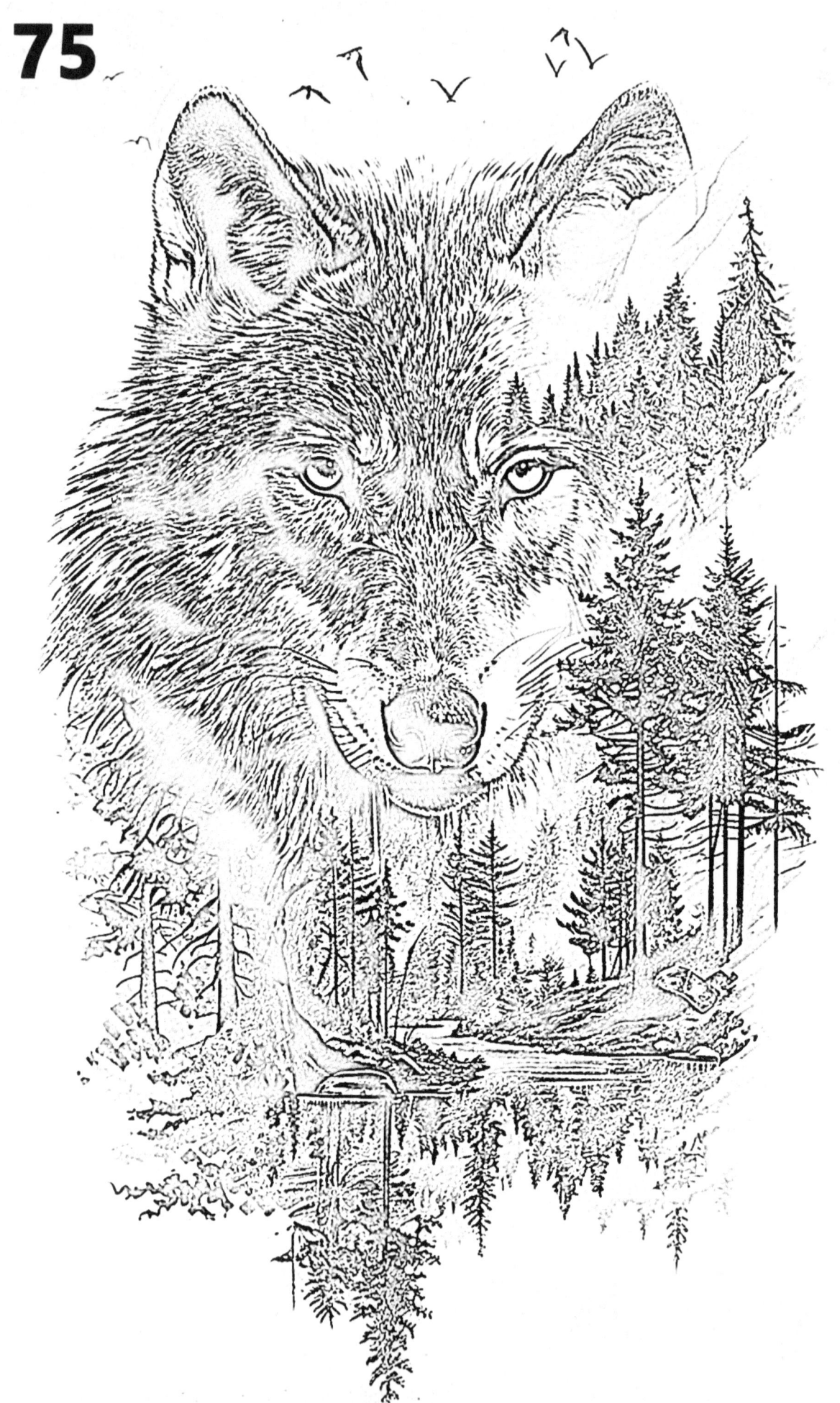

75

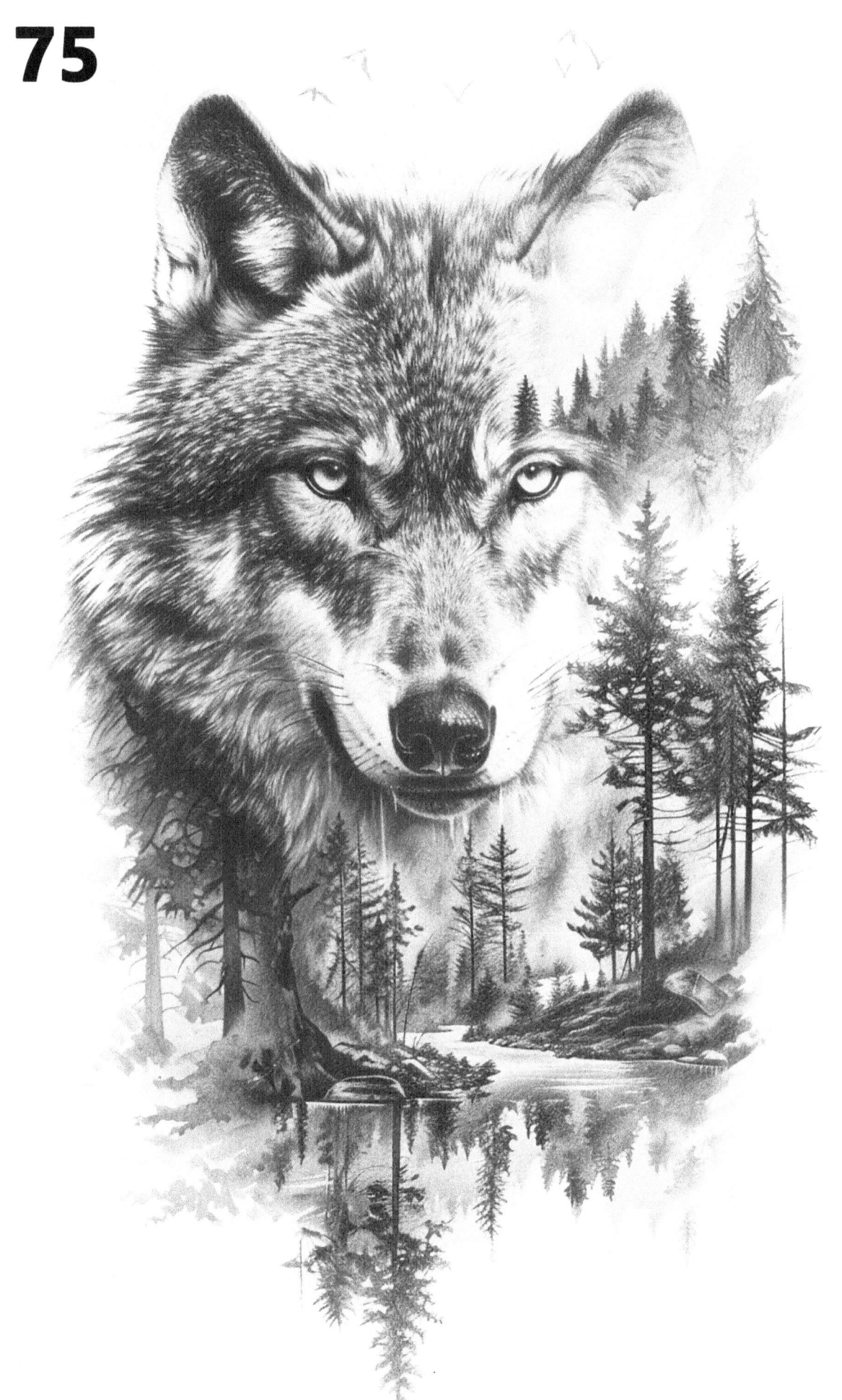

76

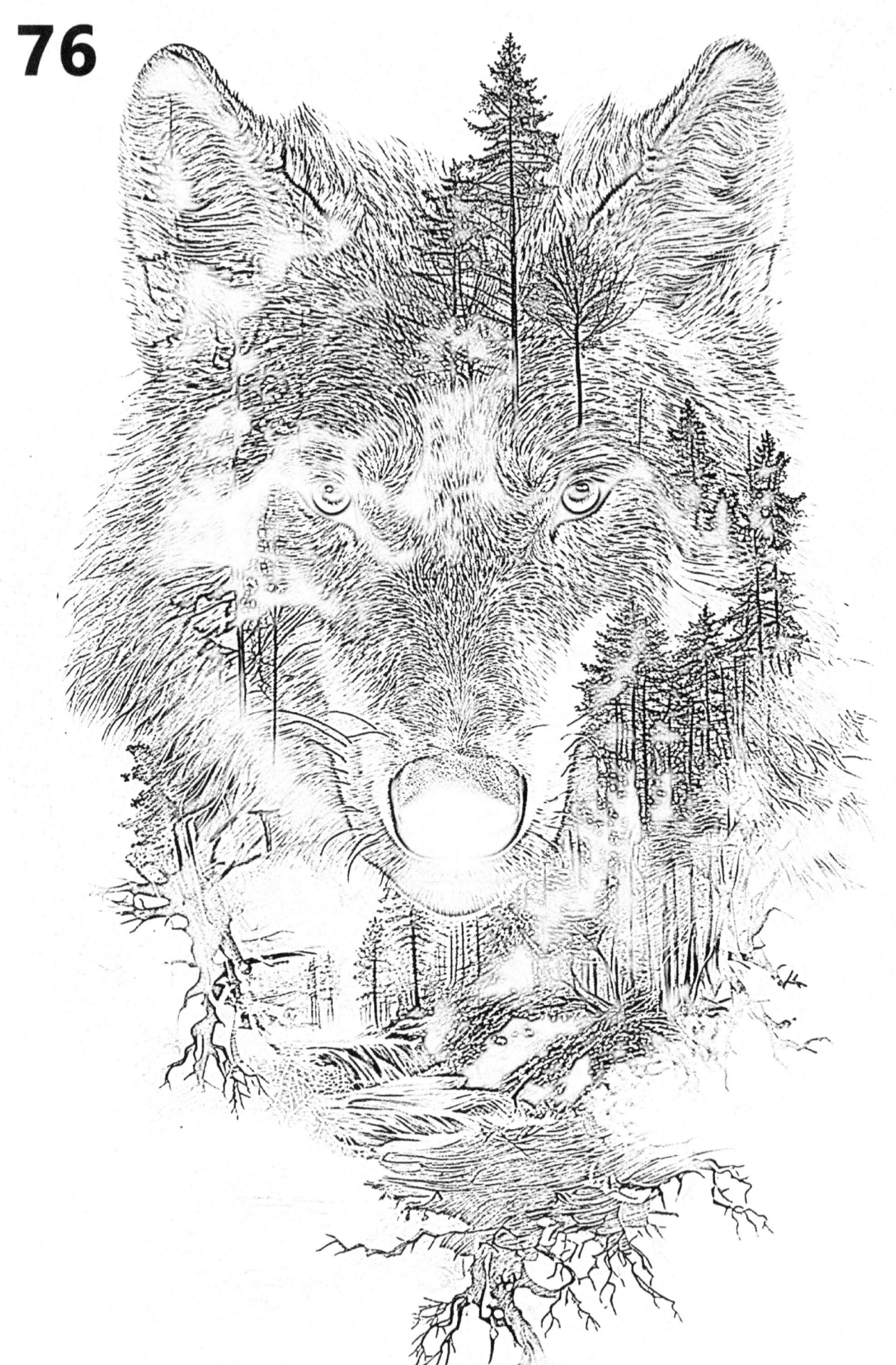

76

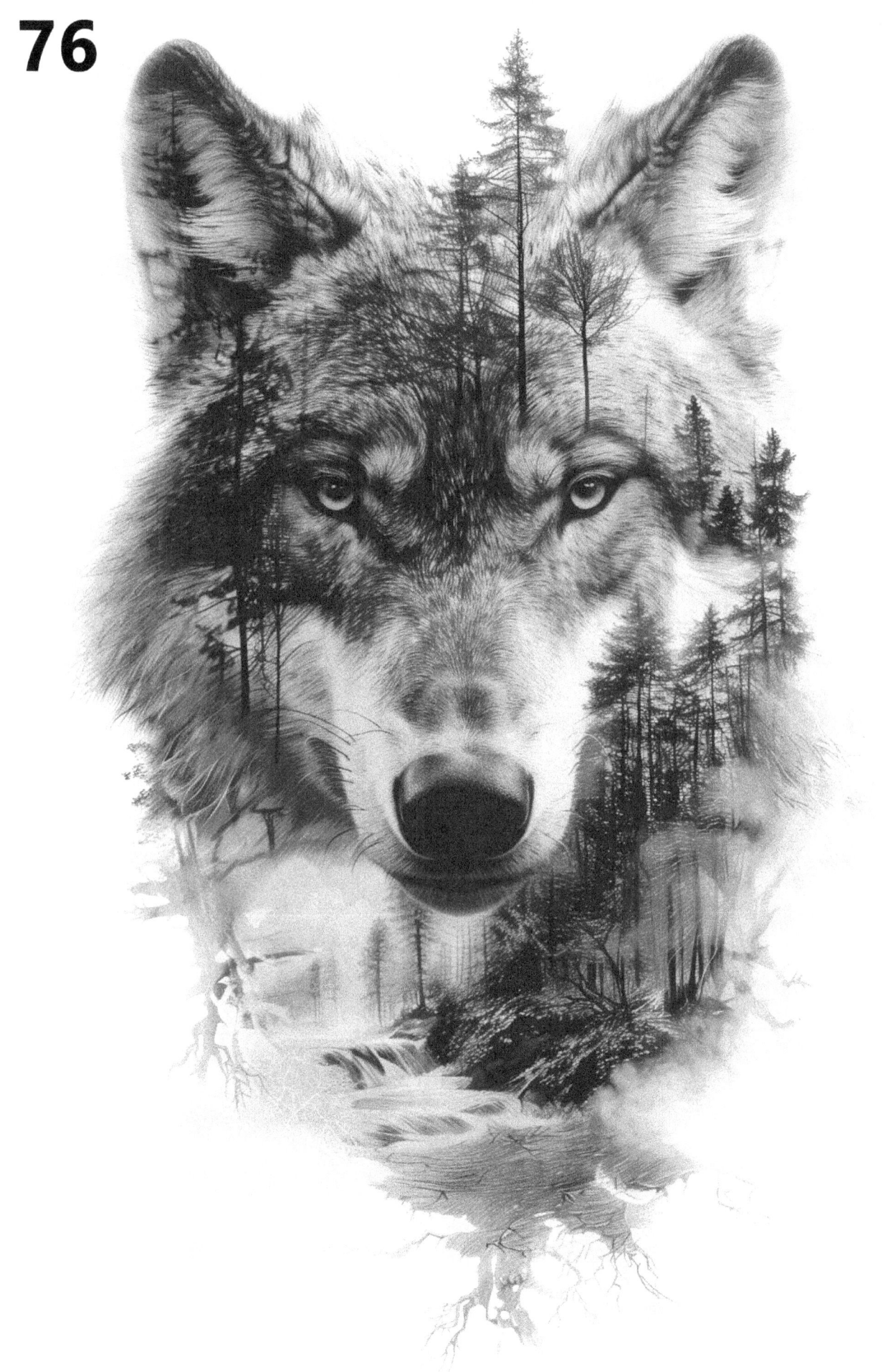

77

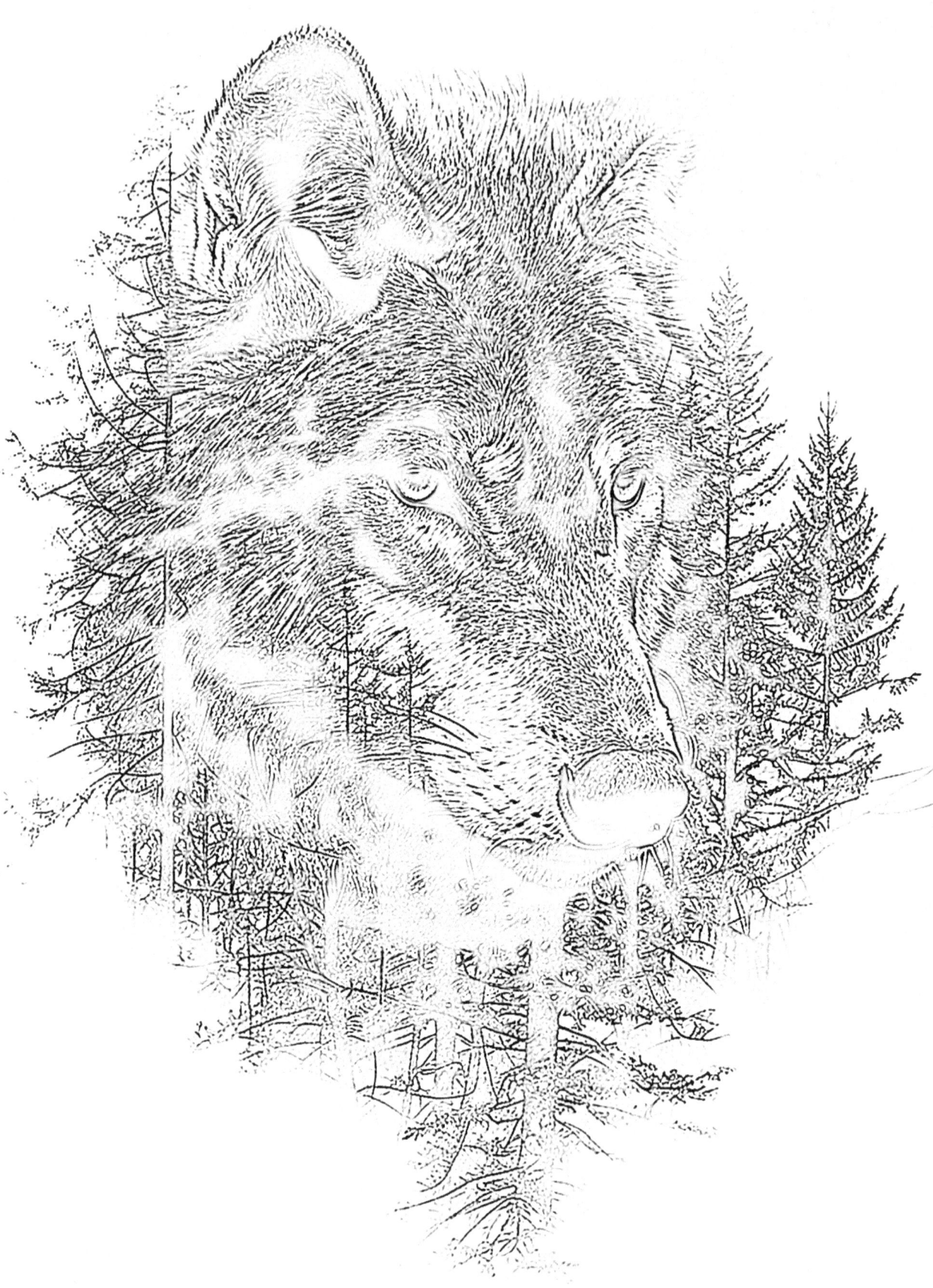

77

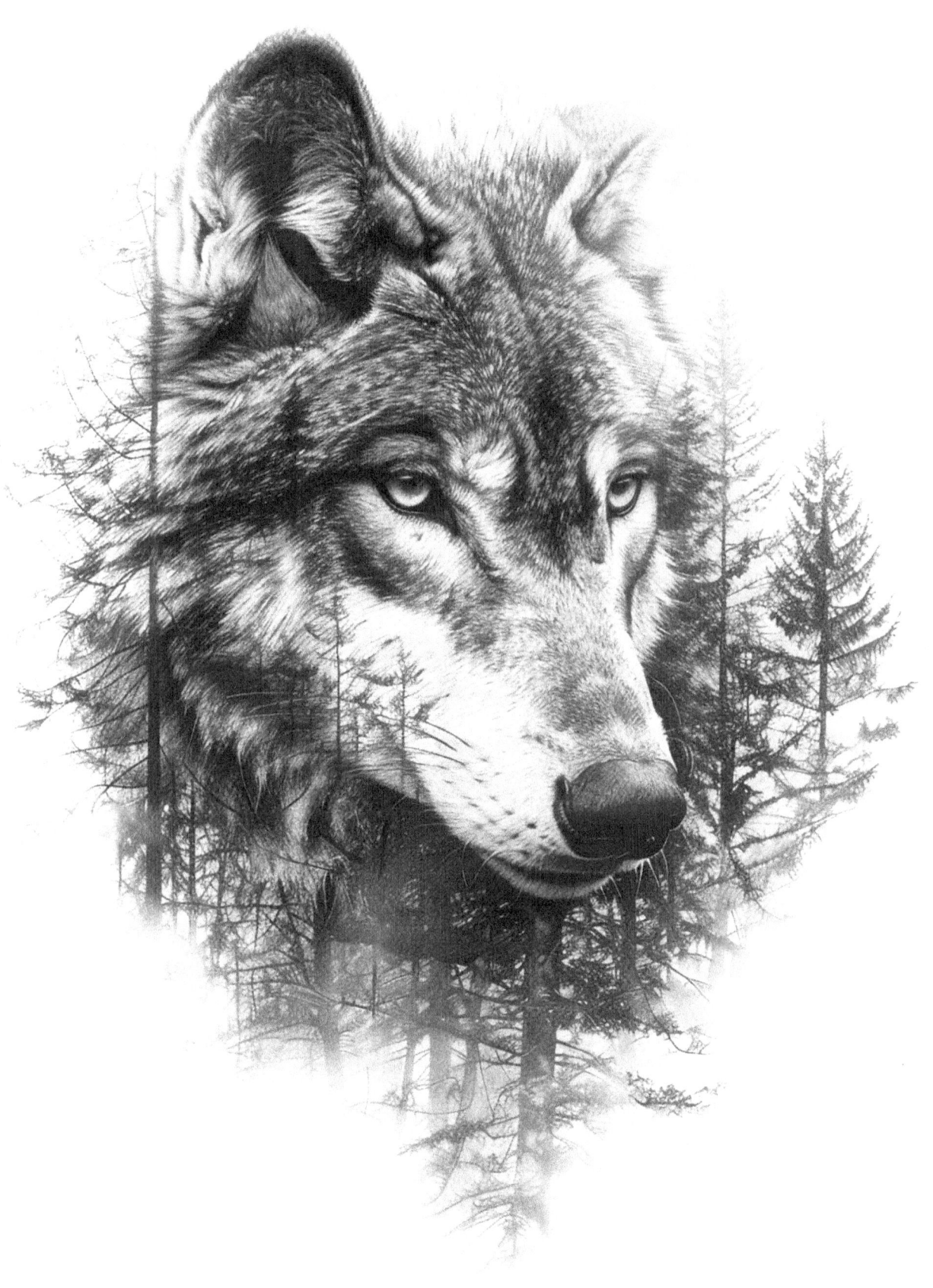

78

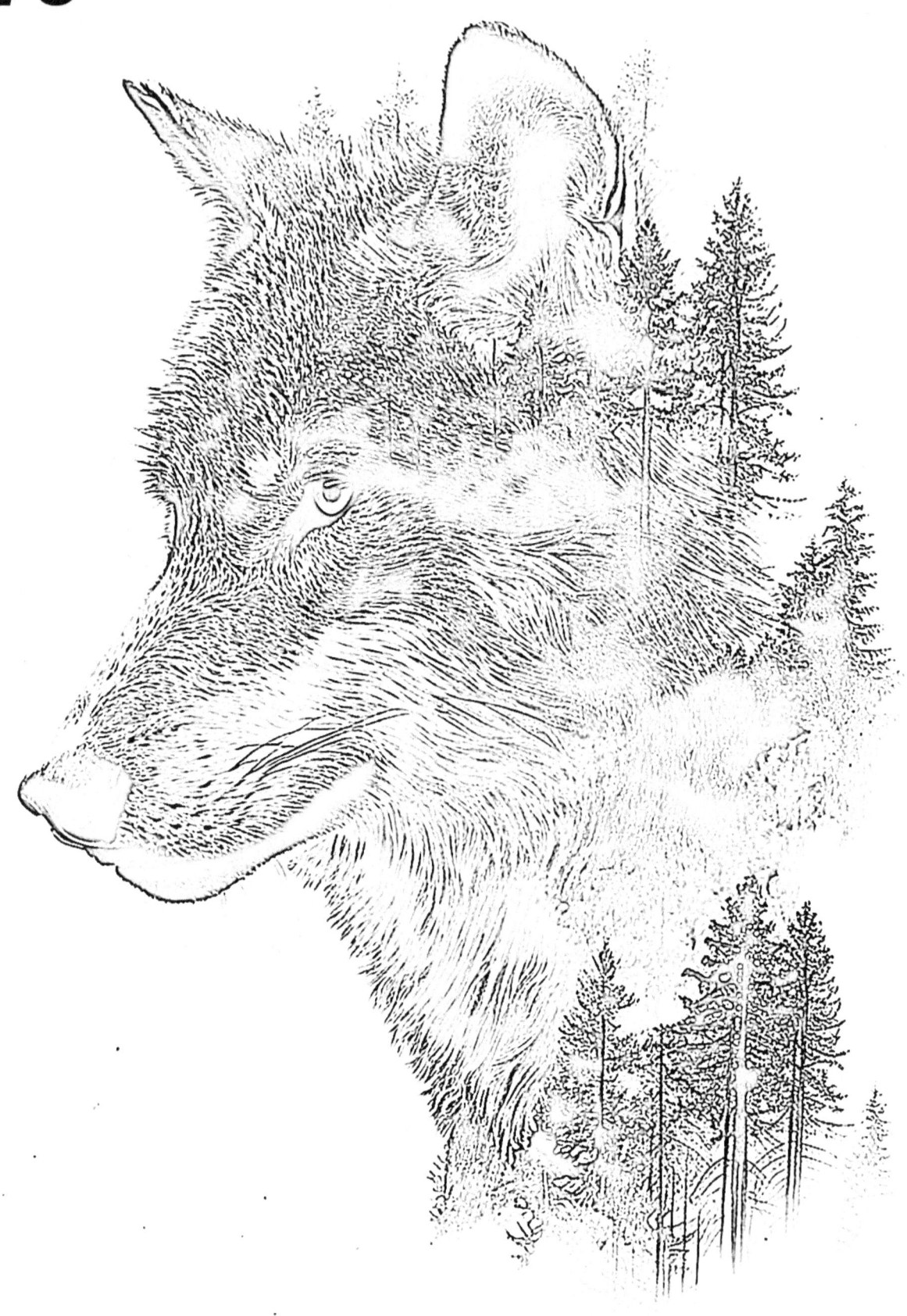

78

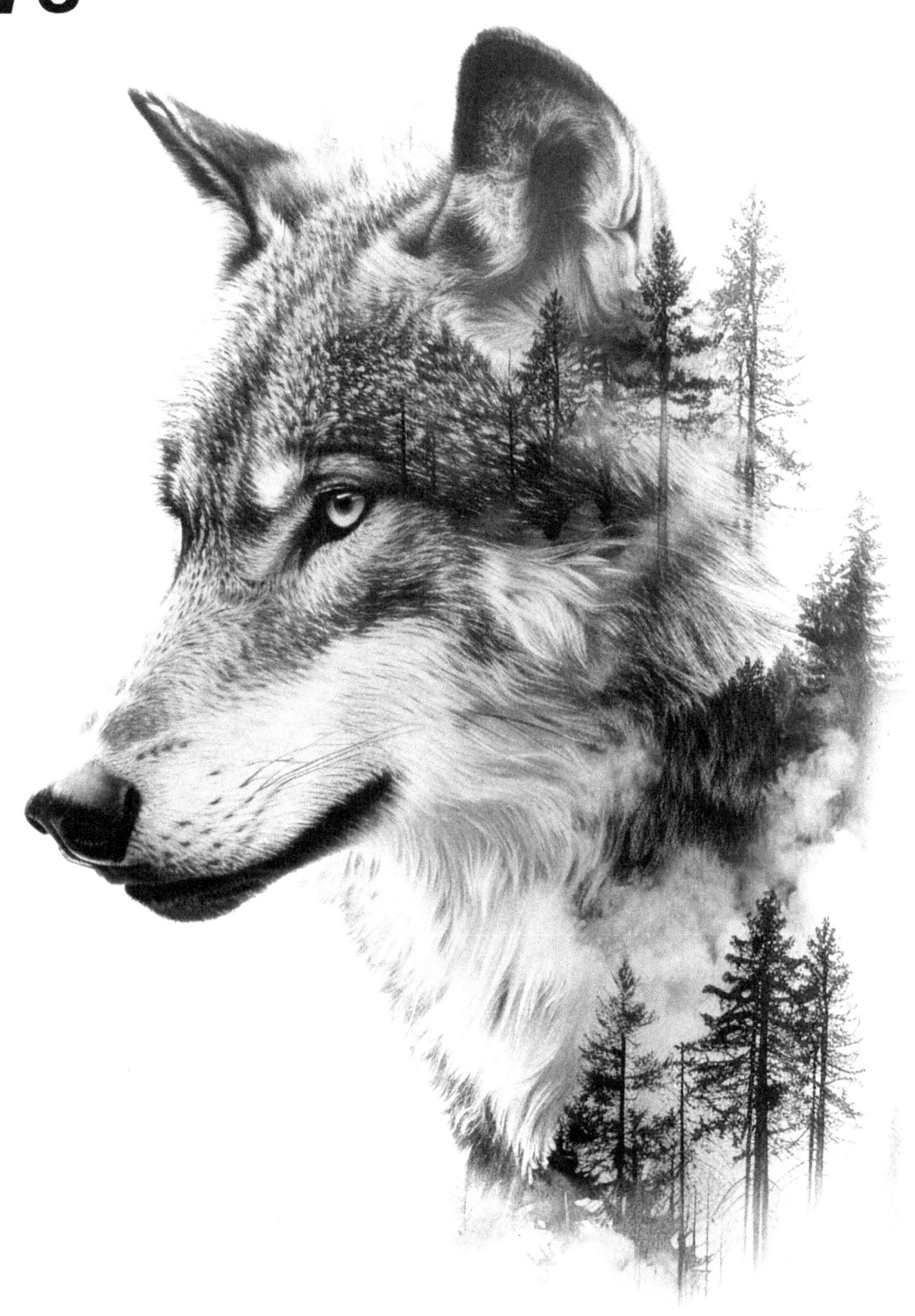

79

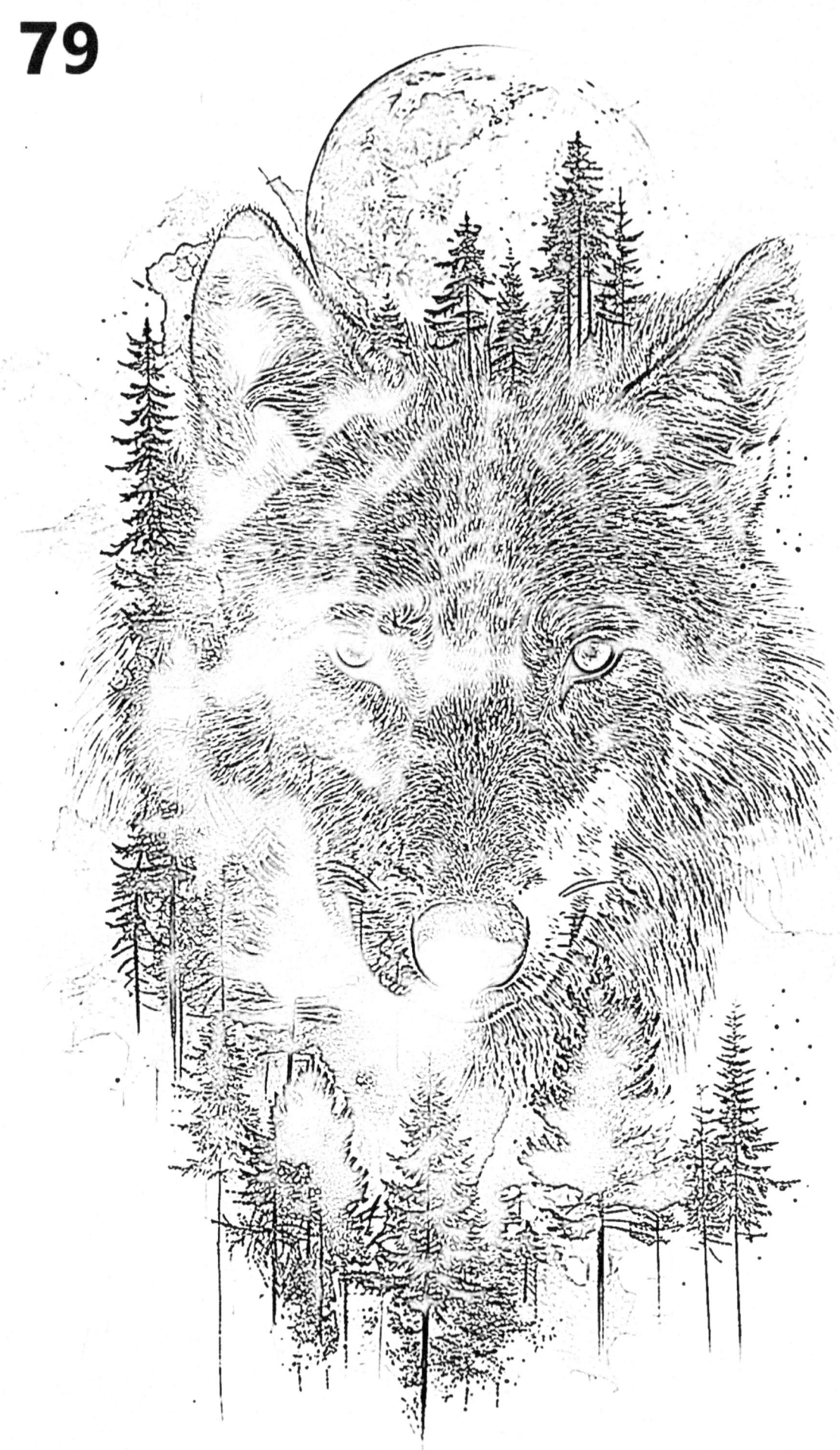

79

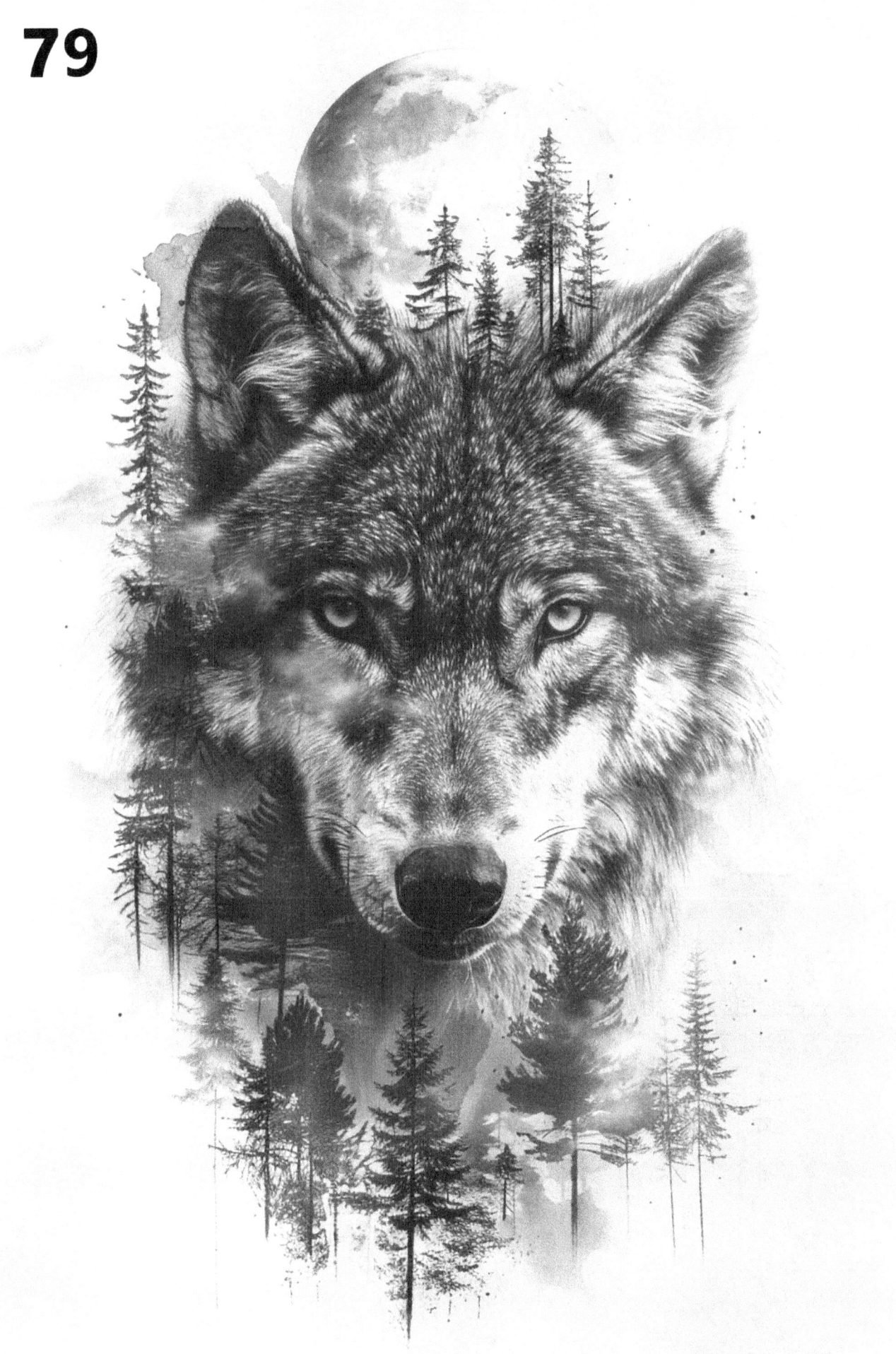

80

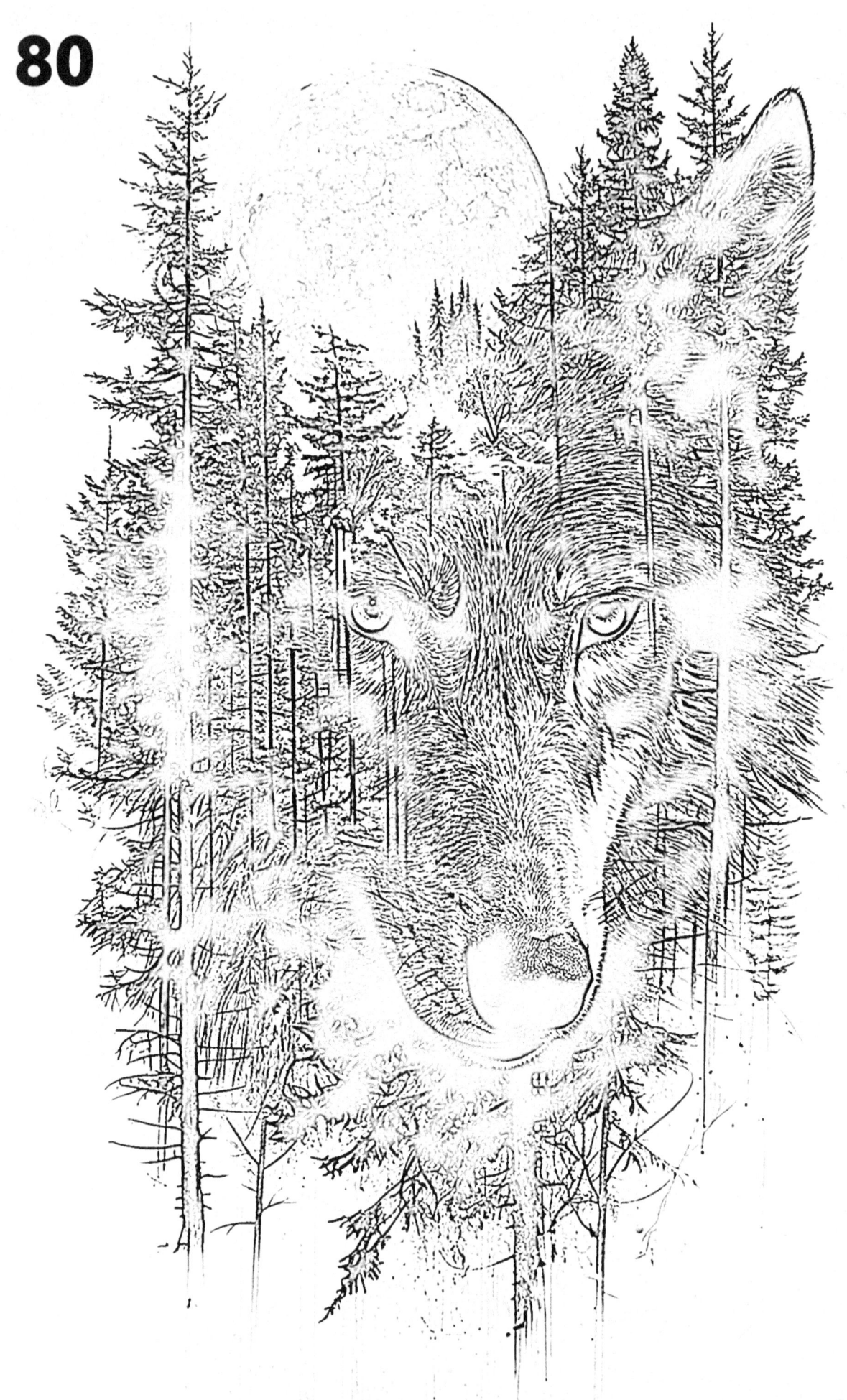

80

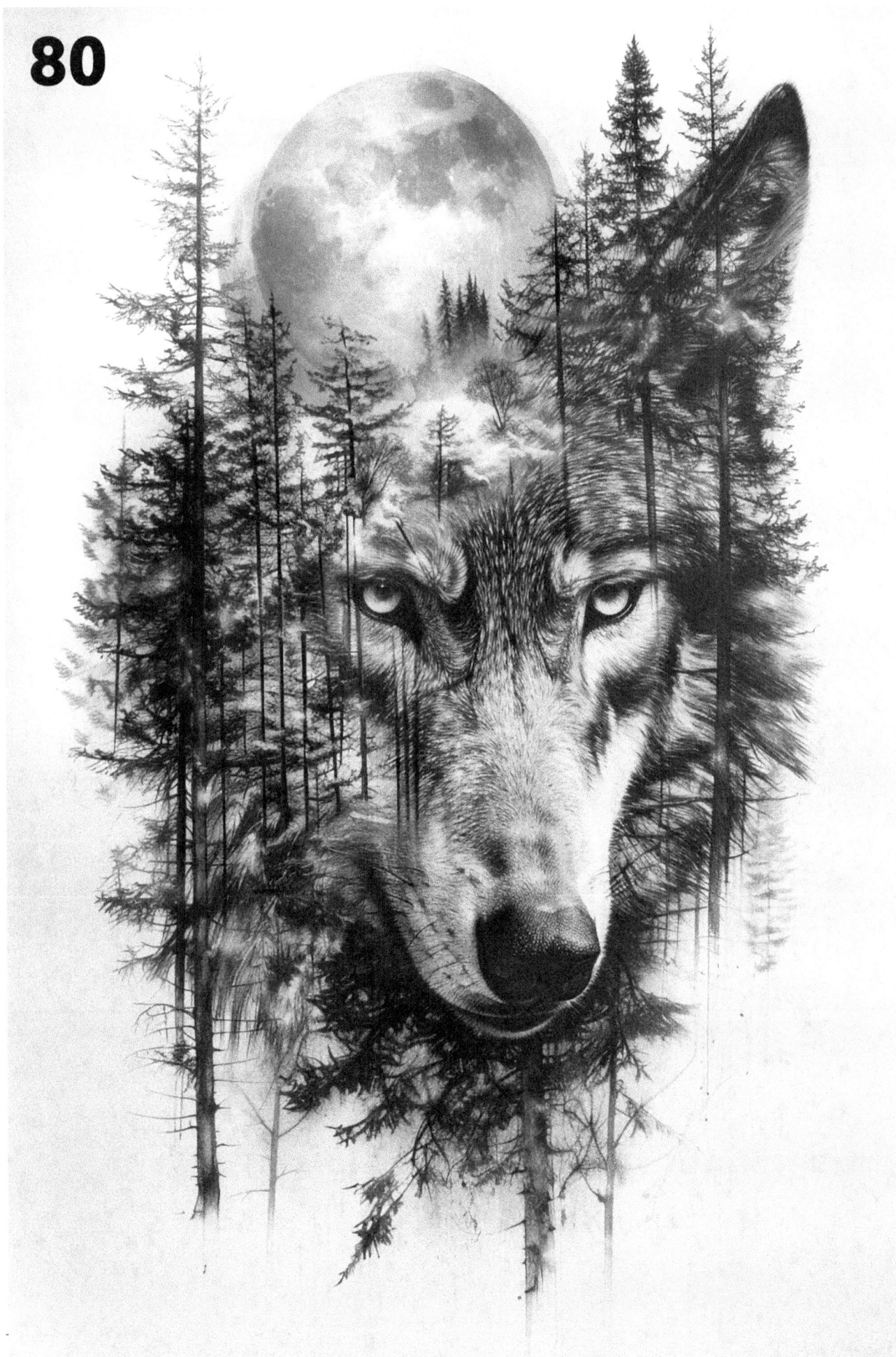

81

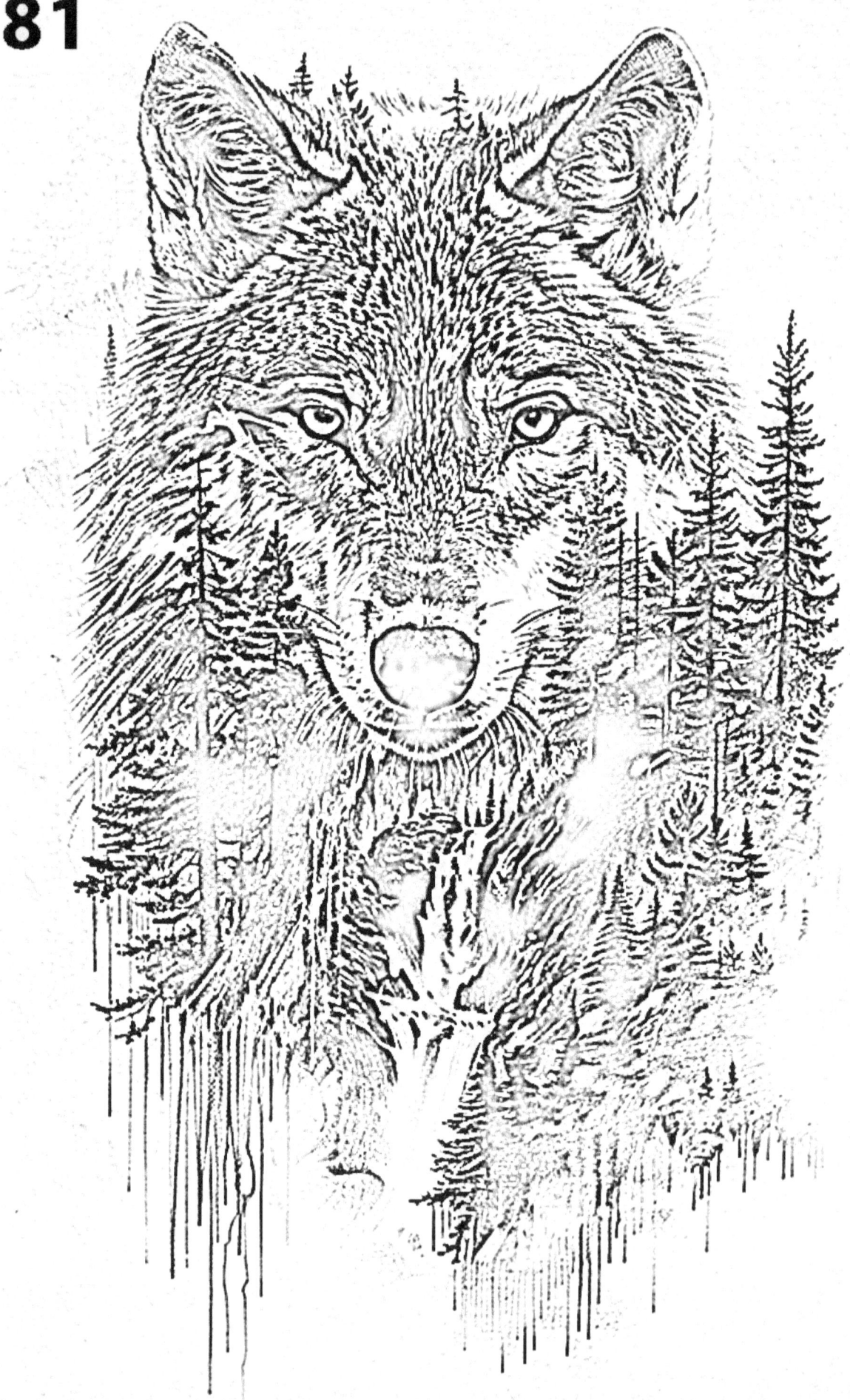

81

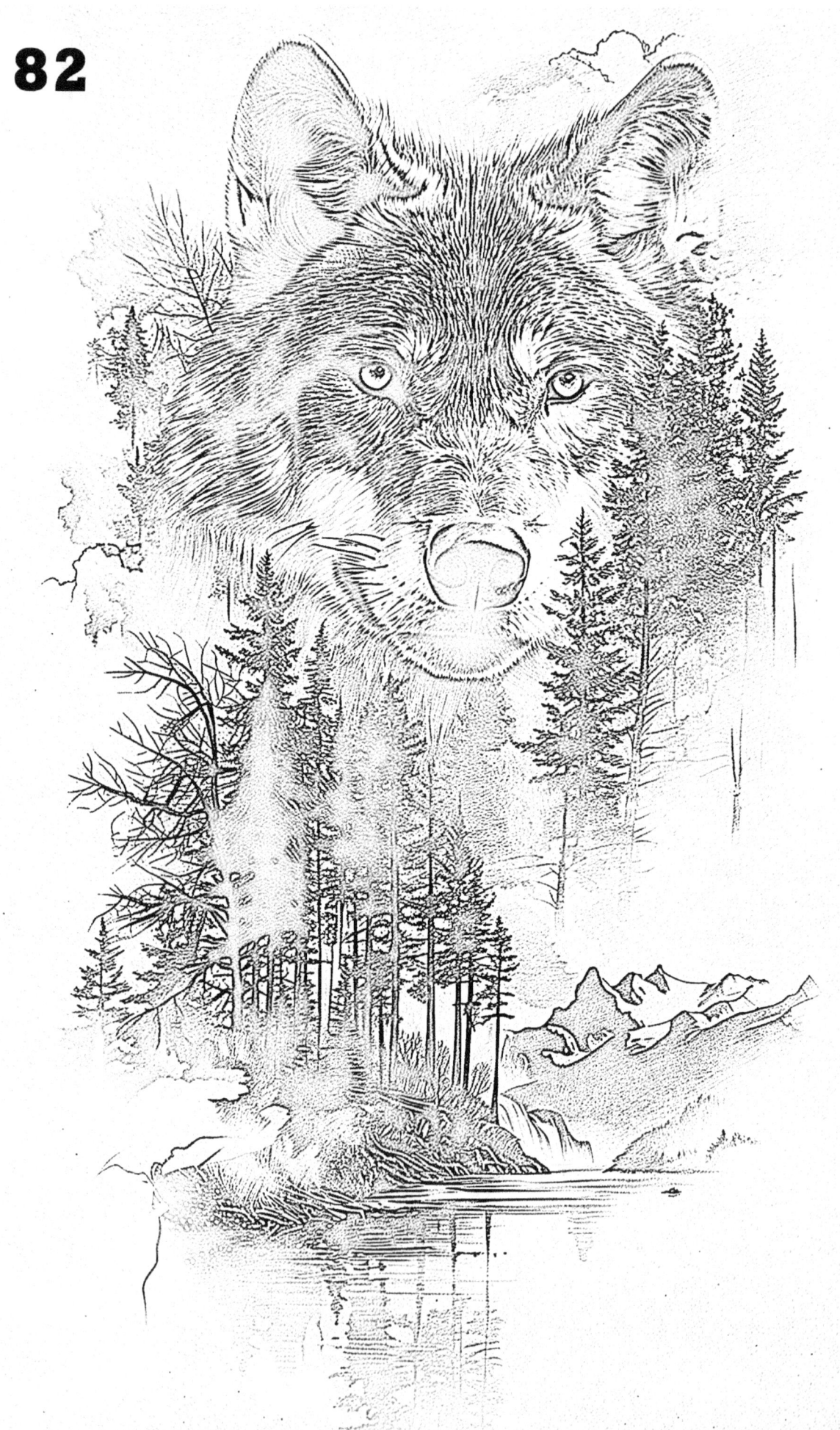

82

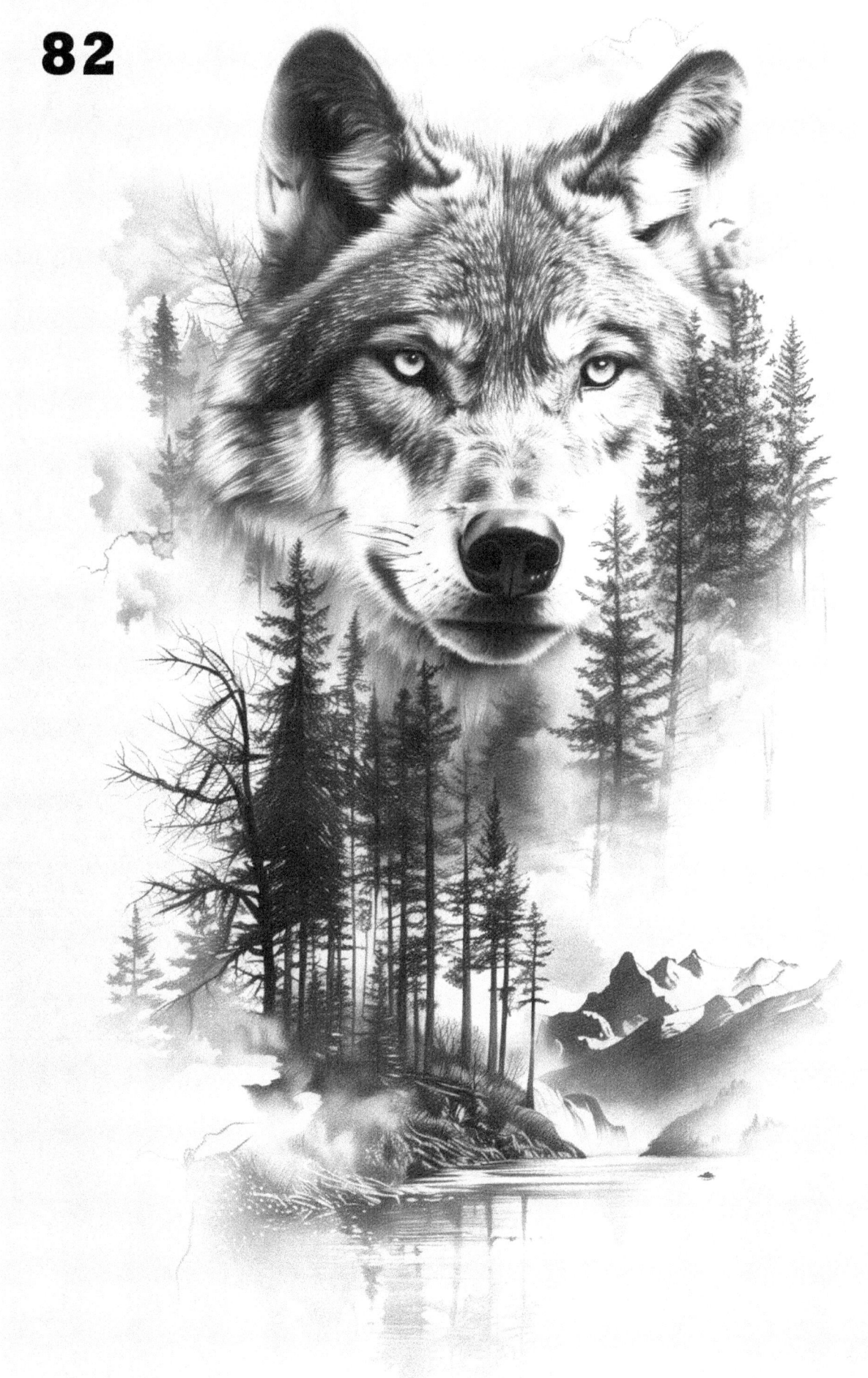

www.ingramcontent.com/pod-product-compliance
Lightning Source LLC
Chambersburg PA
CBHW062105220526
45471CB00010B/3608